Security and Development

GLOBAL DEVELOPMENT NETWORK

Series editor: George Mavrotas, *Chief Economist, Global Development Network*

Meeting the challenge of development in the contemporary age of globalization demands greater empirical knowledge. While most research emanates from the developed world, the Global Development Network series is designed to give voice to researchers from the developing and transition world – those experiencing first-hand the promises and pitfalls of development. This series presents the best examples of innovative and policy-relevant research from such diverse countries as Nigeria and China, India and Argentina, Russia and Egypt. It encompasses all major development topics ranging from the details of privatization and social safety nets to broad strategies to realize the Millennium Development Goals and achieve the greatest possible progress in developing countries.

Titles in the series include:

Testing Global Interdependence
Issues on Trade, Aid, Migration and Development
Edited by Ernest Aryeetey and Natalia Dinello

Political Institutions and Development
Failed Expectations and Renewed Hopes
Edited by Natalia Dinello and Vladimir Popov

Economic Reform in Developing Countries
Reach, Range, Reason
Edited by José María Fanelli and Lyn Squire

China, India and Beyond
Development Drivers and Limitations
Edited by Natalia Dinello and Wang Shaoguang

Health Care Systems in Developing and Transition Countries
The Role of Research Evidence
Edited by Diana Pinto Masís and Peter C. Smith

Global Exchange and Poverty
Trade, Investment and Migration
Edited by Robert E.B. Lucas, Lyn Squire and T.N. Srinivasan

Diversity in Economic Growth
Global Insights and Explanations
Edited by Gary McMahon, Hadi Salehi Esfahani and Lyn Squire

Security and Development
Edited by George Mavrotas

Security and Development

Edited by

George Mavrotas

(DPhil. Oxford), Chief Economist, Global Development Network

GLOBAL DEVELOPMENT NETWORK

Edward Elgar
Cheltenham, UK • Northampton, MA, USA

Published by
Edward Elgar Publishing Limited
The Lypiatts
15 Lansdown Road
Cheltenham
Glos GL50 2JA
UK

Edward Elgar Publishing, Inc.
William Pratt House
9 Dewey Court
Northampton
Massachusetts 01060
USA

A catalogue record for this book
is available from the British Library

Library of Congress Control Number: 2011932942

ISBN 978 0 85793 838 1

Printed and bound by MPG Books Group, UK

Contents

Notes on the Contributors

MAXIMILLIAN ASHWILL is a researcher for the Graduate Program in International Affairs and the Economics of Security Study Group, sponsored by the International Relations and Security Network (ISN). He worked with several NGOs in various conflict and post-conflict areas and is a graduate of The New School International Affairs Program.

AJAY CHHIBBER is U.N. Assistant Secretary General and Director of the United Nations Development Programme's Regional Bureau for Asia and Pacific. He has also served as a Senior Economist at the World Bank and has lectured in economics at Delhi University.

ELIZABETH CHIAPPA is a researcher in the Conflict Prevention project at The New School, New York. She holds a BA from Harvard University and an MA from The New School.

PAUL COLLIER, CBE, is Professor of Economics at the Centre for the Study of African Economies at the University of Oxford. He was director of the Development Research Centre at the World Bank 1998–2003. He is a world-renowned expert on African economics, politics and development issues, such as conflict. He is author of a number of well received and widely read books, including *The Bottom Billion* (2007) and *Plundered Planet* (2010).

SAKIKO FUKUDA-PARR is Professor of International Affairs at The New School, New York. She was Director of the Human Development Report Office at the UNDP and lead author of the UNDP Development Report from 1995–2004. She was the UNDP's Deputy Resident Adviser in Burundi (1985–1987), Principal Economist and Deputy Director at the Regional Bureau for Africa (1986–1991), and Chief of the West Africa Division (1992–1994).

MARK GERSOVITZ is Professor in the Department of Economics at The Johns Hopkins University. He has traveled widely in Africa and Asia as an economic researcher and adviser, and he has been a consultant to the World Bank, the International Monetary Fund, the United Nations Development

Programme and other organizations. From 1992 to 1994 he was the editor of *The World Bank Research Observer* and *The World Bank Economic Review*. In 1993 and 1994 he was the Director of the Center for Research on Economic Development (CRED) at the University of Michigan, Ann Arbor.

MARTIN KRYGIER is the Gordon Samuels Professor of Law and Social Theory at the University of New South Wales. His work is interdisciplinary, and he publishes in a number of areas: among them, comparative legal, political and social theory; politics, law and society after communism; sociology of law; and the history of political and social thought. His research has been published in academic journals across the world.

RACHID LAAJAJ is a Research Assistant at the University of Wisconsin.

WHIT MASON is a non-resident Fellow at the Lowry Institute for International Policy, Sydney. He is also currently the Research and Lessons Learned Project Manager at the Asia Pacific Civil-Military Centre of Excellence in Queenbeyan, Australia.

GEORGE MAVROTAS is the Chief Economist of the Global Development Network (GDN). He is also a Visiting Professor at CERDI, University of Auvergne, Clermont-Ferrand, a Non-Resident Associate Fellow at the Centre of Regional Integration Studies of the United Nations University (UNU-CRIS), Bruges, and an Adjunct Professor of Economics in the Faculty of Economics and Business of the University of the South Pacific, Fiji. He was formerly a Senior Fellow and Project Director at the World Institute for Development Economics Research of the United Nations University (UNU-WIDER) and prior to that on the Economics Faculties of the Universities of Oxford and Manchester. He has published more than 120 papers in leading journals and nine books on a broad range of deveopment issues.

CAROL MESSINEO is a researcher in the Conflict Prevention project at The New School, New York, and is currently a graduate student in the International Affairs Program.

MARTA REYNAL-QUEROL is Affiliated Professor at Barcelona Graduate School of Economics, an ICREA Research Professor and a Research Fellow at the European Research Council-Stg. Professor Reynal-Querol is a member of the editorial boards of the *Journal of Conflict Resolution* and *The Open Political Science Journal*. She is also an Associate Editor of the *Spanish Economic*

Review. She is author of a number of articles on conflict and development in several notable journals.

MICHAEL SPENCE is the William R. Berkley Professor of Economics and Business at New York University Leonard R. Stern School of Business and Senior Fellow at the Hoover Institution, Stanford University. He was awarded the Nobel Memorial Prize for Economic Sciences in 2001 for his contribution to research on the dynamics of information flows and market development. His past positions include Dean of the Stanford Graduate School of Business. He is currently the chairman of the Growth and Development Commission.

GRAEME WHEELER is Managing Director, Operations, at the World Bank. He has also served as Vice President and Treasurer at the World Bank. He was also Deputy Secretary and Director of Macroeconomic Policy and Forecasting at the New Zealand Treasury. His experience also includes tenure as Economic Counselor for the New Zealand Delegation to the Organization for Economic Cooperation and Development in Paris. His publications include a book on Sound Practice in Government Debt Management.

Acknowledgements

This book is the outcome of the Global Development Network's efforts to promote policy-relevant social science research on development. Published as part of the GDN book series with Edward Elgar Publishing, it emanates from the Ninth Annual Global Development Conference held under the theme 'Security and Development: Confronting Threats to Survival and Safety' in Brisbane, Australia (2008).

The Editor and the Contributors to the book are most grateful to the GDN Secretariat staff for general support. The Editor would like also to thank Ann Robertson for outstanding work regarding the copyediting process and for preparing the text for publication. Special thanks also to Alex Pettifer, Editorial Director of Edward Elgar Publishing Ltd. and Emily Neukomm, Editorial Assistant, for the overall support and enthusiasm with which they embraced the whole publication project and for excellent guidance and advice during the preparation process. Finally, many thanks also go to Simon Harding for excellent research assistance.

Chapter 5, 'The Conflict-Development Nexus: A Survey of Armed Conflicts in Sub-Saharan Africa 1980–2005', by Sakiko Fukada-Parr, Maximillian Ashwill, Elizabeth Chiappa and Carol Messineo was originally published in the *Journal of Peacebuilding and Development* (2008) and was included here with the kind permission of the authors and the Journal.

For Myrto and Jason

1. Security and Development: Delving Deeper into the Nexus

George Mavrotas

The overall nexus between security and development poses some formidable questions about the multiple forms of violence that afflict the international community: Why are some places peaceful while others are violent? Is poverty the main cause of civil conflict? What is the role of foreign aid in the whole process of rehabilitation, reconstruction and recovery following conflict? How do natural disasters affect the economic prospects of a country? What can the international community do to stop the spread of infectious diseases? In the current debate on threats to individuals, households and nations, the answers to questions like these could have a huge positive effect on the lives of millions of people worldwide.

There is a broad consensus that poverty fuels conflicts. Indeed, low incomes and sluggish economic growth do have the potential to spark and sustain conflicts; however, the empirical evidence is not particularly robust. A more significant factor is the strength of political and economic institutions, which oversee the distribution of resources. The inequitable distribution of resources is regularly a more powerful driver of conflict than the amount of resources *per se*.[1] Conflicts, including those arising from the struggle for resources, can have disastrous effects on development: civil wars and insurgencies in Africa are costing the continent US$18 billion a year and take 2 per cent off annual growth figures (Guest 2009). The impact is felt directly by the population: Poverty rates are 20 per cent higher in countries that are affected by repeated cycles of violence. The World Bank's Fragile and Conflict-Affected Countries program estimates that the 1.5 billion people who live in countries with high levels of violence are twice as likely to be undernourished and 1.5 times more likely to be impoverished, while their children are three times more likely to be out of school (World Bank 2011). Education is hit particularly hard by violence. Armed conflicts around the world are preventing 28 million school-age children from gaining an education, a figure that represents 42 per cent of the total global un-enrolled school aged population (UNESCO 2011).

But the 'growth impact' of conflict is complex. Conflict does not have a universal and negative impact on growth. The effects differ between countries and may even be markedly different between regions in the same country, depending on factors such as the duration of the war, type of conflict, intensity of fighting and international responses to the conflict (i.e. from direct intervention and humanitarian aid to sanctions). The UNDP Bureau for Crisis Prevention and Recovery states that while countries with long-term conflicts appear to post resilient annual growth, these longer conflicts play a larger role in shackling GDP growth than shorter ones. Figure 1.1 shows the differing effects of conflict on GDP growth for a selection of conflict countries. The diversity of the conflict-growth relationship is demonstrated by the few countries that managed to grow during periods of conflict.

Figure 1.2 shows the number of conflicts by region over time. The graph shows that global conflicts rose from a low of 15 in 1946, doubling by the late 1960s and further rising to reach a peak of over 50 in the mid-1990s. The data also suggest that levels of conflict in different regions are strongly related, as all regions experience similar trends: all regions see peaks in the late 1960s and early 1990s, as well as recent increases from 2006 onward. Despite interlinked trajectories, most conflicts occur in two regions: Africa and Asia, with Europe, the Middle East and the Americas appearing more peaceful.

Conflicts often hinge on the presence and distribution of resources as opposing sides fight to capture resource rents.[2] Poor institutions and bad, often authoritarian, governance may be causal factors. However, democracy is not a silver bullet for peace. Democratic governance may actually make rebellion easier by constraining the capacity of the state to put down the insurgencies that may arise in an attempt to capture resource rents (Collier and Rohner 2008; Collier and Hoeffler 2009). Fear, uncertainty and grievances surrounding elections often provide the catalyst for latent conflicts, as in the Ivory Coast in 2011.

This is not to promote authoritarianism of course – democracy remains a valid goal regardless of its effects on conflict and growth – but rather to suggest that fractured democracies need to become more inclusive and advance all-embracing policy agendas that cut across ethnic groups (Lijphart 2004). Electoral systems that generate stable and inclusive governing coalitions must be chosen (IDEA 2006) in order to avoid ethnic fragmentation and the unequal dispersal of state funds to certain ethnic groups. Equitable distribution of resource-related benefits may prevent grievances from arising in the first place. Furthermore, good management of natural resources can further reduce the risk of conflict by removing potential causes: corruption, economic shocks and potential rebel financing (Collier et al. 2003; Collier and Venables forthcoming).

Figure 1.1 Overall Change in GDP Per Capita during Conflict (%)

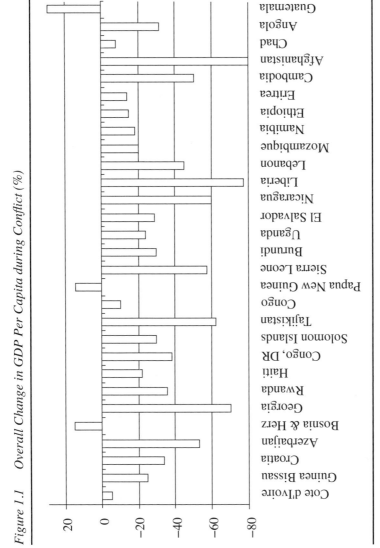

Source: UNDP Bureau for Crisis Prevention and Recovery (2011).

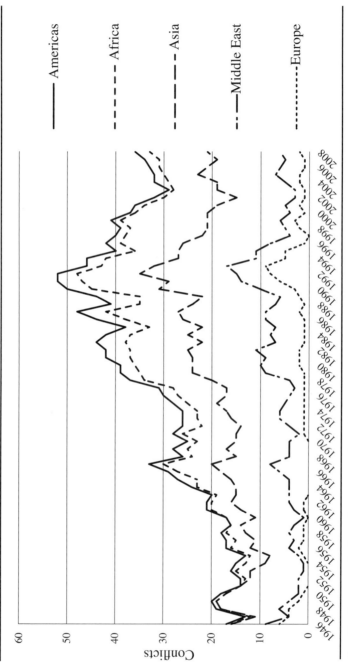

Figure 1.2   Conflicts by Region, 1946–2008

Note: Needless to say, the figure does not cover the political shifts in the Middle East in early 2011.
Source: PRIO 2009

4

Crucial to forging a path out of this trap is a 'rule of law' that is recognized by all sections of the population and understood as the result of contributions from all elements of society, rather than as the preserve of one ethnic or regional group. Understanding the complex factors associated with conflict and the most effective interventions are crucial to improving the social and economic well-being of many poor countries.

The immediate post-conflict period has the potential to kick-start economic growth. The payoffs of aid and technical assistance are considerable, due to the weakening of vested interests, a newfound political will for national unity, stability and a political environment conducive to much needed reforms. However, post-conflict reconstruction interventions have a mixed record (positive in Namibia and Mozambique, less so in many other states). In the case of Africa, the high incidence and long history of state failure – even stable states can quickly topple – and the gap between scholarly knowledge and policy hinder reconstruction efforts (Englebert and Tull 2008).[3]

The role of development aid is therefore crucial in countries emerging from conflict (and beyond). Development aid is one of the few topics in the development discourse with such an uninterrupted and volatile history in terms of interest and attention from academics, policymakers and practitioners alike. As Roger Riddell put it, 'Aid has managed, repeatedly, to reinvent and renew itself after repeated bouts of uncertainty, doubt and pessimism' (2007, 2). Development aid has received a lot of attention since the implementation of the best-known and probably most successful aid program, the Marshall Plan, in Western Europe following World War II. Since then the aid landscape has changed many times, and in recent years a number of key questions have emerged. Does aid work in promoting growth and reducing poverty in the developing world? What is the role of aid in countries emerging from conflict? Can aid buy reforms in recipient countries? Does aid affect governance in recipient countries? Can the lessons of almost a half a century of aid giving be learned?

Foreign aid reached almost US$129 billion in 2010 according to data released by the Development Assistance Committee of the OECD (OECD-DAC) and remains a crucial source of development finance for many countries in the developing world, particularly in the aftermath of the global financial crisis (see Figure 1.3).

Recent years have witnessed various important initiatives in this area, and a number of influential books (though without reaching consensus on the overall effectiveness of aid) have also been published on the subject, including Sachs (2005), Easterly (2006), Riddell (2007), Lahiri (2007), Collier (2007) and Moyo (2008). It also seems that aid allocation is now more developmental and less political after the Cold War. However, issues related to strategic donor behavior and *realpolitik* (Maizels and Nissanke 1984) have not lost importance completely in recent years (Burnell 2004; Kanbur 2006; Mavrotas and Villanger 2006; Lahiri and Michaelowa 2006; Murshed 2009; de Haan and Everest-Phillips 2010 and Browne 2010).

At the same time, aid to fragile states and the crucial issue of structural vulnerability has attracted much attention recently (Collier 2007; Guillaumont 2006, 2009; Fukuda-Parr 2010). A message emanating from recent work on the effectiveness of foreign aid (including aid-targeting to war-torn countries) is that it is not sufficient to scale up aid efforts by raising and transferring more money (see Killick and Foster 2007; Bourguignon and Sundberg 2007a, b; Mavrotas and Nunnenkamp 2007; Barder 2009 and Mavrotas 2010, among others). At least part of the blame for not making a lot of progress on the aid-effectiveness front so far falls on insufficient targeting of sector-specific aid; in this context, unless aid is better targeted, scaling up aid is unlikely to have the desired effects (Thiele et al. 2007). Against this new background for development aid, the overall *modus operandi* of the aid 'architecture' needs also to be re-examined, particularly in view of the various implications of the global financial crisis for both donors and recipients (Mavrotas 2010).

On the other hand, and of great relevance to the overall nexus between security and development, natural disasters and pandemics are currently a pressing threat to the international community. The prevalence of natural disasters has been on an historically upward trajectory. The empirical evidence is strong. Figure 1.4 shows the number of reported disasters per year from 1900 to 2009.

While many disasters are unprecedented and unpredictable, such as earthquakes and tsunamis, many are a byproduct of the growing human impact on natural resources. Many development strategies conceive of natural resources as infinite, an approach that is clearly no longer tenable and can lead to intense resources pressures and largely man-made disasters, such as famines. How best to plan for and respond to hazards is therefore a pressing issue.

Infectious diseases render international borders porous. Pandemics bring with them loss of life and severe economic impacts ranging from higher health-care costs to loss of earnings. Government attempts to restrict the spread of disease are often blunted by resistance from those affected by quarantine restrictions, vaccinations or, in the case of diseases transmitted by animals, culling. Responses are also curtailed by economic considerations. There is widespread agreement that contagious diseases must be tackled multilaterally with international responses to outbreaks because health must be conceived of as a global public good. However, containment efforts rest on the actions of individuals. The task of policymakers is to encourage individuals

Figure 1.3   Net Official Development Assistance (ODA) in 2010

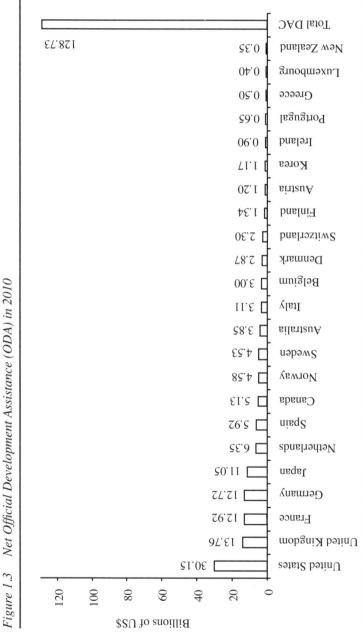

Country	Billions of US$
United States	30.15
United Kingdom	13.76
France	12.92
Germany	12.72
Japan	11.05
Netherlands	6.35
Spain	5.92
Canada	5.13
Norway	4.58
Sweden	4.53
Australia	3.85
Italy	3.11
Belgium	3.00
Denmark	2.87
Switzerland	2.30
Finland	1.34
Austria	1.20
Korea	1.17
Ireland	0.90
Portugal	0.65
Greece	0.50
Luxembourg	0.40
New Zealand	0.35
Total DAC	128.73

Source: Development Assistance Committee of the OECD, 2011.

7

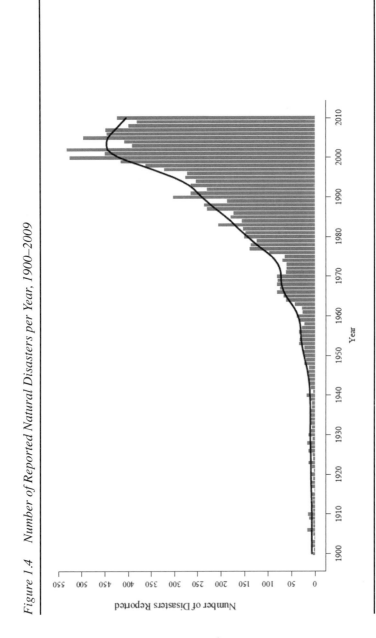

Figure 1.4   Number of Reported Natural Disasters per Year, 1900–2009

Source: World Health Organization Collaborating Centre for Research on the Epidemiology of Disasters Emergency Events Database (2009).

to adopt behaviors that minimize the risk of infection driven by awareness of the immediate personal benefits, while ensuring that individual benefits correspond to wider social benefits. How to achieve this delicate balance remains a complex question.

The contributors to this volume seek to address these important questions. They first identify the nature of the specific threat to security and then go on to offer policy responses to mitigate those threats. Many of the responses recommended go beyond the scope of individuals to call for better national and international-level policies to tackle security threats. The remaining chapters deal with issues such as coping with civil wars and how to avoid them in the first place; how to strengthen the rule of law; responses to natural disasters and halting the spread of diseases across international borders.

In Chapter 2, Nobel Laureate **Michael Spence** lays out the relationship between security and economic development. Those economies with the best post-war performances share numerous characteristics, including engagement with the global economy. Governments play a critical role in creating and maintaining growth. Security, the author argues, is an end in itself, irrespective of its economic impact, but it is vital to the sustainability of growth. However, the security-growth relationship is far from unidirectional. Growth strengthens security by reducing the impact of economic shocks, increasing adaptive capacity and moving countries away from zero-sum game economies, which lead to resource-based conflicts. Growth brings social safety nets, lower unemployment resulting in lower crime rates and improved healthcare, all of which decrease discontentment, instability and the risk of civil conflict. Conversely, high levels of security foster economic growth by providing a safe environment for investment and encouraging investments in human capital, which may take time to come to fruition. Security also provides the conditions for the eradication of problems that have long-term effects on the labor force, such as child malnutrition. Equality of opportunity and outcomes, protection from the downside risks of the global economy and economic security are all vital components of successful economic growth, he concludes.

The global productivity shock has created the most significant and widespread global growth in 40 years, writes **Graeme Wheeler** in Chapter 3.[4] Millions of workers are entering labor markets in emerging economies while technology is transforming lives inside and outside the workplace. Official Development Assistance (ODA) is dwarfed by private cross-border capital flows and remittances, which have seen the foreign exchange reserves of developing countries increase dramatically. High growth rates in emerging economies, coupled with slower growth in the developed world, have meant that the center of economic influence has shifted eastward, a trend that is set to continue. However, several threats to growth persist in developing nations.

First, the poorest typically live in fragile states, often landlocked, with major infrastructure problems, poor governance and chronic instability. Poor-quality public services and nonexistent social mobility mean that a substantial section of the global population remains mired in poverty with little prospect of escape, a situation that has notable implications for security. Second, climate change poses a serious threat to the long-term prospects of the poor in many developing countries. The investments required are massive, argues Wheeler. While targeted assistance can be effective, it is often confounded by other policies, such as US and EU agricultural subsidies. Rather than being a significant financial contributor, concludes Wheeler, the World Bank plays an important role as a provider of expertise data, and strategic advice in order to bring about the knowledge transfers and capacity building necessary to mitigate these threats to security.

Paul Collier discusses political violence in Chapter 4. He sketches out the distinctions between seven forms of political violence: rebellions, coup d'états, pogroms, terrorism, riots, voter intimidation and assassination. Each form has its own particular dynamics, motivations and organizational forms. Given this complexity, he narrows the focus of the chapter to the most 'organizationally demanding' and 'damaging' form of violence: the civil rebellion. Civil rebellions rarely result in rebel victory or lead to positive changes in governance. They also have the potential to become civil wars, which last an average of seven years and can spill over into neighboring states. Preventing rebellions in the first place is therefore an important task. He uses quantitative analysis to investigate the structural causes of these conflicts. The chapter centers on the question as to whether there are factors that make some countries more vulnerable to rebellion than others and what can be done to mitigate the conflict risk from a policy point of view. Policy responses aimed at tackling these structural factors, rather than short-term measures, can be called 'deep prevention'. However, many conflicts are simply recurrences of past conflicts, or 'relapses'. As such, 'emergency interventions' directly following the cessation of hostilities are crucial in preventing further violence. Governments, donors and peacekeeping forces are the three main actors responsible for the success or failure of post-conflict states. All three are interdependent. He goes on to document post-conflict responses involving national governments and the international community, which may reduce the risk of future conflicts. The chapter concludes with a call for further economic analyses of conflict in order to supplement the context-specific expertise of practitioners with a broader analysis. A combination of context-specific knowledge and a holistic view is the best way to prevent future conflicts and the unwelcome return of past hostilities.

Chapter 5, by **Sakiko Fukada-Parr**, **Maximillian Ashwill**, **Elizabeth Chiappa** and **Carol Messineo**, looks at civil conflict in Africa from 1980 to 2005: its trends, developmental impacts, socioeconomic risk factors and policy responses. The authors use quantitative analysis to claim that the state is an inadequate framework through which to view such conflicts, as they are not traditional Clausewitzian wars, but rather complex struggles involving state and non-state actors with a range of overlapping motivations and incentives. Approaches to conflicts frequently retain this unhelpful state-centrism. Contrary to the common understanding of war as 'development in reverse', the authors find that the economies of conflict-ridden countries continued to grow despite internal discord. Social indicators also improved. However, the impacts of the conflicts were largely localized, affecting certain areas more than others, which points to increased regional inequalities, as some areas are decimated while others are relatively untouched. The authors cite unemployment, resource dependency and horizontal inequalities, the youth bulge, environment pressure and natural resource dependence as structural risk factors. Tackling these risks with effective social and economic policies can reduce the danger of conflict, but at present national and international policy does not address these issues. They conclude by stressing the fragility of peace in sub-Saharan Africa and echo the call for an approach that prevents conflict by addressing structural risk factors.

In Chapter 6, **Marta Reynal-Querol** reflects further on the theme of civil conflict. She agrees with the Copenhagen Consensus that civil wars are one of the main challenges to development and that measures to reduce their number, duration and severity would be a priority if their success could be guaranteed or predicated with a significant level of confidence. She then goes about analyzing the causes of civil conflicts and suggests some effective prevention mechanisms. The author weighs up the evidence for the orthodox theory that poverty and other economic determinants cause civil conflict. She concludes that the claim that poverty causes conflict is based on weak empirical evidence. Here Reynes-Querol questions the stance of the UN Millennium Project, *Investing in Practical Development* (2005), which cites poverty as a major cause of conflict. Rather than focus on poverty, Raynal-Querol finds evidence that institutions play a significant role in determining the likelihood of civil conflict. Her findings actively rebut the idea of poverty as a cause of conflict. The strength or weakness of institutions is a far more significant determinant of civil conflict than poverty and other economic determinants. She concludes by discussing the role of institutions in preventing conflict. To understand the causes of civil conflicts future research should concentrate more on institutions and less on poverty and economic development. The author sees this as a positive development as attempts to alleviate poverty through aid have had little success; therefore, a new focus on institutional development opens up fresh and potentially effective channels of intervention for conflict prevention.

Martin Krygier and **Whit Mason** discuss violence and the rule of law in Chapter 7. There are fewer more shocking comparisons in the world, claim the authors, than between peaceful societies where the rule of law predominates and those in which the law is weak and violence is an everyday occurrence. The rule of law means the difference between having the opportunity and confidence to follow one's dreams and being cowed by the looming threat of disorder and duress. The difference between these two kinds of places is apparent to anyone who has experienced both, but it is far harder to account for these differences or – further still – actually do anything about them. Attempts to improve the rule of law rely almost entirely on the technical capacities of the judiciary and other legal institutions. It is assumed that once there is sufficient capability then good, efficient law will follow. However, the authors argue that where there is a 'way' there is not necessarily a 'will': Technical solutions and institution building cannot combat the lack of political will to improve the rule of law. But the old adage does function in its conventional form: where the 'will' exists to strengthen the rule of law, then an institutional 'way' will be found. What policymakers should focus on is how to create an environment in which adhering to the law makes sense for both the powerful and relatively powerless. Fostering the will to behave civilly and supporting the legal order must be the prime objective. Only in societies with soundly balanced institutions, which prevent predatory actions by legal bodies, can people go beyond survival and begin to flourish. In this sense, the technical interventions of Western donors – which often run into billions of dollars – cannot create the conditions necessary to convince people to follow the rule of law. But by listening to the people affected by the absence of the rule of law and trying to perceive the situation from their point of view, it is possible to comprehend what is needed for upholding the rule of law and encouraging civil behavior.

Natural disasters are the focus of **Ajay Chhibber** and **Rachid Laajaj** in Chapter 8. They begin by arguing that the increasing frequency of natural disasters is due to human activity and the nature of development. Disasters have severe and highly visible short-term costs, which can lead to severe long-term costs in countries in which short-term disasters occur on a regular basis. Despite the increasing frequency of disasters, response mechanisms are inadequate and need to be better institutionalized at the local, national, regional and global levels. The authors review the existing evidence, which shows that the frequency of disasters has increased eight times since the 1960s to affect 2 billion people in the past decade. The cost of disasters has risen by 15 times in the same period. In the past four decades the frequency of hydro-meteorological disasters (floods, typhoons and hurricanes) has increased markedly, which the authors link to climate change and such human activities as deforestation, unplanned settlements and coastal development. The short-term financial costs of disasters average as high as 2–15 per cent of GDP in some countries, often more than the total aid flows and even foreign investment; however, there are long-term consequences that can have inter-generational repercussions. Lower food intake leads to stunting, school dropouts and other health problems. The threat of disasters may also encourage risk-averse behavior, which has the potential to lower long-run investment rates. However, on a macroeconomic level the picture is less clear. Disasters can sometimes improve a country's long-term economic outlook by destroying old capital and encouraging new technologically superior investment, the authors argue. Post-disaster aid and reconstruction can also help kick-start growth. The authors conclude by arguing that one-off disasters may have high short-term costs but may have positive long-term economic effects, while smaller more frequent disasters will most likely permanently lower long term economic performance.

In the final Chapter 9, **Mark Gersovitz** discusses the theme of externalities and their incorporation into policies designed to control the spread of infectious diseases. Rarely do people threatened by a disease weigh up all the costs of becoming infected. People do not take into account the implications for other people when they expose themselves to the risk of infection, especially if those other people live in a different country. Given this it is easy to see how externalities arise concerning prevention and therapy. State actors, says Gersovitz, have too narrow a view. They attend only to those within their jurisdiction, ignoring the wider global community and the fact that infectious diseases do not respect administrative borders. Standard incentives and penalties (subsidies and taxes) to discourage becoming infected are ineffective as the risk-taking behavior of individuals is hard to monitor. Moreover, there is a persistent gap between the social benefit and private benefit of remaining uninfected. The challenge facing public officials is to induce individuals to consider the social benefits and costs of their actions, which they would otherwise disregard. This challenge must be met on a continual and sustained basis. Gersovitz quantifies this discussion with a model that combines behavioral economics and epidemiological models of contagion in order to recommend informed, integrated interventions. However, no local or national governments have made significant efforts to inform their citizens of the global social cost of becoming infected. Expenditure on restricting the spread of disease is a global public good, but there is little scope for funders to claim reimbursement from beneficiaries of their investments, medicines and technologies, which are globally available. Multinational and supranational policies are needed to deal with these externalities, the author argues. Similarly, knowledge about contagion from the social sciences, particularly epidemiology, is also a global public good. Contagion is influenced by human behavior as well as biology. Like biological knowledge, the findings of social science should be disseminated and much-needed resources put into the area, Gersovitz concludes.

The chapters in this volume tackle some of the main security challenges facing the international development community. They also go further by putting forward suggestions and recommendations as to how best to deal with these threats. Researchers and policymakers have the difficult task of understanding and responding to a complex and dynamic set of challenges in this crucial area. It is hoped that this volume will help to provide some useful reflections – if not complete answers – relevant to this challenging task and suggest ways for future research in this area.

NOTES

I am most grateful to Simon Harding for outstanding research assistance. The usual disclaimer applies.

1. There exists a voluminous literature regarding conflict over natural resources. The interested reader can refer to Lane and Tornell (1996), Sachs and Warner (1999), Tornell and Lane (1999), Bourguignon and Verdier (2000), Auty (2001), Ross (2001), Collier and Hoeffler (2004, 2005), Robinson et al. (2006), Mehlum et al. (2006) and more recently Mavrotas et al. (2011) among others. See also van der Ploeg (2010) for an excellent recent review of the literature on the subject.
2. See van der Ploeg (2010) and Mavrotas (forthcoming) for a detailed discussion.
3. See also Addison (2003), Murshed (2002) and Dibeh (2010).
4. The chapter was written before the emergence of the global financial crisis.

REFERENCES

Addison, T. (2003), *From Conflict to Recovery in Africa*, New York: Oxford University Press.
Auty, R. (ed.) (2001), *Resource Abundance and Economic Development*, New York: Oxford University Press.
Barder, O. (2009), 'Beyond Planning: Markets and Networks for Better Aid', Washington, DC, Center for Global Development, Working Paper No. 185.
Bourguignon, F. and M. Sundberg (2007a), 'Absorptive Capacity and Achieving the Millennium Development Goals', in G. Mavrotas and A. Shorrocks (eds), *Advancing Development: Core Themes in Global Economics*, Basingstoke: Palgrave Macmillan.
Bourguignon, F. and M. Sundberg (2007b), 'Is Foreign Aid Helping? Aid Effectiveness – Opening the Black Box', *American Economic Review*, **97** (2), 316–321.
Bourguignon, F. and T. Verdier (2000), 'Oligarchy, Democracy, Inequality and Growth', *Journal of Development Economics*, **62** (2), 285–313.

Browne, S. (2010), 'Aid to Fragile States: Do Donors Help or Hinder?', in G. Mavrotas (ed.), *Foreign Aid for Development: Issues, Challenges and the New Agenda*, New York: Oxford University Press.

Burnell, P. (2004), 'Foreign Aid Resurgent: New Spirit or Old Hangover', Helsinki, United Nations University, World Institute for Development Economics Research (WIDER) Research Paper No. 2004/44.

Collier, P. (2007), *The Bottom Billion: Why the Poorest Countries are Failing and What Can be Done About It*, New York: Oxford University Press.

Collier, P. and A. Hoeffler (2004), 'Greed and Grievance in Civil War', *Oxford Economic Papers*, **56** (4), 563–95.

———, (2005), 'Resource Rents, Governance and Conflict', *Journal of Conflict Resolution*, **49** (4), 625–33.

———, (2009), 'Testing the Neocon Agenda: Democracy in Resource-Rich Societies', *European Economic Review*, **53** (3), 293–308.

Collier, P. and D. Rohner (2008), 'Democracy, Development and Conflict', *Journal of the European Economic Association*, **6** (2/3), 531–40.

Collier, P. and A. Venables (forthcoming), 'Managing the Exploitation of Natural Assets: Lessons for Low Income Countries', in G. Mavrotas (ed.) *Natural Resources and Development*, Cheltenham, UK and Northampton, MA, USA: Edward Elgar.

Collier, P., V.L. Elliot, H. Hegre, A. Hoeffler, M. Reynal-Querol and M. Sambanis (2003), *Breaking the Conflict Trap: Civil War and Development Policy*, Vol. 1, New York: Oxford University Press.

Collier, P., A. Hoeffler and D. Rohner (2008), 'Greed and Grievance: Feasibility and Civil War', *Oxford Economic Papers*, **56** (4), 563–95.

de Haan, A. and M. Everest-Phillips (2010), 'Can New Aid Modalities Handle Politics?' in G. Mavrotas (ed.) *Foreign Aid for Development: Issues, Challenges and the New Agenda*, New York: Oxford University Press, pp. 197–221.

Dibeh, G. (2010), 'Foreign Aid and Economic Development in Post-war Lebanon' in G. Mavrotas (ed.) *Foreign Aid for Development: Issues, Challenges and the New Agenda*, New York: Oxford University Press, pp. 179–94.

Easterly, W. (2006), *The White Man's Burden: Why the West's Efforts to Aid the Rest Have Done So Much Ill and So Little Good*, New York: Penguin Press.

Englebert, P. and D. Tull (2008), 'Post-Conflict Reconstruction in Africa: Flawed Ideas about Failed States', *International Security*, **32** (4), 106–39.

Fukuda-Parr, S. (2010), 'Conflict Prevention as a Policy Objective of Development Aid', in G. Mavrotas (ed.) *Foreign Aid for Development: Issues, Challenges and the New Agenda*, New York: Oxford University Press, pp. 123–51.

Guest, P. (2009), Paper Presented at the World Economic Forum on Africa Workshop 'Global Redesign Series: The Cost of Conflict', Cape Town, South Africa, June.

Guillaumont, P. (2009), *Caught in a Trap: Identifying Least Developed Countries*, Paris: Economica.

Guillaumont, P. (2006), 'Macroeconomic Vulnerability in Low-Income Countries and Aid Responses', in F. Bourguignon, B. Pleskovic and J. van der Gaag (eds), *Securing Development in an Unstable World*, Washington, DC: World Bank, pp. 65–108.

IDEA (2006), *Democracy, Conflict and Human Security: Key Findings and Recommendations*, Stockholm: Institute for Democracy and Electoral Assistance.

Kanbur, R. (2006), 'The Economics of International Aid', in S. Christophe-Kolm and

J. Mercier-Ythier (eds), *The Economics of Giving, Reciprocity and Altruism*, Elsevier: North-Holland, chapter 26.

Killick, T. and M. Foster (2007), 'The Macroeconomics of Doubling Aid to Africa and the Centrality of the Supply Side', *Development Policy Review*, **25** (2), 167–92.

Lahiri, S. (ed.) (2007), *Theory and Practice of Foreign Aid*, Amsterdam: Elsevier.

Lahiri, S. and K. Michaelowa, (2006), 'The Political Economy of Aid', *Review of Development Economics*, **10** (2), 177–344.

Lane, P. and A. Tornell (1996), 'Power, Growth and the Voracity Effect', *Journal of Economic Growth*, **1** (2), 213–41.

Lijphart, A. (2004), 'Constitutional Design for Divided Societies', *Journal of Democracy*, **15** (2), 96–109.

Maizels, A. and M. Nissanke (1984), 'Motivations for Aid to Developing Countries', *World Development*, **12** (9), 879–900.

Mavrotas, G. (ed.) (forthcoming), *Natural Resources and Development*, Cheltenham, UK and Northampton, MA, USA: Edward Elgar.

—— (2010), *Foreign Aid for Development: Issues, Challenges and the New Agenda*, New York: Oxford University Press.

Mavrotas, G., S.M. Murshed and S. Torres (2011), 'Natural Resource Dependence and Economic Performance in the 1970–2000 Period', *Review of Development Economics*, **15** (1), 124–38.

Mavrotas, G. and P. Nunnenkamp (2007), 'Foreign Aid Heterogeneity: Issues and Agenda', *Review of World Economics*, **143** (4), 585–95.

Mavrotas, G. and E. Villanger (2006), 'Multilateral Aid Agencies and Strategic Donor Behaviour', Helsinki, United Nations University, World Institute for Development Economics Research (WIDER) Discussion Paper No. 2006.02.

Mehlum, H., K. Moene, and R. Torvik (2006), 'Institutions and the Resource Curse', *Economic Journal*, **116** (508), 1–20.

Moyo, D. (2008), *Dead Aid: Why Aid is Not Working and How There is Another Way for Africa*, London: Allen Lane for Penguin Books.

Murshed, S.M. (2003), 'Civil War, Conflict and Underdevelopment', *Journal of Peace Research*, **39** (4), 387–93.

Murshed, S.M. (2009), 'On the Non-Contractual Nature of Donor–Recipient Interaction in Development Assistance', *Review of Development Economics*, **13** (3), 416–28.

PRIO (2009), *Conflicts by Region 1946–2008*, Oslo: Peace Research Institute Oslo.

Riddell, R. (2007), *Does Foreign Aid Really Work?*, New York: Oxford University Press.

Robinson, J.A., R. Torvik and T. Verdier (2006), 'Political Foundations of the Resource Curse', *Journal of Development Economics*, **79** (2), 447–68.

Ross, M. (2001), 'Does Oil Hinder Democracy?', *World Politics*, **53** (3), 325–61.

Sachs, J. (2005), *The End of Poverty: How We Can Make it Happen in Our Lifetime*, London: Penguin.

Sachs, J. and Warner, A. (1999), 'The Big Push, Natural Resource Booms and Growth', *Journal of Development Economics*, **59** (1), 43–76.

Thiele, R., P. Nunnenkamp and A. Dreher (2007), 'Do Donors Target Aid in Line with the Millennium Development Goals? A Sector Perspective of Aid Allocation?', *Review of World Economics*, **143** (4), 596–630.

Tornell, A. and P. Lane (1999), 'The Voracity Effect', *American Economic Review*, **89** (1), 22–46.

van der Ploeg, R. (2010), 'Natural Resources: Curse or Blessing?', Munich: CESifo Working Paper No. 3125.

UNDP Bureau for Crisis Prevention and Recovery (2011), *The Economic Impact of Conflict*, New York: United Nations Development Programme.

UNESCO (2011), *The Hidden Crisis: Armed Conflict and Education*, Paris: UNESCO Press.

UN Millennium Project (2005), *Investing in Development: A Practical Plan to Achieve the Millennium Development Goals*, New York: UN Millennium Project.

World Bank (2011), *World Development Report*, New York: Oxford University Press.

WHO (2009), *Number of Disasters Reported 1900–2009*, Geneva, World Health Organization Collaborating Centre for Research on the Epidemiology of Disasters, Emergency Events Database.

2. Security and Development: Some Reflections

Michael Spence

This chapter provides a fairly high-speed tour of sustained, inclusive, rapid growth, as it has been developed in the work of the Growth Commission, followed by some remarks on the question of security. Statements made in the first part of this chapter either have implications on security or are related in some way to some aspect of security as it has been defined and set out in the materials for the conference. This chapter focuses on ingredients – not policies – of the sustained high-growth dynamics that we know about, on the role of government and the critical policy and investment activities that seem to support this kind of growth, followed by a brief discussion of security.

The origin of the Growth Commission has several sources, one of which is a decision by Gobind Nankani, then leader and President of the Global Development Network, to organize a review of the growth experience of the 1990s. Its results came out in three books that seek to understand from several perspectives what we learned, what worked, and what did not work and so on. As was the case with many others, this work influenced me a great deal.

The Growth Commission is a forward-looking version of that review – a prescriptive, descriptive, policy-oriented version. We came to realize that what we thought were necessary and sufficient conditions for growth, conditions that probably are close to necessary and sufficient in advanced market economies, did not seem to be sufficient in developing countries, albeit perhaps still necessary – though this is not entirely certain.

There was an enormous accumulation of relevant experiences, ranging from very high growth to stalled growth to failure to jump-start growth, and those were fed into and actually influenced the composition of the Commission. We also felt that the instrumental role of growth and the importance that growth plays in making permanent changes in people's lives had somehow been overlooked. In the Growth Commission we understand completely that growth is not the ultimate objective; rather, growth enables a set of things that are much more fundamentally important to people, such as security, employment opportunities and the ability to be creative, for example.

Sustained high growth takes a very long time to yield the changes developing countries seek. Growth from poor to advanced country status takes a long time, and it takes an extremely long time without high growth rates. It is sometimes hard to think about growth in these terms, but it is important to understand that what the Commission is interested in are journeys that last five or six decades, not episodes that last three or four years.

The mandate of the Commission, mostly self-imposed, is to focus on sustained high, inclusive growth and on the policies, investments and the political underpinnings – leadership and other things – that support it. The goal is to expand the already expanding array of countries that are entering growth accelerations with a pattern of drivers and activities that are likely to make them sustained over time – and 'sustained' in this context means decades.

The primary target audience is the leaders, the policymakers who are trying to develop strategies and policies for growth. This is difficult. Robert M. Solow put it best in an article marking the 50th anniversary of the Solow growth model:

> Some of the literature gives the impression that it is after all pretty easy to increase the long-run growth rate. Just reduce a tax on capital here or eliminate an inefficient regulation there, and the reward is fabulous, a higher growth rate forever, which is surely more valuable than any lingering bleeding-heart reservations about the policy itself. But in real life it is very hard to move the permanent growth rate; and when it happens, as perhaps in the USA in the later 1990s, the source can be a bit mysterious even after the fact. (Solow 2007, 5–6)

This is a fundamental fact. It is much harder, particularly in the developing country context, to produce a permanent or semi-permanent upshift in the rate of growth and keep it going for a long period of time, and even after this happens, it is a bit mysterious as to why it occurred.

One way the Commission tried to understand this was by looking at the cases of sustained high growth where 'high' is defined as 7 per cent on average and 'sustained' is 25 years. That puts them in the upper tail of the distribution, and there are 13 countries that have done that. They are all in the post-war period because, before that, there was not a global economy of sufficiently well-developed, integrated characteristics to sustain this kind of growth. They are surprisingly similar to each other, notwithstanding the differences.

Vietnam and India look very much like they are entering this phase and will be in this category, and there may be many others if the growth accelerations that have occurred in many places, countries and continents actually turn into sustained accelerations; but there is a question about whether they are sustainable.

The common ingredients in these countries are things that tend to happen in the course of growth – without exception. It is important to emphasize that these ingredients are not policies; ingredients, as Solow will point out, can be included in a recipe, but the outcome of the dish depends on the cook.

One of the characteristics – probably the single most important – is that these are growth dynamics that are fueled in part by leveraging the assets in the global economy. The two most important assets are knowledge and demand. A poor, small economy's demand is not big enough and has the wrong composition to drive the kind of growth that we are talking about here.

They all rely on markets, incentives and decentralization, although a developing country is developing in part by building its domestic market, increasing the depth and maturity of its market institutions. This is not a process by which we have a market economy overnight.

All of these economies are characterized by extremely high levels of – by average standards – public and private sector investment. We should pay attention to the public sector investment. Surprisingly, data on public sector investment and its components, like infrastructure, are not very good. Paul Romer thinks this is so because these data are collected for stabilization purposes and do not really focus on long-term investment characteristics and growth.

They are all economies that experience rapid diversification, almost always toward the export sector in part – not exclusively, but in part – and a huge amount of incremental productive employment of formerly underemployed people in traditional sectors. This is a version of the W. Arthur Lewis model running at very high speed.

They all involve structural transformation of the economy, which happens very fast and in a way that is quite threatening to people. A snapshot of a developing economy growing at these speeds may look like something that is just proceeding at a high rate and going up and up, but inside the actual structure of the economy is changing very, very quickly.

They all have resource mobility, especially labor. Labor is changing its location in terms of sector and industry and is changing its location geographically, usually in the process of heading for cities. Hence, rapid urbanization, for all of its chaotic characteristics, has to be enabled and turns out to be an important part of this.

They all have a stable and functional investment environment, which means that the macroeconomic stability and the institutions that support transactions, exchange, contracts and so on may differ from country to country, but they

Figure 2.1a   Growth Rates in China

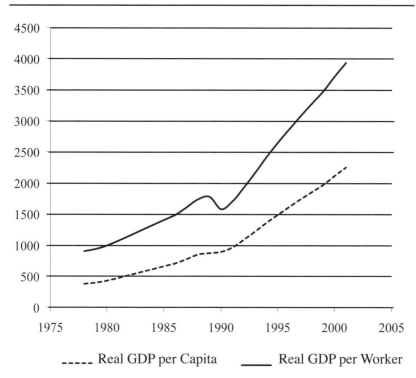

have to be in place. This is sometimes described as having the basic elements of the rule of law in place.

They all rely in the early stages and at repeated points along the way on very effective political leadership. If there is one thing learned in the past few years from interacting with my much more experienced colleagues, it is that leadership and the political economy dimensions of growth are absolutely essential. It is not primarily or exclusively an economic subject. It is a multi-decade process. And the governments that seem to succeed are ones that understand that they have an incomplete understanding of their evolving developing economy. They do not act like they have a perfect model of it but instead engage in activities that you would expect in the face of uncertainty – a pragmatic approach characterized by experimentation.

Further, the countries that grow seem to have as the main objective of policy, at least at the national level, growth – not just trying to get things right. They were really persistent about going after this.

Figure 2.1b   Poverty in Percentages

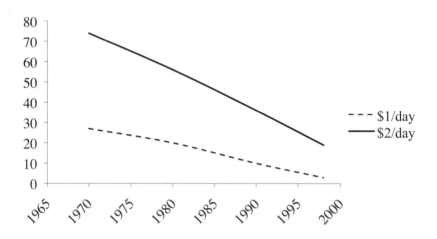

Finally, these are all governments or governance structures that range from democracy to all kinds of things on the other side of the spectrum, but somehow they ended up with a government that prioritizes the interest of all the people as opposed to only a subgroup of the people. To put that the other way around, if one has a government that is not trying to do that, then it will fail on the inclusive front, it will probably fail on the high-speed employment generation process and do something else, and that will be almost fatal with respect to growth.

As an example, look at the Chinese experience. On one hand, post-1978 growth rates have averaged 9 per cent per year (Figure 2.1a). This is remarkable for an entity this size. And on the other hand is a version of the poverty reduction numbers measured absolutely in one and two dollars a day (Figure 2.1b).

In another example, India is chugging along, doing reasonably well and accelerating. India is just about going to track China; it is about 13 years back on the China line, and it will run on the same path unless something interrupts it (Figure 2.2).

Figure 2.3 shows the savings and investment rates of China and India. Twenty-five per cent is a relatively high level, and India's rate is even higher since 2004. At that level, one should expect about 10 per cent as public sector investment, including education. That is not the case in India, and those who spend time there know perfectly well that on a short list of high-priority

Figure 2.2   GDP Per Capita: China and India (constant 2000 US$)

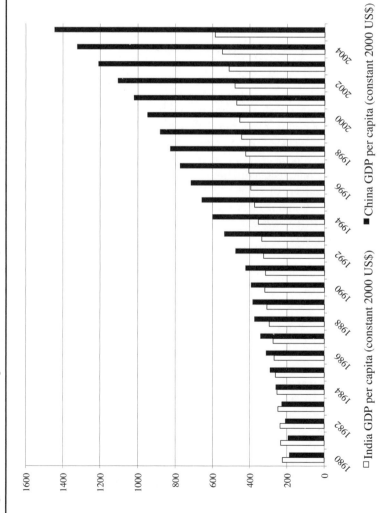

challenges, infrastructure is important. China is almost unbelievable in terms
of the height of these numbers, particularly in the early stages. The government
has a zero or negative discount rate and invests a lot. But at the start, China was
a very poor country, and investing 35 per cent of the GDP per capita at those
income levels is a remarkable achievement (Figure 2.3).

In leveraging the global economy, it is difficult to precisely quantify the
advantages created by knowledge flow. However, with trade it is important
that increased exposure should be done carefully, so that too many domestic
industries are not blown away too quickly. Observing the China pattern,
exports plus imports now run up to the 70 per cent range of GDP, which is
unusual in an economy of that size. In India the exposure is at lower levels,
but accelerating rapidly, so one should expect it will soon be in the 60 per cent
range.

However, there is a very pronounced tendency – and this needs to be
managed, even if everybody is benefiting – for the income inequality to rise, in
part because everyone cannot move at the same time into the modern economy.
In the China case, even at the bottom 5 per cent over a 10-year period, they had
growth in incomes on the order of 60 to 70 per cent higher, which is positive,
but at the upper end, of course, it is three or three-and-a-half times. So the
rising income inequality in the country is a pressing problem along with the
lack of delivery of services at the lower end, particularly in the rural areas. This
is a fairly common pattern, and it needs to be anticipated and managed both in
terms of ex-ante equality of opportunity and ex-post results in terms of income
and basic services.

Shifting to the role of government, this is an area that needs to be discussed
in a forthright way. There are differences of opinion about this. The instinct
behind the 'stabilize, liberalize and privatize' approach is essentially sound.
An early stage of economic development and reform very often has to do with
removing the government as a barrier to economic activity in a whole variety
of ways.

But it is more complicated than that because of model uncertainty, so
probably the answer to governments that do not do all of these things very well
is not to make them as small as possible but to make them as good as possible
and to some extent a bit activist.

The other thing that needs to be said about the role of government is that
it evolves over time. The role of the government in the early stages as market
institutions are being developed is very different than the role of government
in an economy that is approaching advanced, mature status. Handling that
evolution and not doing the wrong thing for too long is very hard.

Lastly, in order to start this process – because it is hard, it is uncertain and it
requires sacrifices – the leadership needs to be there. There has to be a vision

Figure 2.3   Savings and Investment in India and China

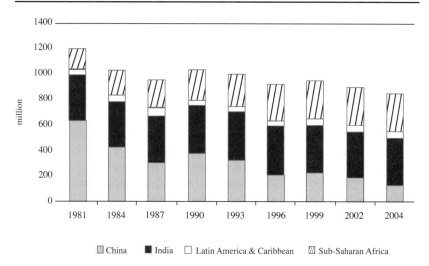

that people can understand and get behind. It does not have to be complete in the sense of this is a 50-year road map, but it has to be compelling. We do not know as much as we need to know about that, but it is very hard to find a case where this was not centrally important at the start and then along the way.

South Korea, for example, was a democracy in name, not practice, during the first 20 or 25 years of its high-speed growth, and the country started out really poor as well. But somewhere in the course of that, the economy created a middle class, and the middle class wanted a voice, and there were basically, as far as analysts who were good at this kind of thing believed, two options – either the people would take politics to the streets or leaders could reform the political system so these people had a voice. Leaders ended up changing the system, and it worked pretty well.

POLICY CHALLENGES

The policy challenges that we have come to believe are very important are a focus on leadership, communication and getting people on board. We think that equity and related issues are a terribly important and integral part of a growth strategy and must be part of the overall plan if it is going to work.

The environment and public sector are also very important. We have learned, not from academia but from experience, that the environment is important and that the 'grow first and then deal with the environment' strategy is a very expensive and bad way to go. It is costly to undo the effect of poor energy policies, poor air quality policies and poor water quality policies, to name a few. The wrong housing gets built. Political situations develop where things are subsidized and become hard to undo. The poster person or entity for this kind of approach is China, which has an enormously challenging problem in undoing such damage.

The other reason for paying attention to environmental issues is that we are entering an era in which we have to pay attention to global warming. The policies that are effective with respect to the environment also make it easier to make the transition to dealing with climate change.

In the area of health, there are many issues – as in security – that people really care about. Health is another item on the list of things that leaders ought to pay attention to when they are worried about growth, but not meant as an instrument. Rather, it is actually part of the objective function.

The other discovery is that in many of these areas, and health is a good example, if it is broken down into parts – control of disease, control of epidemics and other things – it has very different impacts, quantitatively and in terms of channels, on growth. In the deliberations of the Growth Commission, we tried to find the ones that really matter with respect to growth; based on expert testimony and lots of research, it appears that a failure in the area of early childhood nutrition – deprivation of stimulation – has a huge, almost permanent, negative effect on the ability to acquire cognitive and non-cognitive skills. It therefore adversely affects the productivity of the entire subsequent education system that children enter.

In addition to – not in lieu of – it being wrong and unfair, the issue of early childhood nutrition is one, if we had to pick one and put it on a high-priority list of things that need to be seriously addressed, would be at the top of the list. We are entering a world in which the importance of human capital for growth and improvement is higher and higher, and thus this issue in particular should be given careful consideration.

One issue that is under-attended to is competition. People say we will limit competition because of economies of scale and the need to be efficient. This is not true. It turns out that the dynamics of efficiency associated with entry, exit and competition quantitatively overwhelm the static effects. This is something that has been learned over the last few decades.

In the course of the work of the Commission, we talked about industrial policies and export promotion and exchange rates. These are highly controversial and tricky policy areas to enter into. There are issues of capture, issues of competence, issues of doing something for too long and the list goes on. We try to talk about them in a balanced way so that decision makers can think about it and make choices that are sensible.

There are a few really important areas in which governments enable or do not enable the growth dynamics. One is in the way they deal with labor markets. This is a very hard area because there is a legitimate interest in intervening in labor markets to protect labor from adverse things that occur in markets, including concentrated buying power wherever it occurs. But that intervention can easily become a tripwire that stops the flow of people across these boundaries into the more modern sector, a trend seen in many countries.

Urbanization is never a pretty process – it was not in the Industrial Revolution in England, and it is not now – but it is important, and we try to talk a little bit about what policies support this aspect of resource mobility.

Technology and technology transfer is arguably one of the most important issues to consider in growth. It is also one of the things that we have the least to say about. I do not mean nothing, but I mean if we are imagining ourselves talking to a senior policy person in a developing country, and they say, 'Okay, I get it; there are a bunch of processes by which knowledge comes into this economy and gets embedded in people and institutions. Tell us what you know about the policy levers that accelerate and make that process more effective and efficient', we do not have good answers to that request, and it is centrally important.

We also try to deal with small states and resource-rich countries that have special problems turning that resource wealth into something that produces a pattern of sustainable growth. The African countries have a whole variety of problems, including being landlocked, being more than normally exposed to climate change issues and having to deal with tribal and ethnic diversity. These are not completely mediated properly by the governments.

Finally, we try to talk about the very different character of the transition from middle income to high income. This is not going to be the same in the future as it was in the past. There are a number of reasons for this. The global economy is big enough and unregulated enough and risky enough to generate adverse reactions. The best report on the topic is the Pew Research Center's comprehensive October 2007 report on 'Global Attitudes', which suggests that there is really a major backing off from the previous five-year report. The challenge is well-recognized and important. It has to do with income equality, benefits, who benefits, who loses, and it is one that runs across advanced and developing economics.

Global warming also is clearly on the horizon. There is a potential that the need for energy and other resources is going to change our world from the current blissful, non-zero sum game mode back toward the zero sum case; this is a real risk.

Demographics, aging and migration are a huge set of issues. There are a large number of developing countries with sufficiently large numbers of young people entering the labor force that no imaginable growth rate is high enough to absorb. We need to start thinking collectively, and with more effort, about migration policies. Some good proposals already exist, such as migration of a variety of kinds, including migration for work. In economic terms, this is simply taking surplus labor areas and allowing those people, on a basis that should be supervised so it is not exploitative, to go to locations with an excess demand for labor.

In terms of security, the range of issues is breathtaking, from getting to school safely for young girls to crime to conflict and disastrous climate consequences.

We will talk about security in relationship to growth, but to be clear: if people were voting with their wallets or in any other way about security, they would vote for security and give up on the growth. Security is centrally important in the objective function. The linkages between growth and security are important and intersect in almost all the other areas already mentioned. And the focus deserves to be on causes and prevention and response mechanisms on a multinational basis.

Security and growth interact and, like human development and fulfillment, security is one of the most important inputs as well as outputs of growth. On the output side, growth helps with different kinds of security problems.

First of all, wealthier countries have more response mechanisms to deal with economic shocks. Second – and this is much talked about – not only is the effect of global warming and failure to mitigate the effects larger in poorer countries because of the proximity to the tropics, as currently assessed by experts, but the capacity for adaptation is much lower because of the limited resources in developing countries. In an 18 December 2007 lecture at the World Bank, Thomas Schelling basically said the best thing you can do for global warming on the adaptation front is to have economic growth – lots of economic growth. That sounds counter-intuitive for those of us who are worried about all the carbon emissions that are going to come from these rapidly growing countries, but there is an element of truth in that, and I think it is an important point.

Growth by definition takes us away from the zero-sum world and toward the world in which people think that lots of other people can benefit. To the extent that security problems, whether they are conflict or crime or other things, are in part induced by an incentive structure associated with a zero sum, no-growth environment, growth is terribly important.

Growth also provides insulation against shocks and outside influences. Growing countries, once they get to a certain size, start to have a larger voice and control over the multinational environment in which they operate. Safety

Figure 2.4   Number of People Living below US$1 Per Day

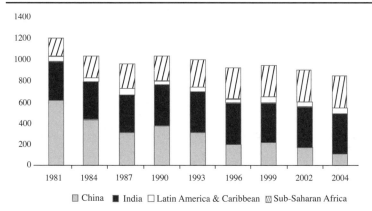

☐ China ■ India ☐ Latin America & Caribbean ▨ Sub-Saharan Africa

nets become more affordable, and growth will help the economic underpinnings of security-related problems, such as youth unemployment. There is more research to do on that, but if a group of highly motivated young people come out of school and find there is absolutely no opportunity in the country, just as a pragmatic matter, that situation is not one to be sustained.

The vulnerable in terms of economic security are surely the poor. There are very large numbers of poor people in China and India still, although they probably are rapidly developing a capacity to provide some sort of protection if they use their policy instruments wisely (Figure 2.4).

Security problems have significant effects on growth so, if the focus is on growth, then one should be concerned about security. Most of the adverse effects that one can detect are effects that have to do with either using up resources because they have to be used up or adverse effects on investment and risk incentives, among others.

As an example, everybody was hoping that the former UN Secretary-General Kofi Annan would successfully reduce violence in Kenya because there were many people at risk and many people being killed. In addition, the violence had the potential to produce a setback in the economic position of a rather important country in Africa in terms of both domestic and foreign investment. This type of setback happened in Indonesia as a result of the turbulence that followed the currency crisis in the late 1990s, and it still has not fully made it back in terms of becoming a place where a wide variety of foreign investors are really comfortable and happy. This is not irreversible, but it is a setback. In a high-growth environment or even in a moderate one, a setback once every decade will knock the growth numbers down to the point where there are serious long-term consequences.

Increasing the risks or knocking down the returns of investment deserves to be highlighted and paid attention to as part of it, even if it is not the main event in human terms.

The reductions in longevity associated with both health and conflict are sufficiently large. There is empirical work that shows that it reduces investment in human capital and – that is, they are not just correlated, but that appears to be the channel – it also reduces investment and other things.

Finally, we might want to talk a little more than we have about energy security and global warming. It is pretty clear that there is a kind of scramble. First of all, the underlying situation is that demand has risen fast, but supply has not responded accordingly. Maybe it was unable to. The elasticities of supply and demand have not kicked in, so we are not quite sure what the long-run effect is, but on the downside, we are here with high prices and the potential to have energy sources cut off, and this has produced a scramble for energy security that has a prisoner's dilemma-like structure. We would all be far better off, with one notable exception, if we agreed to have open energy markets and use the price system and adapt to it, but that is not what is going on right now. There are real risks associated with this that people talk about, and it is not yet centrally on the multinational policy agenda yet.

The qualifying factor is that developing countries that are not resource-rich are experiencing rising food, commodity and energy prices and feeling quite a lot of pain from that. There is a real conflict between what is good for the system in the long run and the need to protect people from the adverse effects of this in the short run. This issue presents a security problem on the economic/natural resources front.

In thinking about developing a sensible global agenda to deal with mitigation issues, there are several roadblocks. Primarily, it is difficult to integrate the developing world into this in a way that produces an efficient pattern globally and in a way that is fair. We have not made much progress on that front partly because of an inability to distinguish between efficiency in where the mitigation occurs and who pays for it, which are two different dimensions. If these two dimensions are merged, then we have a problem of being efficient in terms of mitigation and determining what would be considered fair is a problem without a solution. Transfers must be a part of the solution.

The good news is that carbon emissions and per capita incomes are very closely related. If the population grew uninterrupted by another 55 per cent, in certain countries and in the world, we would have a disaster. But it turns out that, with the notable exception of Canada and the United States, a country can grow after a certain threshold and have pretty high incomes without noticeably increasing its carbon emissions. Therefore, if we can get everybody at that

Figure 2.5   Carbon Emissions and GDP Per Capita (1960)

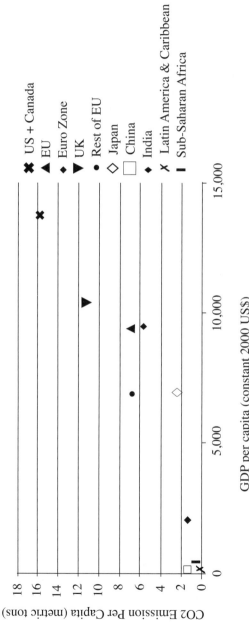

threshold, but through technology lower the cost, then the countries at the bottom end can actually grow (Figure 2.5).

Finally, this global governance problem and the current credit crisis, which is an instance of the former, is real. The current situation in the global financial markets is extremely risky. It is not just a possible U.S. recession; it is the credit lock-up and the inability to get past the transparency fog that surrounds it that is producing this downward spiral. This has two implications. First, we need to be more effective in inventing ways to preside over this on a multinational basis. Second, developing countries are particularly vulnerable because of the absence of things to fall back on. These countries, with a few exceptions, need to build into their strategies and policies elements of insurance and protection. The reserve run-up for the countries that have been able to do it is precisely that kind of behavior.

REFERENCES

Pew Research Center (4 October 2007), World Publics Welcome Global Trade – But Not Immigration: 47-Nation Pew Global Attitudes Survey.

Schelling, Thomas (2007), 'What Development Economists Need to Know about Climate Change', World Bank PREM Seminar Series, 18 December.

Solow, Robert M. (2007), 'The Last 40 Years in Growth Theory and the Next 10', *Oxford Review of Economic Policy*, **23** (1), 3–14.

3. Globalization and the Challenges of Inclusion and Climate Change

Graeme Wheeler

The world economy had hit a rocky patch, when the conference leading to this book convened in early 2008. Stock markets were volatile and economic risks were on the downside. But as we survey the global economic landscape from that perspective, we need to bear in mind the longer-term background and trends.

The fact is, we live in extraordinary times – times of unprecedented opportunity for many in the developing world. Powerful global forces are driving economic convergence, and global poverty is declining more rapidly than ever before.

THE POWER OF GLOBALIZATION

A global productivity shock has helped generate the strongest and most broadly based global growth for 40 years. Investment ratios and profit shares are at historic highs in many countries.

Hundreds of millions of workers in emerging market economies, their productivity enhanced by the global transfer of skill-enhancing technologies, are joining the global work force. Technology – and especially information technology – is transforming lives. Cellular technology has become a major development tool, and information technology (IT) inputs in services and manufacturing rise exponentially as the cost of storing, processing and transmitting information approaches zero. Recent evidence suggests that the pace of technology transfer to developing countries is accelerating, especially for newer technologies.

Fueling these developments are record volumes of private net cross border capital flows and private remittances. Having more than doubled over the past three years, these combined annual flows total around US$1 trillion – about 10 times annual official development assistance.

Trade also is a powerful catalyst. Trade flows have expanded at twice the rate of industrial production, and developing economies' share of world exports of manufactured goods doubled to 25 per cent in just 15 years. And major shifts in wealth to commodity producers in developing countries are underway. Developing countries now supply 60 per cent of global crude oil production, and more than two-thirds of lead, zinc and copper production. Their overall terms of trade have improved by 14 per cent since 2004.

Some important developing countries are also benefiting from a 'demographic window' – rapid labor force growth and declining dependency ratios. Labor has become more mobile, with around 3 per cent of the world's population living outside their country of birth, although this has often been a mixed blessing for small, poor, developing countries.

Governments have played a valuable role by improving the quality of their economic policy and the overall business climate. Government balance sheets have strengthened with improved fiscal settings, debt forgiveness, greater access to global capital markets and the build-up in foreign currency reserves. Developing country foreign exchange reserves now total US$4.6 trillion – an increase of 90 per cent in special drawing rights (SDR) terms over the past three years. And it is now easier to do business in some Eastern European and former Soviet bloc countries than in many Western European economies. The result – a boom in new business formation.

That said, the process of catch-up and convergence remains highly differentiated. It can also be a slow process. In 2007, Brazil's per capita income grew by 3.5 per cent – its fastest in 12 years. Assuming U.S. per capita income continues to grow at its secular trend, it would take 190 years for Brazil to catch up with the United States. On the other hand, if China maintains high rates of per capita income growth, it could catch up in around 40–50 years, even though its per capita income is 40 per cent of Brazil's.

WILL SLOWING OECD ECONOMIC GROWTH DERAIL DEVELOPING ECONOMIES?

Will these development prospects be derailed by slowing economic growth in OECD countries, high food and energy prices, and persistent global payments imbalances?

Clearly, there are risks. Economic activity in the industrial world is slowing as credit conditions tighten and households rebuild savings and strengthen their balance sheets. The risk of a marked U.S. slowdown has increased and, if realized, this would be transmitted to the rest of the world through the usual trade and financial linkages, including changes in investor risk appetites.

Some developing countries are already badly affected. The terms of trade losses due to commodity price changes over the past four years exceed 10 per cent of GDP in five African countries.

However, while supply and demand imbalances suggest that oil and other commodity prices might remain high for several years, the impact on global output and inflation is likely to be significantly different from the early 1970s and 1980s.

Industrial economies are now much more resilient. Almost all countries have significantly reduced the energy intensity of their output. OECD central banks have had more than two decades' experience in building credibility and maintaining low inflation, and fiscal and debt management policies have improved in most economies.

Developing countries are also more resilient, though I would not agree with the more extreme version of the 'decoupling' theory. There is now a rising middle class in many developing countries that is able to generate demand and purchasing power to fuel domestic growth. The newly unveiled Tata Nano automobile shows how business is beginning to respond to this trend, which is essential for the longer-run 'rebalancing' of the global economy.

While global interdependence has increased, so too have intra-regional trade and investment flows. East Asia, for example, is less vulnerable to a U.S. economic slowdown given regional trading patterns, high savings ratios, diversified investment strategies, and the possibility of rebalancing demand.

EMERGING MARKETS EXPAND THEIR INFLUENCE

Between 2004 and 2007, developing countries grew at over 7 per cent and OECD countries at around 2.5 per cent. The next two decades will continue to see major shifts in global economic influence.

East and South Asia, with their favorable demographics, high savings and investment ratios, economies of agglomeration and rapidly growing middle classes will be a critical growth pole of the global economy.

Although recent work suggests that China and India may be 40 per cent smaller on a purchasing power parity basis than previously thought, this represents only five years' output growth at current rates. Capital flows from this region will assume even greater importance. At the official level, surplus savings from China, in particular, have helped finance savings and investment imbalances in key industrialized countries. And recently, sovereign wealth funds and government-owned banks in Asia and the Middle East have injected US$50 billion of capital to help shore up Western banks.

As the rapidly growing Asian middle class and large institutional savers seek to diversify their portfolios and take on additional foreign currency exposure, they will become important investors in corporate equities in industrialized countries, further strengthening their global links.

Two decades from now, Eastern Europe, Asia and Latin America will have made huge inroads into alleviating poverty, reflecting the increasing integration of these regions into the global economy and stronger domestic institutions.

These developments are all part of a longer-term process that will likely see China, India, Russia and Brazil become key members of an expanded G-7 by the middle of the century. Increasingly, we will examine their policy settings and corporate performance in assessing global economic conditions and rely on them as important providers of aid assistance.

TWO KEY CHALLENGES

The powerful forces of demographics and the globalization of trade, investment, technology and labor will drive these fundamental transitions, even through shorter-run traumas in the global economy. But two major long-run threats hang over these dynamic influences. First, are the political and economic pressures associated with exclusion and growing inequality in many countries, along with the sheer magnitude of global poverty. The second challenge will be climate change.

Left Behind

The catalyst of globalization will only be sustainable if it can create opportunity and benefits for all. This challenge extends well beyond the Millennium Development Goals. There are signs that income distribution and inequality in most developing countries have been increasing, a change in pattern from previous decades. Over the past decade, three times as many countries witnessed widening, rather than diminishing, income inequality and in several instances, these deteriorations were large.

Most developing countries have enjoyed strong growth in recent years – but several have not. Per capita income in low-income countries grew by 5 per cent on average in the five years to 2006. However, in the bottom nine countries, it averaged –2 per cent per annum.

In development speak, the poorest on the planet – those consuming less than US$1 per day in purchasing power parity (PPP) terms – are referred to as the bottom billion. Although with the recalculation of poverty numbers that will follow the recent international review of per capita GDP calculated on a PPP basis, this group will probably number well in excess of a billion.

For this group, poverty is so severe that life is a struggle for survival. They are politically and socially disenfranchised, comprise predominantly women and young children and are discriminated by ethnic, sectarian, religious and political divisions.

They often live in fragile states wracked by years of repetitive civil conflict, in landlocked countries with major infrastructure problems, and in countries with massive governance challenges and endemic corruption – often exacerbated by windfall revenues from natural resource endowments. Even though urbanization is accelerating, the vast majority (70 per cent) of the poor continue to live in rural regions. Their countries often have low levels of investment and experience an exodus of skilled workers. One-fifth of African-born doctors, for example, work outside Africa, and 80 per cent of skilled Haitians live overseas.

For the poorest, cycles of poverty are self-reinforcing. They have fewer opportunities to escape poverty and, with low-quality or no public services, lag others in health care and education. They suffer higher rates of crime and violence, and they are the greatest victims of corruption. Average life expectancy for the group is 50 years and one in seven children die before the age of five. In El Salvador, for example, a child born to a well-educated mother has a 2.5 per cent chance of dying before her first birthday. This probability climbs to 10 per cent if the mother has no formal schooling.

Africa currently has the highest proportion of extremely poor, and its share is increasing, partly because of the number of fragile and conflict-affected states. Less than 25 per cent of Africans have access to electricity, the region lags every other zone in terms of the Millennium Development Goals, and the challenges of governance, institution-building, and establishing functioning markets are more acute than in other regions.

It is clear that powerful global forces are bypassing a large proportion of the global population. Globalization does not work for this group, which is becoming increasingly disconnected from global society. And even with growth, the pressures will increase. Over the next 25 years, the world's population will increase by around 2 billion people – 95 per cent of whom will be in the developing world.

Compare the age pyramids for Sub-Saharan Africa and the Middle East with that of high-income countries. Fifty-four per cent of the population of Sub-Saharan Africa is under 20 years of age, compared to 24 per cent in high-income countries. Some 40 per cent of the population of the Arab world is aged under 15.

A world where a large proportion of the population remains trapped in extreme poverty and unable to share the benefits and opportunities of globalization carries unacceptable costs in terms of human suffering, economic losses, political tensions, and such circumstances have important potential implications for security within countries and across borders.

Climate Change

Climate change is the second major threat to long-term prosperity. The need to moderate and manage climate change is central to every aspect of economic growth, development and poverty reduction, and its policy dimensions embrace issues of equity, ethics and security.

The challenges are enormous. Drought, for example, now affects twice the area of the earth's surface than it did 30 years ago. Modeling the distribution of world climate risks (e.g., drought, floods, storms, rising sea levels) shows overwhelmingly that low-income countries are the most vulnerable to the impact of climate change, and the extreme poor are the most seriously affected. This was borne out during the 1990s, when 2 billion people in developing countries were significantly affected by climate-related disasters, compared to less than 25 million in developed countries. Climate change will be felt most acutely in Africa, where 95 per cent of farming is rainfall dependent, and also in low-lying areas like Bangladesh, the Netherlands and small island states.

Access to safe drinking water and irrigation is a related and huge development challenge, and an increasing source of tension between countries. Chronic water stress affects nearly 800 million people worldwide. In two decades' time, 3 billion people – or around 37 per cent of global population – are projected to be living in countries below the current water stress threshold.

COLLECTIVE SOLUTIONS ARE NEEDED

Addressing the challenges of inclusive and sustainable economic growth and global warming will require an unprecedented degree of international cooperation and goodwill.

Country ownership of growth and poverty-reduction strategies, and their taking responsibility for building a sound governance environment, are critical. Growth and employment creation are the main avenues of poverty alleviation, and these can only be sustained in the longer term through private sector investment and integration into the global system.

Some of the investment requirements are enormous, like the US$60 billion required over the next 15 years to help develop Mumbai. But often, real incomes and welfare can be improved by providing basic infrastructure and access to seeds, livestock and fertilizers for farmers or through community-based development involving women's self-help groups, and the availability of micro-credit.

Initiatives that provide well-targeted development assistance and debt relief can be enormously valuable. But they can easily be undermined by other interventions. OECD agricultural subsidies, for example, total around US$350 billion annually and are as large as the entire agricultural exports of developing countries.

International cooperation on climate change will be essential. Today's greenhouse gas problems are mainly generated by developed countries, whose energy use per capita is about 5 times that of developing countries. But over the next two decades, predictions suggest that it will be the developing countries that are responsible for around 70 per cent of the predicted increase in greenhouse gas emissions. These countries recognize that the levels of greenhouse gas emissions that helped generate wealth in industrial countries cannot be sustained, but they also have urgent development needs.

Collective action can generate powerful benefits. Agreements are more easily negotiated when all parties face a common threat or can all benefit from collective action, such as responding to the threat of avian flu, strengthening the international financial architecture, and investing in regional transport corridors and river basin developments.

Yet, we also see how difficult reforms and collective actions can be when domestic politics assume overwhelming importance. Despite a common location, history, customs, food and culture, South Asia remains the least integrated region in the world. Countries that have opened up trade with the rest of the world still remain closed to each other.

ROLE OF THE WORLD BANK GROUP

In the face of these powerful forces and enormous challenges, the World Bank Group has a modest financing role. It currently commits around US$35 billion annually in loans, grants, equity investments and financial guarantees to governments and businesses.

Reflecting the effects of globalization, important changes in the composition of the World Bank's borrowers are occurring. Within a decade, the Bank's current 21 investment-grade borrowers are unlikely to have a significant borrowing relationship with the Bank. Today's better-performing IDA countries will be the IBRD borrowers of the future.

But the Bank Group is much more than a financial intermediary. It has important strategic assets in terms of convening power, development databases and expertise, and it draws upon them to deliver strategic advice, transfer knowledge, induce learning and build capacity.

Building on these assets, the Group is addressing the challenges I have discussed. Increasingly, it is focusing its efforts around six strategic areas where inclusion, equity and climate change are prominent. These are the needs of fragile and conflict-affected states, the poorest countries, middle-income countries and countries from the Arab world. Cross-cutting themes will expand the Group's engagement on regional and global public goods and in knowledge, learning and capacity building.

The World Bank Group will scale up successful development initiatives and build stronger partnerships with countries and institutions. It will place more emphasis on developing innovative products and programs, building more effective markets and helping to develop a consensus for action on key global issues. In the area of climate change, for example, we worked with Turkey on CAT (catastrophe) bonds and plans to expand this effort to other countries. The Group has set up carbon markets and has recently launched a Carbon Forestry Partnership Facility to combat deforestation.

Using our convening power, we have helped Caribbean countries to pool their resources and establish a Catastrophic Risk Insurance Facility that has considerably reduced insurance costs and made its first pay-outs in 2007. We are actively working with donors to explore new trust fund facilities to help countries improve their technology and to better adapt to climate change. The 2010 World Development Report brings together evidence and good practice relating to the climate change agenda.

We are also expanding our work with poor countries and fragile states. Our convening power and scope for providing a country-based platform for development of the poorest has also been reflected in the recent record contributions to the IDA 15 – with the Group itself being among the largest donors, dedicating US$3.5 billion for 2008 to 2011. We play an important role in designing debt relief efforts and helping to clear arrears – most recently in Liberia. And through the Stolen Asset Recovery Initiative, we are helping governments build on the experience of others in retrieving stolen funds.

CONCLUSION

Even though we may have short-term concerns about the global economy, enormous opportunities will open up over the next two decades. Global forces can help sustain productivity growth, deliver hundreds of millions of people from poverty, and bring rising prosperity to a rapidly growing middle class.

But for this to happen, the catalysts of trade, investment, capital flows, technology and migration need to flourish, and the improvements in policy settings and business climate in developing countries need to be accelerated.

Collective action from the countries concerned and the international community is needed to ensure that the poorest are not trapped in inescapable poverty and become political, economic and social outcasts. Climate change is more than an immense development challenge. It is a major threat to all our economic and political systems and requires vision, courage and leadership to address it.

4. Prevention of Threats and Emergency Responses: Challenges to Policy Making

Paul Collier

All forms of political violence constitute 'threats' that potentially pose a challenge to policymakers. Fortunately, the threat that dominated the first half of the twentieth century, international warfare, is now very rare, despite the intense global focus on the wars in Afghanistan and Iraq after 2001. The key forms of political violence that concern developing countries are largely internal to each country. Even with this restriction, political violence takes seven main forms: rebellions, coups d'etat, pogroms, terrorism, riots and related forms of street protest, voter intimidation and assassinations. Each of these is distinct and needs separate analysis: abstracting from any differences in motivation or objective, they take very different organizational forms. It makes little sense to try to cover all of them in a single chapter, so I will focus on the one I regard as the most important. However, first I briefly sketch why each is distinctive.

A rebellion requires the formation of a private, non-government, army. Although a coup d'etat may have the same objective of capturing control of the state, it uses the government's own army. Pogroms use the government's instruments of violence, whether army or police, against its own defenseless citizens. Terrorism is a strategy of the weak: it requires only modest resources but does not have the potential to threaten the state. Riots depend upon mass mobilization and so depend upon the coordination and willingness of many participants. Voter intimidation requires only that politicians hire gangs of thugs and direct them at identifiable opposing voter groups. Finally, assassinations are technologically the least demanding, requiring only individual evil.

Of these, the most organizationally demanding and also by far the most damaging is rebellion, a form of political violence sometimes referred to as 'armed struggle'. Rebellion is the only form of political violence that can escalate into a civil war. Although civil war is a term used loosely in popular discourse, in social science it has been given a more precise meaning, defined in terms of the scale and structure of the violence and the characteristics of the participants. Specifically, violence must be of a sufficient scale, conventionally set as at least 1,000 battle-related deaths, and of a specific structure, with at least 5 per cent of these deaths are suffered by each side. The participants must include both a government and a non-government army drawn from the same state.

Rebellion is also the most costly form of political violence by a large margin. The average civil war lasts for around seven years, is highly destructive, inflicts high spillover costs on neighboring countries and leaves a legacy of persisting economic, social and political malfunction. Compared, for example, with coups d'etat, rebellions are vastly more costly – yet less effective – means of achieving regime change. Only around one of every five rebellions end up with a rebel victory. Thus, even if these successful rebellions were to lead to major improvements in governance, *ex ante*, the expected consequences of rebellion are likely to be highly adverse. Hence, there is a strong case for regarding the threat of rebellion as something that is to be discouraged. This chapter examines how a predisposition to rebel can be reduced. Differently expressed, how can civil war best be prevented?

To answer this question I first consider the evidence on the structural causes of civil war. By structural, I mean to abstract from the detailed sequence of political events that are inevitably the antecedents to any particular rebellion. Are there preconditions that make some countries systematically more prone to rebellion than others? Are any of amenable to policy changes? These potential channels then become the menu for 'deep prevention'. Around half of all civil wars are post-conflict relapses – the risk of conflict is far higher in the years following a civil war. One implication is that post-conflict situations constitute opportunities for 'emergency responses'. After surveying the structural causes, I explore a range of risk-reducing rapid post-conflict responses.

DEEP PREVENTION

Why are some places more prone to war than others? If we could answer this question, we might be able to do something about it: some of the factors that elevate the risk of civil war might be things that could readily be put right. My approach to answering this question is statistical. I take all the countries in the world over as long a period as possible and try to find what accounts for why civil wars break out in some places at some times but not in other places at other times; in other words, why some places are dangerous. The core of my approach is to try to predict whether a country descends into civil war on the basis of its characteristics prior to the conflict.

There are many pitfalls in this approach, but the key problem is the lack of data. Records of the civil wars themselves are not the problem. Astonishingly, a small team at the University of Michigan, the university that pioneered the quantitative analysis of political phenomena, has built a record of all the world's civil wars since 1815. There is even now a rival list built up in Oslo. But for most of this period there is very little other data to match against these outbreaks of civil war to try to explain them. For example, few or these countries even have reasonable economic data prior to 1960. Even if all the other data were available, prior to 1960 for many years virtually all of the contemporary low-income world was part of a colonial empire, which kept the lid on internal conflict. Even for the post-1960 period, the countries that are most likely to have a civil war also tend to be those most likely not to have adequate data on other characteristics: they are the dots and blanks in the global data tables produced by various international organizations.

My first serious attempt to apply this approach was with Anke Hoeffler in 'Greed and Grievance in Civil War' (2004). This paper used 53 civil wars and around 550 episodes during which a civil war could have occurred. This was far from ideal, and global developments since that paper have helped in three distinct ways. Here I report on our latest work (Collier, Hoeffler and Rohner, 2008). The most obvious way is that there has been more time in which civil wars have occurred or, more encouragingly, might have occurred but did not. Anke and I work in five-year episodes, and whereas our previous analysis only took the story up to the end of 1999, we are now able to take it up to the end of 2004. Indeed, this is a very strategic additional five years because that period was distinguished by a major effort by the international community to settle wars, allowing us to test whether it also reduced the incidence of outbreaks. But time has helped us in other ways as well. Scholars have quantified phenomena that were not previously measured and filled in the gaps in previous estimates, so that our dataset for the past is now much nearer to being complete. We have also got better at doing the work. For example, we have used Gary King's AMELIA program to fill in the blanks of missing data by randomly assigning a range of different numbers. We used this to check that our core results derived only from those numbers that were genuine. Another way in which we improved was better to control for endogeneity. For example, one of our core results was that low-income countries are more likely to have outbreaks of civil war. But is this more than just a correlation between low income and civil war: the two phenomena tending to occur together? Why do we think it is causal? We measure income at a time prior to the outbreak of the civil war: A causes B because A occurs before B. But is this enough? There are three ways in which it could be spurious. First, the civil war could be anticipated. If you know that you are living in a country at risk of violent conflict, then you are less likely to invest and so the country will tend to be poor as a result of the potential outbreak of war. Instead of A causing B, B is causing A! Second, the country might have some characteristic not included in our analysis that keeps causing civil wars. For example, Jonas Savimbi launched two civil wars in Angola. Since civil war destroys the economy, by the time of the second civil war Angola was poor: low-income preceded that second civil war even if it did not cause it. So, some off-stage C variable keeps causing B, and B causes A. Third, some phenomena are likely both to lower income and also to increase the risk of civil war. Both bad governance and difficult terrain could have both effects: bad governance might destroy the economy and give people cause to rebel, and difficult terrain might retard growth and provide rebels with safe havens. C causes both A and B. So, just because A occurs before B is not enough to conclude that it causes B. Gradually, economists have become better at guarding against these problems, introducing steps that leave fewer and fewer ambiguities. In our more recent work we have used more of these safeguards: indeed, having more observations makes it easier to do so because the safeguards generally need large samples. We got rid of the 'Savimbi' problem by restricting the analysis to the prediction of first-time civil wars. In part, we reduced the bad governance and difficult terrain problem by controlling for them, and by including as many characteristics as possible in the analysis. We addressed the problem of anticipated conflict by replacing the actual level of income with the level predicted by a few geographic characteristics that influence income but do not directly affect proneness to civil war. Even with these safeguards there is room for doubt, but at least we now have results based on comprehensive data – at its maximum over 1,600 episodes during which 84 civil wars broke out.

Although we are economists, we have tried to be agnostic as to what might 'explain' proneness to civil war, and so we have included a wide range of possible causes drawn from explanations across the social sciences. In addition to various characteristics of the economy, these include aspects of the country's history, its geography, its social composition and its polity. Let me be clear about what we do not include: we are not interested in the personalities and immediate political circumstances leading to the conflict. All wars have multiple 'causes': one reason why Saddam Hussein invaded Kuwait in 1990 was that the Kuwaiti leadership was sufficiently impolite to doubt whether the Iraqi leader had been born in wedlock. Such things matter for a proper understanding of any particular war but clutter up and detract from our understanding of civil war as a phenomenon. In trying to prevent war I suppose that it is useful to know that insulting psychopaths is not a good idea, but my approach has been to try to find structural characteristics that expose a country to risks and could, over time, be changed.

STRUCTURAL CAUSES OF CIVIL WAR

So what actually 'caused' these 84 civil wars? Table 4.1 reports our core results.

Poverty and Stagnation

First, the economy matters. Low-income countries are significantly more at risk even when we control for as many of the possible spurious interpretations as possible. Poor is dangerous. Nor is it just the level of income – it is also the rate of growth. Given the level of income, societies that are growing faster per capita are significantly less at risk of violent conflict than societies that are stagnant or in decline. In one sense this is hopeful; it tells us that economic development is peace-promoting. The truly difficult issue about the peace-enhancing effects of economic development is to sort out which of a number of possible routes might account for it. I suspect that there is no single magic route that could be isolated and promoted distinct from overall economic development. My guess is that there are multiple routes, such as jobs, education, hope, a sense of having something to lose and more effective state security services, all of which contribute something.

DEPENDENCE ON NATURAL RESOURCES

The level and growth of income are not the only aspects of the economy that matter for violence. Dependence on natural resources also increases risks. This proposition is supported by the grim evidence of resource wars: timber in Liberia, diamonds in Sierra Leone, a wonderland of minerals in the Congo. It is also now supported by statistical analysis of the where violence occurs within countries. For example, in Angola the violence tended to be concentrated in the diamond areas. It is also evident why natural resources might increase proneness to violence. They provide a ready source of finance for rebel groups, they provide a honey pot to fight over, and they enable the government to function without taxing the incomes of citizens, which gradually detaches it from what citizens want. Nevertheless, this is probably the most controversial of our results: some scholars have argued that it is purely an oil effect, and others insist that we have run foul of a particular variant of the endogeneity problem.

With our new data we duly tested whether oil was the real story: as far as we can see it isn't. We do find, however, that with sufficient natural resources a country becomes safe: Saudi Arabia and the other super-rich Gulf states are peaceful: they can afford good security systems and they can buy off opponents.

Table 4.1 Proneness to Civil War

	Risk of war
Economy	
ln GDP per Capita	−0.203
	(1.63)*
GDP per Capita Growth (t−1)	−0.145
	(3.70)***
Primary Commodity Exports (PCE)	7.133
	(1.84)*
PCE squared	−14.058
	(1.82)*
History	
Peace	−0.057
	(5.96)***
Former French African Colony	−1.020
	(1.74)*
Social Characteristics	
Social Fractionalization	2.323
	(2.88)***
Proportion of Young Men	17.423
	(1.67)*
ln Population	0.284
	(2.93)***
Geography	
Mountainous	0.015
	(1.94)*
Observations	1063
Pseudo R^2	0.28
Log Likelihood	−187.58

Note: Logit regressions, dependent variable: war start. Absolute value of z-statistics in parentheses. *significant at 10% level, ** significant at 5% and *** significant at 1% level. All regressions include an intercept (not reported).
Source: Collier, Hoeffler and Rohner (2008).

The endogeneity problem is trickier. It arises because we measure resource dependence by the ratio of primary commodities to income. That inevitably creates a problem because countries that, for whatever reason, have low income will tend to have a high ratio of primary commodity exports to income, simply because the denominator is small. Some scholars have recently tried to get around this problem by replacing our measure with a newly available measure: the value of natural resources in the ground. The World Bank released estimates, country-by-country, giving a snapshot for the year 2000. Unfortunately this runs into another form of the endogeneity problem. Any estimate of natural resource reserves depends upon what resource extraction companies have found through prospecting. Prospecting is costly, so 'proven reserves' is an economic concept as much as a geological one. It is only worth doing in places where the company's rights of extraction are secure. Between 1960 and 2000 prospecting tended to avoid societies that were at civil war as well as places where there was a serious risk of war. Think what this implies. The places with few proven natural resource reserves in 2000 will tend to be those with the worst prior history of civil war. The scholars who followed this approach duly announced with a confident fanfare that possessing large endowments of natural resources actually makes a society safer.

COLONIAL EXPERIENCE

So much for the economy, let's turn to history. Analysts tend to first look toward a country's colonial history to explain a civil war. However, neither the length of time that has elapsed since independence, nor the particular former colonial power, seems to matter. I do not want to push this too far: it is quite evident that Portuguese decolonization was disastrous: Angola, Mozambique, East Timor, all went straight into civil war. But the Portuguese empire was relatively small, and neither the British nor the French empires, which were the two major ones, show any distinctive patterns. The empire-free countries of Ethiopia, Liberia and Sierra Leone all eventually collapsed into terrible civil wars as well.

Cold War History

The other aspect of history that many scholars have got excited about is the Cold War. Quite evidently, in some instances civil wars were aided and abetted by each side. But even the effect of the Cold War is controversial. While it is clear that the superpowers intervened in civil wars, it is less clear that they caused them. Indeed, they may even have made had an offsetting effect: if any petty war had the potential to scale up into the Third World War the superpowers might have tried to prevent conflicts from occurring. We tested for this by investigating whether the post-Cold War period has had a significantly different incidence of the outbreak of civil war than we might otherwise expect. Basically, it doesn't. There was a brief, significant surge in violence in the first few years after the end of the Cold War, but from 1995 onward the world has been back to normal.

Past Civil Wars

The one aspect of history that really seems to matter is a previous history of civil war. Once a country has had a civil war it is much more likely to have another war. However, this is ripe territory for the endogeneity problem. Suppose that there is some characteristic of the country that makes it prone to violence but which we have missed: perhaps the people are just inherently violent. Statistically, this will appear as one war 'causing' another, whereas actually the same underlying factor is causing all of them. We got around this problem by measuring the number of years since the last civil war and testing whether that, or the mere fact of having had a previous civil war, was decisive. It turned out that it was only the length of time since the previous war that mattered: the risk of further conflict gradually declined with the passage of time. This looked more like a risk of violence caused by the previous violence than by something underlying and constant.

Social Structure

Using the expanded data, we found ethnic and religious divisions to be the most relevant aspects of social structure. We had previously found that ethnic and religious diversity had ambiguous effects. If there was a division between one dominant group, with around half or more of the population, and minority groups, then the risk of violence increased considerably, but otherwise diversity made a society safer. This was good news for the highly diverse societies in which no group was large enough to be dominant. While it was good news, it looks to have been wrong. We now find that the relationship is more straightforward: diversity increases the risk of violence. As far as we can tell, ethnic and religious diversity compound each other: having three ethnic groups and three religious groups has the same consequences as if it had nine ethnic groups. It is as if each of the ethnic groups was further chopped up into three religious groups.

Another aspect of the social structure that seems to affect the risk of violence is the proportion of young men in the population: young men, defined as those aged between 15 and 29, are dangerous. The effect is large: a doubling in the proportion increases the risk of conflict from around 5 per cent over a five-year period to around 32 per cent. However, there are a few caveats here. It is very hard to distinguish statistically between societies with many young men and those with many young women: other than in China the two tend to go together. In most rebellions the fighting is done almost exclusively by young men, but not always: famously the Eritrean People's Liberation Front was one-third female. And it is also very hard to distinguish between societies with a high proportion of young men of fighting age and those that simply have rapid population growth.

A final aspect of the society that matters is its size. The risk of conflict increases with population, but the relationship is much less than proportionate. A doubling in the size of the population increases the risk of outbreak of civil war by only one-fifth. This implies that if two identical countries were merged, abstracting from all the nationalism that would of course be provoked, the risk of a civil war breaking out somewhere in the combined territory would fall. Suppose that previously there was a 10 per cent risk in each country, so that the risk that there would be a war *in one or other* of the countries was around 20 per cent. Now, the risk of a conflict in the new super-country is only a fifth higher than that in either of the former countries individually: that is, the risk is 12 per cent. So, the risk of war has *fallen* from 20 per cent to 12 per cent. I think that this is because there are scale economies in security. Most of the countries that emerged with the dissolution of empires were too small to reap adequate economies of scale in security. At the end of the twentieth century, the prevailing political pressure is for nations to get smaller. Eritrea exited from Ethiopia, Yugoslavia split up into six different countries, East Timor split from Indonesia. In 2011, Southern Sudan voted to withdraw from Sudan. Stepping back from the historical particularities of these struggles for nationhood, is the drift in the right direction?

Geography

So much for social structure: how about geography? Anke and I had already tried to investigate whether particular types of geography were well-suited for rebellion. The most promising idea seemed to be that of the safe haven, and two aspects of the landscape seemed likely to facilitate: forests and mountains. Forests were relatively easy to measure: the Food and Agricultural Organization had global measures, country-by-country. We investigated the hypothesis and could find no effect. But there was no equivalent measure for mountains. There were crude proxies such as the highest point in the country, but these seemed to miss the point as to what rebel groups would actually find useful: they did not want to perch on the top of Everest; they wanted rugged terrain where government forces would not be able to find them. We commissioned a specialist geographer to build a quantitative measure of the proportion of a country's terrain that could reasonably be called mountainous. This measure has since become widely used and in our new work we indeed find it to be significant: mountains are dangerous.

Political System

Governance seems to be the most likely source of violent conflict. We investigated a range of political science variables, but focused on the one most widely used by political scientists, an index known as 'Polity IV'. This is a 21-point scale ranging with the autocracies ranged on -10 to 0 and the democracies ranged on 0 to $+10$. In our core regression we could find no effect.

Now let me investigate more deeply the effect of the political system on the threat of political violence. Whereas entered directly into a regression the polity has no significant effect, once introduced as an interaction term it becomes significant (see Table 4.2 sources). The effect of the polity depends upon the level of income. In societies already at or above middle-income levels, the more democratic is the society the less prone it is to civil war. Unfortunately, in contrast, in low-income societies democracy significantly increases the risk of civil war, and indeed of most other forms of political violence. The threshold level of income below which democracy increases risks is $2,700. All the societies of the 'bottom billion' (Collier 2007) are well below this threshold. It is, of course, an important matter to discover why democracy tends to be so problematic in low-income societies. However, it would involve too large a detour from my main theme and so I refer you to my book, *The Bottom Billion* (2008). My concern here is simply to reinforce the point that, unfortunately, in the low-income societies, democracy does not look as though in itself it is the solution to the problem of proneness to civil war. Democracy is desirable for other reasons, and there is scope radically to improve the practice of democracy in low-income countries, but expecting it rapidly to become the solution to violence when to date it has intensified the problem would be to let our illusions triumph over the evidence.

IMPLICATIONS FOR PREVENTION STRATEGIES: THE FEASIBILITY HYPOTHESIS

Given this evidence on the structural causes of civil war, what are the implications? There remains a considerable leap from evidence to interpretation, and from interpretation to policy. Some interpretations become implausible

Table 4.2   Democracy and Proneness to Civil War

	(1)	(2)	(3)	(4)	(5)	(6)	(7)
		Interaction	Time		Dummy	Dummy	Civil war
	Normal	term	effects	2SLS	logit	probit	data
GDP per capita (−1)	−0.000	0.000	0.000	0.000	−0.000	−0.000	0.069
	(5.30)***	(1.76)*	(1.87)*	(3.71)***	(1.37)	(1.47)	(0.37)
Democracy (−1)	−0.014	0.046	0.078	0.134	0.263	0.152	4.462
	(0.69)	(1.97)**	(3.44)***	(3.52)***	(2.15)**	(2.28)**	(2.36)**
GDP per cap. (−1) * Democ (−1)		−0.000	−0.000	−0.000	−0.000	−0.000	−0.609
		(5.63)***	(5.79)***	(5.03)***	(1.97)**	(1.92)*	(2.22)**
Population (−1)	0.046	0.052	0.059	0.058	0.283	0.158	0.197
	(7.18)***	(8.05)***	(9.37)***	(7.99)***	(8.60)***	(8.64)***	(1.76)*
Mountainous Territ.	0.001	0.001	0.001	0.002	0.010	0.005	0.019
	(2.75)***	(3.33)***	(3.47)***	(3.86)***	(4.35)***	(4.20)***	(2.34)**
Noncontig. Territ.	0.231	0.242	0.214	0.273	1.228	0.663	
	(8.80)***	(9.21)***	(8.40)***	(9.26)***	(9.99)***	(9.48)***	
Oil Exporter	−0.035	−0.066	−0.039	−0.135	−0.363	−0.180	
	(1.38)	(2.52)**	(1.56)	(4.04)***	(2.47)**	(2.30)**	
New State	−0.119	−0.125	−0.073	−0.130			
	(1.12)	(1.19)	(0.69)	(1.18)			
Instability (−1)	0.049	0.041	0.036	0.027	−0.230	−0.139	
	(1.35)	(1.11)	(1.02)	(0.71)	(1.21)	(1.35)	
Ethnic Fract.	0.132	0.145	0.158	0.187	0.762	0.417	
	(3.60)***	(3.96)***	(4.47)***	(4.44)***	(4.06)***	(4.03)***	
Religious Fract.	−0.235	−0.226	−0.209	−0.198	−1.007	−0.560	
	(5.22)***	(5.03)***	(4.82)***	(4.20)***	(4.33)***	(4.35)***	
Other control variables	No	No	No	No	No	No	Cf. note
Constant	−0.542	−0.674	−0.884	−0.837	−6.635	−3.748	−7.974
	(5.22)***	(6.35)***	(7.69)***	(6.72)***	(11.96)***	(12.33)***	(2.80)***
Estimation method	OLS	OLS	OLS	2SLS	Logit	Probit	Logit
Observations	4379	4379	4379	4228	4348	4348	871
(pseudo) R-squared	0.06	0.07	0.14	0.05	0.12	0.12	0.25

Note: Dependent variable: Guerrilla warfare. Abs. value of z-statistics in parentheses. *significant at 10% level; **significant at 5% level; ***significant at 1% level. (−1) = first lag. Instruments included in column (4) for the instrumentation of GDP per capita and of the interaction term: Post Cold War, Rural Population, Distance from USA, Land in Tropics, Island, Number Neighbors, Population in Tropics, Coast. In column (7) the other control variables of the core model of Collier, Hoeffler and Rohner (2006) have been included (not displayed): Growth, Primary Co. Exports (PCE), PCE squared, Peace, Former French colonies, Social fractionalization, Young men.
Source: Collier and Rohner (2008).

in the face of the statistical evidence, but we are not yet at the stage where only one interpretation is possible. With that caveat I propose the *feasibility hypothesis*.

By its nature a civil war is politicized. Each side tries to justify itself both to the domestic population and to the international community. Although there are at least two sides, the decisive side is the rebel group. All governments – with the sole exception of Costa Rica – have armies. Usually, the government has a monopoly on the capacity for large-scale violence constituted by an army. The defining feature of the outbreak of civil war is that this monopoly is challenged: a private organization within the society builds its own army. No government can tolerate the existence of a private army on its soil; so even if it is the government that 'fires the first shot', it is the creation of the rebel army that defines a civil war. Because observers and analysts tend to focus on *why* the civil war is being fought, studies tend to focus on what *motivates* the rebel group to form an army. My own previous work fed this perspective: it questioned the conventional view that rebels were motivated by a sense of grievance, introducing the idea that they might also be motivated by greed. But it was essentially a refinement within the motive-based explanation for rebellion. I have now moved on from this view.

It seems to me that the key explanation for rebellion comes not from asking why it happens but *how* it happens. Usually rebellion, at least on a scale needed for civil war, is simply not feasible. The definition of civil war that I have used, which is conventional, is that a least 1,000 people are killed in combat. Using this definition, the average civil war lasts around seven years. So, we are looking for rebel organizations that can kill and be killed on a large scale and yet survive for years. Rebellion on this scale faces two major hurdles. One is money: a rebellion is going to be expensive. Someone has to pay for the guns, and someone has to pay for the troops. Often people think that a rebellion is just another form of political protest: people fight when they can't vote.

However, rebellion is not simply a variant on other forms of political opposition. Compare the finances of a medium-sized rebel group, the Tamil Tigers, and a major opposition political party. As rebel groups go, this is not out of the ordinary: Northeastern Sri Lanka, where it operates, lacks high-value natural resources; this war is not financed by diamonds. I choose the Tamil Tigers only because unusually its finances have been reasonably well studied. Its annual revenue is around $300 million. This is around 28 per cent of the GDP of Northeast Sri Lanka, although most of the money is generated outside Sri Lanka from donations by Tamils abroad. For a political opposition party I decided to look for a rich one. I chose the British Conservative Party, one of the longest-surviving and most successful political parties in history, which, being on the political right, is able to tap readily into the support of the better off. I chose the election year of 2005, when presumably its revenues were relatively high. This information was more accessible than that of the Tamil Tigers: its revenue was around $50 million. So, one of the best-financed political opposition parties in the world had an income one-seventh that of a medium-sized rebel movement. Recall that the revenue of the Tigers was 28 per cent of the area they sought to control; expressed in that way the British Conservative Party was not one-seventh the size of the Tigers it was one ten-thousandth. There is no simple passage from political opposition to private army: there is a cliff face in the form of a financial barrier. Most would-be rebels just cannot muster the money regardless of their motivation. The other hurdle is military. Under most circumstances, if a small group of young men arm themselves and oppose the government army, either they confine themselves to the irritant of terrorism and aimed primarily against civilians or they die. Only if they are faced by a militarily weak government do they stand much chance of survival. In Zaire the rebellion led by Laurent Kabila hung on for many years, safe because Mobutu Sese Seko had undermined all the organs of government, even the army.

So what is the feasibility hypothesis? It is that in explaining whether a rebellion occurs, motivating factors are of little importance compared to the circumstances that determine whether it is feasible. The tough version of the hypothesis, which I am reluctant to adopt but which I suspect is close to the truth, is that where a rebellion is feasible it will occur: the rebel niche will be occupied by some social entrepreneur although the motivation might be anything across a wide range. Civil war is predominantly studied in political science departments, and so naturally enough they interpret the motivation as political: sometimes it surely is, although even political motivations might stray quite some distance from 'social justice'. Even rebellions that look entirely justified can sometimes be called into doubt. Take the rebellion, or rather rebellions in Darfur. Quite evidently the government of Sudan is awful, and its conduct during the conflict has been murderous. But at least part of the initial impetus for the Darfur rebellion was the settlement of the rebellion in the South. The Sudanese People's Liberation Army, which fought the rebellion in the South, won some remarkable concessions from the government in the North: its own government, a substantial share of the oil revenue, gilded by the promise of huge aid inflows from donors, together with the promise of a referendum on full independence six years after the onset of peace. No sooner was this deal signed than the contingent from Darfur that had been fighting for the Sudanese People's Liberation Army returned home and launched its own rebellion. You can certainly see why, with that precedent, rebellion might be attractive, at least for its leadership. The leader would become a president, and the others would become ministers: secession has its rewards. The rebellion is, of course, justified in terms of the atrocious sufferings of the Darfur people. But to date the consequences of the rebellion for the people of Darfur have been catastrophic: surely far worse than any plausible alternative scenario. Either the rebel leadership radically misjudged the consequences of its actions, or it was not genuinely motivated by the welfare of the people of Darfur. I do not know enough to judge between these alternatives, but when the government was eventually coaxed to the negotiating table, the key rebel organizations refused to attend. It is hard to see how a refusal to negotiate can be in the best interests of the people of Darfur.

Sometimes the motivation for rebellion seems to be religious, with the rebel group more akin to the fringe religious groups such as the Branch Davidians in Waco, Texas, or the People's Temple in Jonestown, Guyana, but with the violence turned outward. For many recruits the motivation may well be the lure of violence: only a small minority of any society are psychopathic, but these people are likely to be in the front of the queue for rebellion. The statistical results do not prove the feasibility hypothesis, but they are consistent with it. I used the results to simulate the risks of conflict in two hypothetical territories, in which rebellion was easier in one territory than in the other. I varied only five characteristics. One was very mountainous, the other was flat. One had a high proportion of young men; the other had a low proportion. Both had a population of 50 million, but one consisted of a single country whereas the other was split into five identical countries, each of ten million. One was dependent upon natural resource exports, the other not. The fifth difference I will discuss below. All the other characteristics were the same and set at the average for all the countries in the analysis. The easy rebellion territory produced a risk of conflict in one or other of its countries of 97 per cent: this territory was basically so dangerous that it was condemned to perpetual conflict. The difficult rebellion territory produced a risk of only 0.3 per cent: basically it was safe, even over a century it was highly unlikely to fall into violence. Dramatic as these differences are, most of the differences in characteristics could, at a stretch, be interpreted in terms of motivation. For example, the population of mountainous areas may be poorer than the rest of the country and storm down from the mountains periodically. While I do not want to discount these other interpretations, I think it is striking that the most obviously grievance-related characteristics, such as the polity, do not seem to make much difference to risks, whereas these characteristics that at least have plausible interpretations in terms of feasibility have such a large effect.

If the feasibility hypothesis is right, it has a powerful implication: violent conflict cannot be prevented by addressing the underlying problems; it can only be reduced by making rebellion more difficult.

One reliable way of reducing the risk of civil war is rapid economic growth. Recall that growth works twice over: it directly reduces risk, and by cumulatively increasing the level of income, it gradually further reduces risk. So, economic development is probably the best 'deep prevention' policy. However, economic growth can be supplemented by strategies that more directly make rebellion more difficult. Rebellion requires two key inputs: guns and money.

To date the attempt to limit the flow of guns through arms embargoes has largely failed. DellaVigna and La Ferrara (2007) show why and what can be done about it. They use information from financial markets to investigate compliance and embargo-busting behavior by arms-exporting firms. Once an embargo is put in place, companies that were previously exporting arms to the country should lose money, so the price of their stock should fall. They find that for arms exporters in Organization for Economic Cooperation and Development (OECD) countries this indeed happens: these firms are complying with the embargo. In contrast, they find that in non-OECD countries the stock price of arms exporters significantly increases. Evidently the armaments firms in these countries are using the embargo as an opportunity to gain market share by displacing the embargoed supplies from the OECD. The large non-OECD countries are thus the weak link in the international system, preventing arms embargoes from being effective. In effect, the large middle-income countries have been free-riding on the international system for their own commercial benefit but at the expense of the security of low-income countries. However, as DellaVigna and La Ferrara point out, precisely the technique that they have used to discover this result, namely the analysis of 'events data', can be adopted by the United Nations to police future embargoes.

The complementary attempt to limit the flow of finance to rebel groups has been more successful, but it has been narrowly focused on revenues from the illicit trade in diamonds. The Kimberley Process now certifies the source of diamonds and has made rebel finance from this source considerably more difficult. In principle, the same approach can be extended to other commodities. However, rebels also get revenues from very different sources and further policy interventions would probably be more effective if targeted at these sources. For example, the primary source of the massive financing for the Tamil Tigers is contributions from the Tamil diaspora living outside Sri Lanka. Whereas in the case of arms embargoes the guilty parties are the governments of the middle-income countries that are failing to restrain their companies, in the case of diaspora financing of rebel groups the guilty parties are the governments of the OECD countries that are failing to restrain their residents. The problem is evidently that imposing effective legal restraints upon the behavior of diaspora groups would be politically costly for the leaders of

OECD governments, whereas all the benefits would accrue to reduce violence in low-income societies.

Both the failure to enforce arms embargoes and the continuing flow of finance to rebel groups from diasporas illustrate the gulf between the posturing rhetoric of concern now routine among political leaders outside the bottom billion and the reality of short-sighted interpretations of self-interest.

IMMEDIATE RISKS AND EMERGENCY RESPONSES

Around the Millennium the international community began to pay serious attention to the running sores of long-lasting civil wars. Peace conferences were called, pressure was put on the various sides and a whole series of peace settlements achieved: Sri Lanka, Burundi, Southern Sudan, Sierra Leone, Angola, the Democratic Republic of Congo, Bosnia and Kosovo. While this was a splendid achievement, post-conflict situations are fragile; to date around 40 per cent of them have reverted to violence within a decade. In total these reversions account for around half of all the world's civil wars. So, maintaining the post-conflict peace more effectively than in the past would be the single most effective way of reducing civil war.

What Makes Peace Endure?

In statistical terms it is much harder to determine what makes peace endure than to discover the overall causes of civil wars, mainly because of the smaller number of pertinent observations. You discover what causes civil war by comparing the 84 outbreaks of civil war against the 1,560 episodes when peace was maintained. You discover why a post-conflict peace breaks down by comparing the handful of situations in which a post-conflict peace broke down against the handful in which it did not. They are only a handful partly because there simply are not that many of them and also because by the time peace arrives data gathering has collapsed so that there is no information to analyze. Only by 2006 had we built a sufficiently large sample of 66 countries to be worth investigating. The techniques needed to study the post-conflict question are also different. To discover how the risk of reversion to conflict evolves year-by-year during the post-conflict decade the appropriate technique is 'hazard functions' rather than logits.

Let's start with democracy and elections. The standard approach of the international community to the end of a civil war is to insist on a democratic constitution, followed after a few years by an election. This is what I refer to as 'the theory of legitimacy and accountability' at its clearest. Peace will be secured by an election because the winner will be recognized as legitimate by the population, making violent opposition more difficult. Not only will the elected government be recognized as legitimate, the democratic process will ensure that it will need to be inclusive and so there will be less reason for grievance: the government will be accountable to its citizens. Not all political scientists go along with this line of argument. Some think that post-conflict democracy and elections will actually be divisive, polarizing the population along ethnic lines and so making the reversion to conflict more likely. So, there we have the two political science positions: they cannot both be right, and so it is time to look at the evidence.

We first checked whether the type of polity made a difference. Again we used the 21-point scale of the Polity IV index, searching along it to see whether any part of the range was significantly safer than any other. We did not like what we found. There was a portion of the range that was significantly safer, but it was the range of intense autocracy: between −10 and −5. Within this range the risk of reversion to conflict dropped from 40 per cent, which was the overall average, to around 25 per cent. Outside that range there was a corresponding increase in the risk of conflict reversion from 40 per cent to an astounding 70 per cent. To think concretely, and to take examples that occurred sufficiently recently not to be driving the results, in the early years of the new millennium both Angola and Sri Lanka made it to peace. Angola continued to be one of the most repressive regimes on earth, whereas Sri Lanka was a long-established democracy. The peace in Angola has held firm, and I expect that it will continue to do so. The peace in Sri Lanka has already fallen apart: rich-country governments have heaped the lion's share of the blame on the Sri Lankan government rather than on the Tigers, just as they tended to blame the government of Colombia for the resumption of the war against the FARC, and the government of Uganda for the running war against the Lord's Resistance Army. I am ready to admit that all three of these governments have probably made mistakes, but what is manifest is that all three of them are saintly when compared with that of Angola.

Next, we pressed on to the effect of elections, introducing them into our hazard model of the post-conflict decade. While the two political science hypotheses could not both be right, they could both be wrong. They were: a post-conflict election *shifts* the risk of conflict reversion. In the year before the election the risk of going back to violence is very sharply reduced: the society looks to have reached safety. But in the year after the election the risk explodes upward. The net effect of the election is to make the society more dangerous. Why do post-conflict elections have this effect? Well at this point we have to leap off the statistical results and start to speculate. Here is my guess. In the run-up to an election there is a strong incentive for the parties to participate: after all, this is the route to power. Energies get diverted into campaigning and risks fall. But then comes the election result. Someone has won, and someone has lost. Of course, if this were a genuine democracy the winning party would say the sort of things that winning parties usually say in genuine democracies: we will govern on behalf of all the people. If it was a genuine democracy the losing party would say the sort of things that losing parties usually say in genuine democracies: we accept the result and will be a loyal opposition. Post-conflict situations are not usually like this. The winner gleefully anticipates untrammeled power: no checks and balances here. The loser anticipates their fate under the thumb of their opponents and knows that there is but one recourse: back to violence.

Let's take a real post-conflict situation: the Democratic Republic of Congo. The international community held the key cards in this situation: the government was up to its eyes in debt, was chronically short of revenue and lacked an effective army. So, it had little choice but to acquiesce in holding a post-conflict election after a three-year interlude during which the victorious rebel leader, President Kabila I, was assassinated and his son inherited the throne. The election was to be in two rounds, somewhat like that in France, with the second and decisive round set for 29 October 2006. The international community was sufficiently confident of the legitimacy and accountability model that it set the date for the withdrawal of its peacekeeping forces as 30 October 2006. If our results were right, in one sense the strategy of the international community was understandable. If the DRC ran to form, the year before the election would be remarkably peaceful, creating the impression that the society was now over the period of high risk. In the event, the aftermath of the election became so violently unstable so rapidly that instead of troops being flown out, more had to be flown in. Within a few months there was a shoot out between the private army of Jean-Pierre Bemba, who lost the election, and the government army of Kabila II, the incumbent winner. Bemba's forces lost, and he himself sought protection in an embassy before fleeing to Europe where he is now in exile. His exit has not restored order: the Democratic Republic of the Congo continues to be dangerous.

Since international peacekeeping is both enormously expensive and highly unpopular with developed-country electorates, there is strong pressure to 'bring the boys home' as soon as there looks to be no need for them. So, it is not surprising that the post-conflict election should be used as the 'milestone' for troop withdrawal. Or, in the more familiar sound byte, elections are the 'exit strategy'. But, if you think about it, our results suggest that a post-conflict election is inappropriate as a 'milestone'. Of course, it depends whether peacekeeping works: if it doesn't work then the boys might as well be brought home. So, it is time to turn from elections to peacekeeping.

The United Nations provided us with data on its peacekeeping operations. Somewhat to our surprise we got clear results: peacekeeping seems to work. Expenditure on peacekeeping strongly and significantly reduces the risk that a post-conflict situation will revert to civil war. Of course, this raises the standard concern as to whether such results are spurious because of endogeneity. For example, if the troops are systematically sent only to the safer post-conflict countries they will appear to be successful in keeping the peace, but it will not be causal. And so we tried to find something that would explain the allocation of peacekeeping troops but which was unrelated to the risk of conflict reversion. Whatever we tried, we were unable to get a good explanation for the allocation of troops. This is consistent with the political science literature: Doyle and Sambanis (2006) conclude that the political decision process that assigns troops to post-conflict situations is so complex as to defy being modeled. The various members of the UN Security Council who take the decision are involved in such Byzantine horse-trading that any particular decision is close to being random. This explained why we were unable to find good predictors and also suggested that we were not facing a severe problem of endogeneity. Nevertheless, we were able to make one helpful check. The decision as to how many troops to send into a post-conflict situation can conceptually be split into two stages: first, should troops be sent at all? Second, assuming that decision was affirmative, how many should be sent? We introduced this into our analysis and found that the decision to send troops at all was associated with a significantly higher risk of reversion to violence, whereas conditional upon any troops being sent the more that were sent the safer was the society. The most plausible way of interpreting this is that troops tend to be sent to places that are more at risk. We cannot tell whether the same is true of the decision as to how many troops to send. If, in fact, troops are sent in the greatest numbers to the most dangerous places then our results, which implicitly assume that they are assigned randomly, will understate their real effectiveness. The true story would be that places with many peacekeepers have a lower rate of reversion to conflict despite intrinsically being more at risk. So, our assumption that their numbers are unrelated to intrinsic risk may well be conservative.

Even if international peacekeeping is effective it is expensive and unpopular. Some of the post-conflict governments get indignant about the intrusion: the Department of Peacekeeping Operations of the United Nations, DPKO, has become the new International Monetary Fund, a challenge to the unrestrained sovereignty on governments keen on asserting their power. It is also understandably unpopular with the electorates of the countries that supply the troops: no one wants their son or daughter to be exposed to the risks of peacekeeping.

Is there an alternative? I could think of two other possibilities. The first is what is known as 'over-the-horizon' guarantees. It is what the British government has done in Sierra Leone. For the past few years there have only been 80 British troops stationed in the country, but the government has been given a ten-year undertaking that if there is trouble, the troops will be flown in overnight. Perhaps this has helped stabilize the society. Sierra Leone is, at least in terms of reversion to violence, a major success. It has even weathered post-conflict elections and a change of government successfully. The problem with the Sierra Leone example is that it is just that: it is only one example. You cannot perform a statistical analysis on one observation and so there is no way of knowing whether in general such guarantees would be effective. Or is there?

There was one past analogy to what the British are now doing in Sierra Leone. The French had provided security guarantees to their client countries in Africa for years. In fact, with the typical logic of international 'coordination' they had abandoned it only just before the British started to do it. The French security guarantees were informal, but they were most surely for real. They were backed by a series of French military bases across Francophone West Africa. They had started with independence and rolled on until the French government got caught up trying to implement its informal guarantee defending the Hutu regime in Rwanda in 1994. The French came disturbingly close to propping up a regime implementing genocide.

After that President Jacques Chirac ordered a rethink and announced a new policy toward Africa: military intervention began to look anachronistic. The first test of this new policy was the coup d'etat in Côte d'Ivoire in 1999. Previously, France would have put down this coup, but President Chirac vetoed it. So, we can date the credible prospect of French intervention from Independence until the mid-1990s. After their military catastrophe of Dien Bien Phu in Vietnam, the French were in no position to extend their military guarantee across the whole of the Francophone world, it was basically credible only in West and Central Africa for around 30 years. This was, however, a large enough group of countries, for a sufficiently long period to be amenable to statistical analysis. The key question was whether this guarantee had actually reduced the incidence of civil war. As shown in Table 4.1, the effect is powerful and significant.

The French guarantee appears to have reduced the risk of a civil war breaking out in these countries by nearly three-quarters relative to what it would otherwise have been. But was the military guarantee the reason for this remarkable reduction in conflict? Could it have been something else associated with the French presence? The most likely alternative was culture in its broadest sense. Perhaps something about being exposed to French colonization had made these countries more peaceful? We tested whether there was something pacifying about exposure to French culture by checking whether the same risk reduction that had occurred in Francophone Africa also occurred in the rest of *La Francophonie*. The is answer is no: the enhanced security was unique to West and Central Africa, the region covered by the French military bases. While there is always the possibility that it was not the French security guarantee but something especially successful about the interaction between France and Africa that did not occur elsewhere, to my mind this is reasonably convincing. Over-the-horizon guarantees look as though they work. Whether or not a territory is covered by the French informal guarantee is the fifth characteristic in the simulation of easy-rebellion versus difficult-rebellion territories presented in the previous section.

The other obvious alternative to peacekeeping troops is that the post-conflict government should provide its own defense. Most post-conflict governments are well-aware that they are living dangerously, so they barely reduce their military spending from the level prevailing during the conflict. The question is whether in post-conflict settings this high military spending is effective in bringing down the risks of violence. Our analysis of the effect of government military spending on post-conflict risk is shown in Table 4.3. Evidently, there is a severe problem of endogeneity. Military spending will be increased in response to the risk of conflict. However, we were able to find good instruments for military spending, as set out in Collier and Hoeffler (2008). So instrumented, we found that government military spending in post-conflict situations significantly and substantially *increased* the risk of further conflict. Thus, in marked contrast to international peacekeeping, armed force supplied by the government itself was counterproductive. This effect was unique to post-conflict situations: in the more usual context of peace high military spending by the government did not increase the risk of rebellion. Why should military spending so backfire? Our explanation is that the decision of the government to spend a lot inadvertently signals to citizens that it is planning to rely upon repression, and that this signal forewarns those rebels who have recently put down their arms that they were unwise to do so. However, there is surely room for other explanations.

It is time to move on from the politics and the military. What else drives post-conflict risks? Again the economy matters. The lower income is the higher is the risk of conflict reversion and the slower is economic recovery the higher is the risk. Both of these have implications. If low-income countries face higher risks of conflict reversion, other things equal the international community should be allocating peacekeeping troops disproportionately to those post-conflict situations with the lowest income. This would, indeed, provide a useful rule-of-thumb to cut through all the horse-trading that Doyle and Sambanis (2006) found to be dominating the decision on the Security Council. A further implication is that, again other things being equal, strategies

Table 4.3   Duration of Post-War Peace

		Duration
Economic		
	Per capita income	−0.427
		(1.72)+
	Per capita income growth	−3.548
		(2.21)*
Political		
	Democracy	1.230
		(2.43)*
	Democracy missing (dummy)	1.752
		(2.68)**
	Regional autonomy	−1.561
		(1.43)
	Regional autonomy missing (dummy)	−0.253
		(0.50)
	Election shift	−0.709
		(1.97)*
	1st election	
Social		
	ln Diaspora	−0.333
		(2.82)**
	Diaspora missing (dummy)	3.464
		(2.46)*
	Ethnic diversity	−1.038
		(1.24)
	Ethnic diversity missing (dummy)	−15.198
		(0.01)
Peacekeeping		
	ln UN peace keeping expenditure	−0.405
		(2.38)*
	No UN PKO	−3.714
		(2.16)*
	UN data missing (dummy)	−3.886
		(2.09)*
Time		
	Years 4+ of peace	−0.475
		(1.12)
Log Likelihood		−66.821
Number of episodes		74
Number of failures		33

Note: Absolute value of z-statistics in parentheses, *significant at 5% and **significant at 1% level. All regressions include an intercept (not reported).
Source: Collier, Hoeffler and Rohner (2008).

that enhance the economic recovery are going to be peace-enhancing: raising growth and cumulatively augmenting the level of income. Before discussing how post-conflict economies can be rebuilt, let me conclude on the factors influencing post-conflict risks.

The story so far is that the post-conflict decade is dangerous and that there seems to be no clear political quick fix. In particular, elections and democracy, at least in the form found in the typical post-conflict situation, do not seem to bring risks down. Nor does the military efforts of the post-conflict government: they make things worse. Economic recovery works but it takes a long time. The one thing that seems to work quickly is international peacekeeping, but it is politically difficult to sustain peacekeeping for the length of time needed for the economy to recover. Is it necessary? There remains one possibility: perhaps the key risks occur early in the decade, followed by a safe period. Perhaps: so we investigated it. The risk does seem gradually to decline. However, although time heals, its effects seem to be decade-by-decade rather than year-by-year. The first four years are perhaps somewhat more dangerous than the next six, but the effect is not statistically significant. Within the post-conflict decade we can find no safe period.

Implications for Emergency Strategies

So what does the above analysis of post-conflict risks imply for policy priorities? I consider the implications for post-conflict governments and the international community in turn.

Post-conflict governments

Perhaps the overarching implication for post-conflict governments is that economic recovery is vital for security and so it should receive serious and sustained attention. Typically, post-conflict governments spend most of their time fussing about issues of political design and national defense. While this is understandable, I think it is misplaced. There is no magic political formula that will secure the peace, and a high level of military spending is counterproductive: the military budget should be slashed, as it was in Mozambique, one of the most successful post-conflict recoveries.

What specific economic policies might a post-conflict government adopt that would speed recovery beyond the conventional list of policies that apply to all governments? Why should post-conflict economic policies be distinctive? I think that there is one sector that is critical to the pace of recovery and yet typically receives no policy attention: the construction sector. This sector typically becomes a bottleneck. There are three key reasons why the construction sector matters.

First, the construction sector supplies the non-tradable capital goods that are essential for recovery: that is why the recovery phase is referred to as 're*construction*'. Many capital goods are internationally tradable and so can be imported, but the construction sector provides infrastructure such as roads and buildings, items that cannot be imported. The need to reconstruct the economy rightly induces an inflow of aid, and this creates a sharp increase in demand for precisely those capital goods that the economy must itself produce rather than import.

Second, the construction sector uses as one of its inputs a large number of unskilled and semi-skilled young men. Creating productive jobs for young men is critical to risk-reduction. Recall that the higher the proportion of young men in a society is, the higher the risk of conflict; this is a large effect. The conventional shadow pricing literature routinely considers circumstances in which the shadow price of labor should be set below the market wage. However, post-conflict situations are distinctive in that the shadow price of the labor of young males is highly *negative*. The only practical alternative to providing young men with jobs in the construction sector is for the government to employ them, either unproductively in the civil service or dangerously in the army.

Third, during civil war the construction sector contracts far more drastically than other sectors of the economy due to a corresponding collapse in investment. The society is engaged in destruction rather than construction. By the end of the conflict the construction sector has withered away, in two key respects. The number and size of firms in the sector will have shrunk so that the economy lacks organizational capital in the sector. Furthermore, the sector-specific skills for construction will have diminished. One of the most famous concepts in economics is 'learning-by-doing', the analysis of productivity improvement introduced by Nobel Laureate Kenneth Arrow. In the context of civil war the construction sector suffers an analogous process of productivity decline: 'forgetting by not doing'.

The implication of these three points is that economic policy should focus on easing the rapid expansion of the construction sector. Otherwise the sharp increase in demand for construction output merely pushes up a steep supply curve, yielding a price boom but not an output boom. When supply expansion fails, severe increases in unit costs and traffic jams result. For example, the cost of school construction in Liberia doubled during the first year of reconstruction. Traffic jams in the capital cities of post-conflict countries arise because it is much easier to expand traded capital goods, namely vehicles, than non-traded capital goods such as roads.

While construction had to be performed domestically, it is now possible to import all construction services. Most notably, Chinese construction companies operate with virtually 100 per cent import content. With this style of operation the construction supply curve becomes horizontal – unit costs need not rise at all. However, the severe price paid for this option is that no jobs are generated. Properly costed at shadow prices, construction contracts undertaken through the Chinese mode of operation would quite probably not be competitive.

Leaders can take a number of steps to address these issues. First, they can apply the techniques of shadow pricing to construction contracts. Second, they could break the skills bottleneck through an early focus on training in the mundane construction skills. For example, the establishment or expansion of colleges of construction technology should probably be a first-year priority in any post-conflict situation. Allied to this is the need to organize an influx of these skills from abroad, partly so that the trainers are available. But also so that skills bottlenecks can initially be broken by foreign labor: each foreign skilled worker can scale up the employment of local unskilled workers. The huge attention devoted to humanitarian needs routinely produces an influx of volunteers from organizations such as Doctors without Borders. This humanitarian response needs to be matched by an economic response: a 'Bricklayers without Borders'! Skills are not the only constraint on the expansion of construction. A second is the ability to import bulky critical inputs such as cement. Typically, the port facilities will have atrophied and so the construction boom rapidly encounters shortages of these key inputs. So, alongside skills, an early priority is to tackle both the infrastructure and management of port facilities. A third common cause of bottlenecks is malfunction in the market for urban land. Construction requires ready access to urban land. Thus, a third early priority is legislative reform both to facilitate private actors to purchase the land needed for private construction and to permit swift government compulsory purchase of land needed for public infrastructure.

The international community

For the international community the overarching implication is that it has a large and critical role to play in reducing the very high risks facing post-conflict societies. It has three instruments, all of which should be deployed: peacekeeping, money and conditionality.

Peacekeeping is effective and it is necessary. The entire decade is risky, and the only other strategy that reliably brings risks down, economic recovery, is slow. In other work I have attempted a cost-benefit analysis of peacekeeping, measuring the benefits by an estimate of the costs of civil war multiplied by the reduced risk of its occurrence (Collier, Chauvet and Hegre 2008). We find that even on conservative estimates of the costs of civil war, peacekeeping is highly cost-effective. Since security is a sine qua non for development, in post-conflict situations it should be seen as a development instrument with a high pay-off. It may be that on-the-ground peacekeeping can phase into an over-the-horizon guarantee, but such guarantees are only likely to be effective if they are credible, implying a dedicated military force on standby with clear instructions for combat already agreed.

Aid seems to be particularly productive in the post-conflict context (Collier and Hoeffler 2004). This is not surprising: post-conflict recovery was the initial rationale for the international aid agencies. There are various explanations as to why the economic benefits of aid in post-conflict settings are distinctive. The most obvious is that there is a particularly acute need for the rehabilitation of infrastructure. Another obvious reason is that since the capacity of the civil service has usually massively degraded and skilled people have emigrated, technical assistance is unusually helpful. A less obvious reason is that during civil wars governments resort to desperate economic measures, notably the inflation tax. This leaves a post-conflict legacy of reduced confidence in the currency. Adam, Collier and Davies (2008) shows that governments use some post-conflict aid to reduce their reliance upon seigniorage, in effect investing in rebuilding confidence in the currency, in the process also rebuilding the long term revenue yield from seigniorage. A further likely rationale for post-conflict aid is to enable the government to impose only light taxation. During the conflict economic activity will have retreated into informality, and so part of the recovery process is to reformalize the markets. High taxation is a disincentive to this process. Nor is the civil service in a fit state to raise taxation effectively. Typically, with the rise of opportunistic behavior during a conflict, standards of conduct by tax collectors will have deteriorated, as too will any sense of moral obligation to comply with the tax regime. Again, a prolonged period of building a habit of compliance through light taxation is likely to be helpful and aid can finance the resulting revenue losses. Since post-conflict economic recovery is a long-term process, a large aid inflow will likely be needed throughout the post-conflict decade.

Finally, the post-conflict context warrants 'governance conditionality'. By this I mean to distinguish it from 'policy conditionality': governments should have clear and sole responsibility for the choice of economic policies. However, a civil war demonstrates that the society finds self-governance highly problematic. Around half of the costs of a civil war accrue to neighboring countries, and so these neighbors have legitimate interests that should be protected by the international community, acting on their behalf. Clear red lines are needed that post-conflict governments should not be permitted to breach. The most important such red line concerns military spending.

Around 11 per cent of aid leaks into military spending. This is not surprising. Typically, the governments of developing countries choose to spend about 10–20 per cent of their revenues on the military, and there are many ways in which aid can evade earmarking. One cost of the leakage is evidently the diversion of aid from its proper uses. If 11 per cent of aid leaks into an activity that is unproductive, then all the beneficial effects of aid are attributable to the remaining 89 per cent. Were it possible to prevent leakage, the amount of aid available for beneficial uses would thus be augmented by around 12 per cent (11/89). However, the main cost of the leakage is that in augmenting military spending it is inadvertently increasing the risk of reversion to violence. On my estimates this is a large effect that severely reduces the net benefit of post-conflict aid. Since aid inflows are large in the post-conflict phase, around half of all post-conflict military spending by the government is inadvertently being funded by donors. This gives donors both a clear right and a clear responsibility to restrain such spending. Given the many routes by which aid is fungible, the only way to do this is directly through a cap on the military budget, combined with insistence upon thorough forensic accounting of the budget process to prevent military expenditures being reclassified.

A new global compact
Three distinct actors are thus jointly responsible for the success or failure of post-conflict recovery: the government, the providers of peacekeeping forces and the donors. All three are interdependent; for example, without a peacekeeping commitment aid will be less effective, yet without a commitment to prolonged aid peacekeepers have no credible exit strategy. What is therefore required is a Global Compact setting out mutual responsibilities. The agency best placed to forge and enforce such a compact is the new Peace-Building Commission of the United Nations. Such an approach, emphasizing the importance of clear, mutual responsibilities, is very much in the spirit of current international development cooperation. The innovation is to recognize that post-conflict situations are distinctive and so require distinctive emergency responses. Precisely because emergency responses need to be swift, it is important to have an agreed course of cooperative action in place as a model before each particular situation arises instead of depending upon ad hoc deals reached reactively.

CONCLUSION

In this chapter I have tried both to display a method and to propose policies.

The method is the application of quantitative economic analysis to a range of behavior that is usually not interpreted as economic, namely violence. Over the past half-century economic analysis has been applied to an increasingly wide range of behavior. Nobel Laureate Gary Becker pioneered this approach by showing that both criminal and family decisions were amenable to standard techniques. The extension to violence is entirely within this spirit. Economists are now working across the entire range of political violence: there are theories and quantitative analyses of everything from coups through voter intimidation, to assassinations. I have focused on civil war because it is the most costly phenomenon and is concentrated in the poorest countries. While I have concentrated here upon my own work, there is now a large literature that follows the same quantitative and analytic approach. However, the entire subject of political violence analyzed as an economic phenomenon is still at an early stage: there is much for young economists to do and major advances in datasets that are making it feasible.

The value of the approach is that it generates insights that have been missed by policy practitioners. The continuing high incidence of civil war, especially the high rate of reversion to conflict in post-conflict societies, demonstrate an alarming degree of practitioner incompetence. The world can surely be made much better than this. Of course, practitioners know a lot that economic analysts miss: they have situation-specific expertise. The responsibility of economists is to supplement this stock of highly specific expertise with a more general analysis. This guards against practitioners both over-generalizing from their particular experience and interpreting complex information so as to conform to their prior expectations.

REFERENCES

Adam, C., P. Collier and V. Davies (2008), 'Post-Conflict Monetary Reconstruction, *World Bank Economic Review*, **22** (1), 87–112.

Collier, P. (2008), *The Bottom Billion: Why the Poorest Countries are Failing and What Can be Done About It*, New York: Oxford University Press.

Collier, P. (2008), *Wars, Guns and Votes: Democracy in Dangerous Places*, New York: Random House.

Collier, P., L. Chauvet and H. Hegre (2008), 'The Security Challenge in Conflict-Prone Countries', in Bjorn Lomberg (ed.), *Global Crises, Global Solutions*, 2nd ed., New York: Cambridge University Press, pp. 58–103.

Collier, P. and A. Hoeffler (2004), 'Greed and Grievance in Civil War', *Oxford Economic Papers*, **56** (4), 563–95.

—— (2006), 'Military Expenditure in Post-Conflict Societies', *Economics of Governance*, **7** (1), 89–107.

—— (2007), 'Unintended Consequences: Does Aid Promote Arms Races?', *Oxford Bulletin of Economics and Statistics*, **69** (1), 1–27.

Collier, P., A. Hoeffler and D. Rohner (2008), 'Greed and Grievance: Feasibility and Civil War', *Oxford Economic Papers*, **56** (4), 563–95.

Collier, P. and D. Rohner (2008), 'Democracy, Development and Conflict', *Journal of the European Economic Association*, **6** (2/3), 531–40.

Collier, P., A. Hoeffler and M. Söderbom (2008), 'Post-Conflict Risks', *Journal of Peace Research*, **45** (4), 461–78.
DellaVigna, S. and E. La Ferrara (2007), 'Detecting Illegal Arms Trade', Cambridge, MA, National Bureau of Economic Research (NBER) Working Paper No. 13355.
Doyle, M. and N. Sambanis (2006), *Making War and Building Peace: United Nations Peace Operations*, Princeton, NJ: Princeton University Press.

5. The Conflict–Development Nexus: A Survey of Armed Conflicts in Sub-Saharan Africa, 1980–2005

Sakiko Fukuda-Parr, Maximillian Ashwill,

Elizabeth Chiappa and Carol Messineo

Sub-Saharan Africa is at the core of today's global challenge of armed conflict, a challenge that is inextricably related to development. Most of the armed conflicts of recent decades have occurred in the region (Human Security Report Project 2006) and continued violence in several countries, the tenuousness of the peace in others and the legacy of violence pose significant peace, security and development challenges.

This chapter will provide an overview of the nexus of poverty/development and armed conflict in Africa. After reviewing trends, the chapter explores two sets of links between conflict and poverty: the consequences of war on development and poverty; and the socio-economic structures as risk factors for war. The final section considers how these links have been addressed in development policy by examining recent Poverty Reduction Strategy Papers (PRSPs).

TRENDS

Since 1980, more than half of the countries of Sub-Saharan Africa have experienced armed conflict, sometimes multiple conflicts taking place simultaneously in different parts of the country involving different parties, sometimes lasting for decades interspersed with periods of 'peace'. Table 5.1 charts 126 wars in 32 countries that are recorded in the UCDP/PRIO Armed Conflict Dataset.[1] There was a general rise in the number of wars in this period but a decline between 2002 and 2005, from 14 to six, with a corresponding decline in the number of battle deaths from 8,200 to 2,400 (Lacina and Gleditsch 2005; Human Security Report Project 2006). This trend should be treated with caution because it covers only four years, with many of the political, social, economic and structural factors of war still unresolved.

All but six of these 126 armed conflicts were intrastate or civil wars. Many continued for decades interspersed with repeated attempts at settlement and often involved multiple parties pursuing different goals. Other, less intense 'minor wars' lasted two years or less (Gleditsch et al. 2002; Harbom et al. 2006). The majority have been driven by attempts to control the state, and only a few involved secessionist groups seeking autonomy for a territory (Gelditsch et al. 2002). Many wars have spilled across national boundaries and developed into sub-regional conflicts in areas such as the Great Lakes, Southern Africa, Mano-River Basin and Central East Africa.

Today's armed conflicts in Africa defy the analytical frameworks used in the study of war and security. These conflicts correspond more closely to the concept of 'new wars' as they are motivated by both political and private economic objectives, co-mingle state and non-state actors with local and external allies, and involve violence perpetrated against unarmed civilians by state armies, non-state militias and organized criminal networks (Kaldor 2007; Reno 2005). Kaldor notes that

> although most of these wars are localized, they involve a myriad of transnational connections so that the distinction between internal and external, between aggression (attacks from abroad) and repression (attacks from inside the country), or even between local and global, are difficult to sustain. (2007, 2)

Non-State Wars

Most definitions of war, including the UCDP/PRIO dataset used in this chapter, include formally organized, contested combat against the state. This excludes armed conflicts between non-state actors such as communal violence, conflict between rival guerilla groups and warlords, state-sponsored violence against unarmed civilians and acts of terrorism. Data on non-state conflicts have only begun to be collected in recent years. Between 2002 and 2005, there were 77 non-state conflicts in Sub-Saharan Africa, compared with 17 state-based conflicts. The number of fatalities was smaller (12,834 compared with 20,655) (UCDP Non-State Dataset v. 4.1). These non-state wars differ in character from state wars – they may be 'low intensity', employing unconventional weapons and tactics without regard for traditional political or military codes of conduct (WHO 2002).

Table 5.1   Comparison of State-Based and Non-State Conflicts in Sub-
             Saharan Africa, 2002–2005 (> 25 battle deaths per year)

Countries with Non-State-Based Armed Conflict	Number of Conflicts Between Nonstate Warring Parties	Fatalities Non-State Conflicts	Number of State-Based Conflicts	Fatalities State-based Conflicts
Burundi	1	97	2	2440
Cote d'Ivoire	4	583	2	1200
Congo, DR	6	5298	0	0
Ethiopia	8	517	3	2210
Ghana	1	36	0	0
Kenya	1	68	0	0
Madagascar	1	79	0	0
Nigeria	17	3050	2	552
Somalia	25	1944	1	–
Sudan	7	688	4	8028
Sudan, Uganda	1	142	–	–
Uganda	5	332	3	6225
Total Sub-Saharan Africa	77	12834	17	20,655
Total Global Non-State Conflict	101	17832	–	–

Source: UCDP Non-State Conflict Dataset v. 4.1.

Casualties and Human Costs

Conventional definitions of casualties count deaths on the battlefield. While the 126 wars described earlier resulted in approximately one million such deaths, the toll would be multiples of this number if all 'war deaths' were counted (Lacina and Gelditsch 2005). Battle-death estimates do not include state-sponsored violence against unarmed civilians, such as the Rwandan genocide, in which 800,000 people perished, and communal violence between non-state groups, such as the 1994–95 ethnic violence of Northern Ghana, which saw 15,000 fatalities (Jönsson 2007). It also excludes the depredations of militias on unarmed men, women and children that have characterized much of the violence in Sierra Leone and Angola. Many additional non-combatants have died of malnutrition and disease. For example, between 1998 and 2004 in the Democratic Republic of Congo, an estimated 3.9 million people died from all conflict-related causes of mortality (Coghlan et al. 2006). Lacina and Gleditsch (2005) found battle-death estimates to be a consistently small fraction of total war death estimates – that include civilian battle deaths and deaths from disease and famine provoked by war, and deaths due to criminal and unorganized violence – ranging from less than 2 per cent in Ethiopia to 29 per cent in Mozambique.

In addition to death and injury, rape, deliberate mutilation, forced conscription of children and the use of landmines exact long-term costs and inhibit recovery from war. The overall legacy of violence constrains post-conflict reconciliation and political accommodation. Violent armed conflict ignites humanitarian crises and disrupts human security in all its personal, economic and political dimensions (Collier et al. 2003; Stewart et al. 2001).

Massive dislocation of people from their homes, livelihoods and communities is another human cost; over the survey period (1980–2005) more than 4 million Africans had to flee their countries (UNHCR 2007). In two of the most dramatic cases, as much as 40 per cent of the population of Rwanda fled their homes in 1994, and 14 per cent of Burundi's people in 1993. In 2005 there were an estimated 12.1 million internally displaced persons (IDPs) in 20 African countries – more than twice the total for the rest of the world – including 5.4 million in Sudan, 2 million in Uganda and 1.7 million in the DRC (Eschenbächer 2006). Unlike refugees, IDPs do not cross an international border. As of 2005 in Sub-Saharan Africa there were 1.9 million people in 17 protracted refugee situations, defined as situations where 25,000 or more people are in exile and reliant upon external assistance for at least five years (UNHCR 2007).

Large-scale forced migration increases mortality and morbidity (WHO 2002; Van Damme 1995). Protracted refugee encampments create security problems and conflict between burdened host countries and their neighbors. Refugee populations may include those sympathetic to the irredentist challenges of ethnic minorities in the host country. Camps often harbor insurgent militias and may facilitate small-arms trafficking, drug smuggling and other illicit trade (Jacobsen 2002; UNHCR 2006). In host countries, concentrations of refugees may exacerbate environmental problems, including deforestation and land and water pollution and overuse (Jacobsen 1997, 2002; Black and Sessay 1997; Black 1994).

CONSEQUENCES OF ARMED CONFLICT ON POVERTY AND DEVELOPMENT

Civil wars have been called 'development in reverse' (Collier et al. 2003, 13). They divert resources away from productive economic activities and from public expenditures for social goods that advance development. They incur direct human costs as described, but also longer-term developmental costs through loss of household assets, destruction of infrastructure essential for both human well-being and for successful agriculture and commerce, and loss of confidence in institutions leading to lawlessness and capital flight (Stewart et al. 2001).

However, evidence from the 126 wars in this survey show that the consequences of armed conflict on development are far from simple; the costs not only vary from one country to another, but are also uneven within countries. Within a given country the entire population does not always suffer the cost of war equally, and in the aggregate, the economy does not always falter. Figures 5.1, 5.2 and 5.3 show the evolution of economic output (GDP) and human survival (Under-Five Mortality Rate) during war years. They show a precipitous economic decline in Liberia, Sierra Leone, DRC, Eritrea, Burundi, Djibouti, Mozambique and several other countries. Only nine of the 22 countries for which data are available show GDP that was lower at the end of the war than at its onset. For 13 other countries, GDP was higher at the end of the war. For some, such as Angola and Rwanda, there were dramatic declines at the height of the fighting followed by recovery. But several countries sustained GDP growth while fighting continued, such as in Sudan, Chad, Senegal, Ethiopia and Niger.

Some examples illustrate why war does not always lead to decline in national development. In both Sudan and Chad, oil has fueled economic growth even though armed conflicts have left thousands dead and millions displaced. In Guinea and Uganda, the fighting has been geographically isolated – in the South and Southeast in Guinea and in the North in Uganda – without compromising overall growth at the national level. These positive macro-indicators are pernicious in that they mask both widening inequality and human suffering.

Civil war may be development in reverse, but the country is not the best unit of analysis. By disaggregating development indicators along regional or group lines, it is possible to track the deleterious consequences that conflict may have on some segments of a country's population despite positive aggregated indicators for the country as a whole. From 1990 to 2004, while armed conflict raged in northern Uganda, the country's HDI improved from 0.411 to 0.502, childhood immunization rose from 45 per cent to 87 per cent and access to

Figure 5.1   GDP Decreases* During Conflicts 1970–2005 (in Constant US$) Excluding Conflicts of One Year

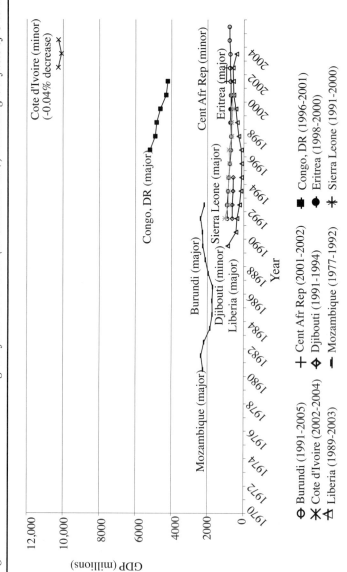

⊕ Burundi (1991-2005)   ✛ Cent Afr Rep (2001-2002)   ■ Congo, DR (1996-2001)
✷ Cote d'Ivoire (2002-2004) ◈ Djibouti (1991-1994)   ● Eritrea (1998-2000)
➤ Liberia (1989-2003)   ▬ Mozambique (1977-1992)   ✳ Sierra Leone (1991-2000)

*Note: GDP decreases defined by GDP lower last year of conflict compared with first year.

76

Figure 5.2   GDP Increases* During Conflicts 1970–2005 (in Constant US$) Excluding Conflicts of One Year

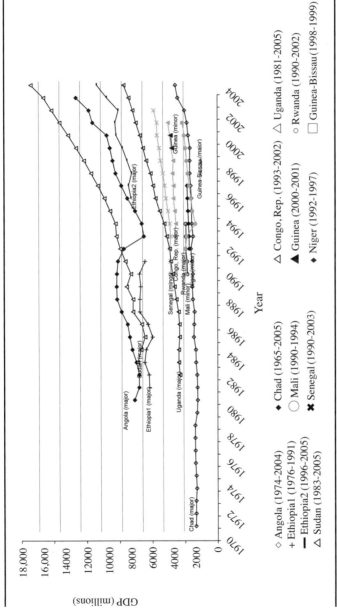

◇ Angola (1974-2004)   ◆ Chad (1965-2005)   △ Congo, Rep. (1993-2002)   △ Uganda (1981-2005)
+ Ethiopia1 (1976-1991) ◯ Mali (1990-1994)   ● Guinea (2000-2001)   ○ Rwanda (1990-2002)
— Ethiopia2 (1996-2005) ✖ Senegal (1990-2003)   ◆ Niger (1992-1997)   ☐ Guinea-Bissau (1998-1999)
△ Sudan (1983-2005)

Note: GDP decreases defined by GDP lower last year of conflict compared with first year.

Figure 5.3   Under-Five Mortality Rate Decreases* During Conflicts 1970–2005 Excluding Conflicts of One Year

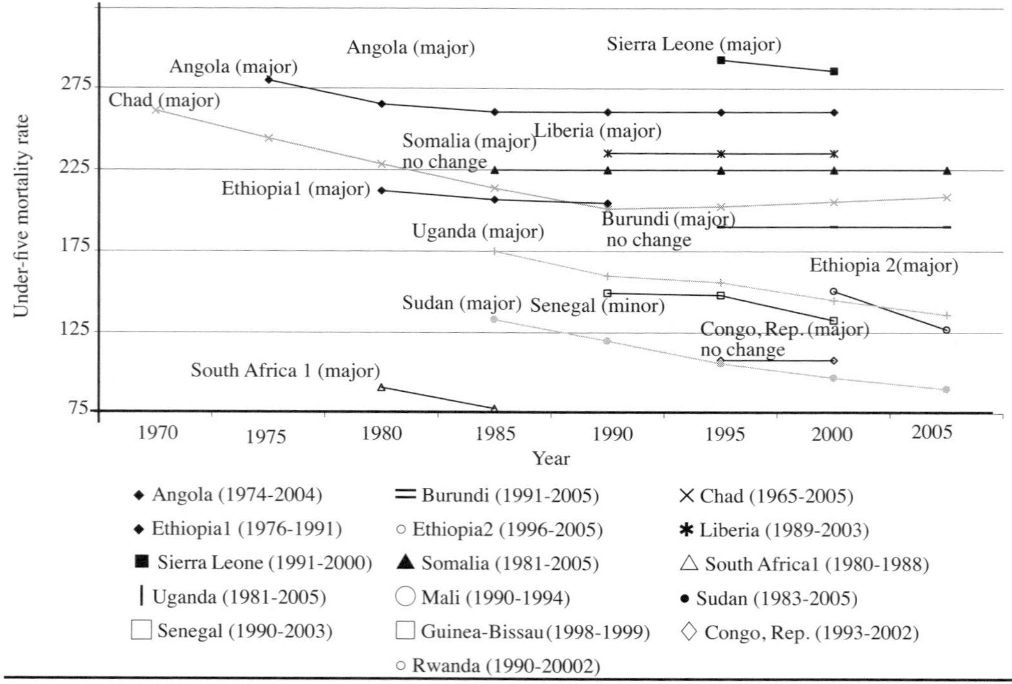

Legend:

- ◆ Angola (1974-2004)
- ◆ Ethiopia1 (1976-1991)
- ■ Sierra Leone (1991-2000)
- | Uganda (1981-2005)
- □ Senegal (1990-2003)
- ≡ Burundi (1991-2005)
- ○ Ethiopia2 (1996-2005)
- ▲ Somalia (1981-2005)
- ○ Mali (1990-1994)
- □ Guinea-Bissau (1998-1999)
- ○ Rwanda (1990-20002)
- ✕ Chad (1965-2005)
- ✳ Liberia (1989-2003)
- △ South Africa1 (1980-1988)
- ● Sudan (1983-2005)
- ◇ Congo, Rep. (1993-2002)

*Note: Defined by under-five mortality rate being lower at last year of conflict (or closest data point, taken at five-year increments) as compared with the beginning of the conflict.

78

clean water improved from 44 per cent to 60 per cent (UNDP 2007). Yet these national numbers severely misrepresent the stark and widening regional inequalities. In 2005–2006, Uganda's national poverty rate was 31.1 per cent, while northern Uganda's poverty level was 60.7 per cent (Uganda Bureau of Statistics 2006). In addition, the Under-Five Mortality Rate remained three-to-four times higher in the northern conflict areas than in the non-conflict areas (World Health Organization 2005) and the adult literacy rate, which stands at 77 per cent in central Uganda, is a mere 47 per cent in northern Uganda (Nawaguna 2007).

STRUCTURAL CONDITIONS AND WAR RISKS

Traditionally, studies of armed conflicts relied on historical and political factors to explain why wars emerge, persist, recur or end. However, in response to the increasing concentration of civil wars in poor countries, new research in the 1990s began to focus on the socioeconomic conditions that are associated with the frequent occurrence of war. This rich and diverse literature of cross-country statistical and qualitative studies identified a series of social and economic conditions that may exist in a country and that appear to favor the emergence of armed conflict. These factors are not mutually exclusive, however, and may coexist and may be mutually reinforcing (Fukuda-Parr 2007; Murshed 2007). Moreover, while political and historical factors may be the proximate factors that drive war, structural risks are root causes. Were these factors relevant for the 32 countries considered here?

Chronic Poverty

Several of these studies found strong correlation between per capita income and the incidence of conflict, implying that GDP growth would help reduce war risk (Collier et al. 2003). All of the 32 countries are among the world's poorest, with large proportions of their population surviving in extreme poverty. The 2005 per capita GDP for these countries ranged from $91 to $997, and HDI in 2004 ranged from 0.311 to 0.532. The proportion of people surviving in extreme poverty, measured by the international threshold of $1 a day (PPP), ranges from 15 per cent to 78 per cent for the 21 countries for which estimates are available from 1996 to 2005. In this respect, these 32 countries are no different from the other 12 countries of the region that remained conflict-free but are also poor.

A more interesting question is whether economic decline and a general worsening of poverty preceded the onset of war. Historical accounts of civil war often attribute serious economic mismanagement and misrule by the ruling regime as one of the causes of an insurgency, such as in DRC, Liberia or Sierra Leone. Economic decline prior to the onset of war was registered in 13 of the 32 countries, where per capita income was lower at the onset of war than five years previously (Figure 5.4); and for nine of these, GDP growth averaged less than 1 per cent annually over that period. But this was not a generalized pattern; in 13 countries for which data are available, per capita GDP was higher at the onset of the war than five years previously (Figure 5.5), and average annual growth rate was over 1 per cent. Under-5 Mortality rates were also improving during the years preceding the war for most countries.

Overdependence on Natural Resources

Collier and Hoeffler (2002) argue that overdependence on natural resources increases war risk, with greatest risk reached when primary commodities comprise a 32 per cent share of GDP. Several of the 32 countries are highly dependent on natural resource exports, including Cameroon, Congo Republic, Cote d'Ivoire, Ghana, Guinea, Guinea Bissau and Liberia, where primary commodity exports exceed 15 per cent as a share of GDP. If oil is included, Angola, Nigeria and the Congo are also highly resource dependent. However, the majority of the 32 countries are not so highly dependent on primary commodity exports. In 2000 Cote d'Ivoire's share of primary commodities to GDP was 31.6 per cent (UNCTAD *Commodity Year Book 2003*); two years later war broke out.

Overdependence on minerals can be a risk factor in two ways. First, groups take up arms to seek control of a country's natural resources. Second, once war starts, control of mineral resources becomes a lifeline for the warring parties. In Sierra Leone during the civil war (1991–2000), Revolutionary United Front rebels financed their insurgency through profits from the diamond trade. In Angola's civil war (1975–2002), both the government and rebels sustained themselves by exploiting natural resource wealth (Gamba and Cornwell 2000). The National Union for the Total Independence of Angola rebel group did so with diamonds, and the Popular Liberation Movement of Angola-led government did so with oil (Le Billon 2001; International Crisis Group 2003; Sherman 2000). In the civil war of Cote d'Ivoire, where primary commodity exports reached almost 32 per cent of GDP in 2000, the role of natural resources (i.e., cocoa) in sustaining violence is more ambiguous. In addition to the examples listed above, it is clear that competition over control of the oil wealth has been a factor in the conflicts in Nigeria's oil-rich Niger Delta.

Figure 5.4   Per Capita GDP Declines Five Years Prior to Onset of Armed Conflict

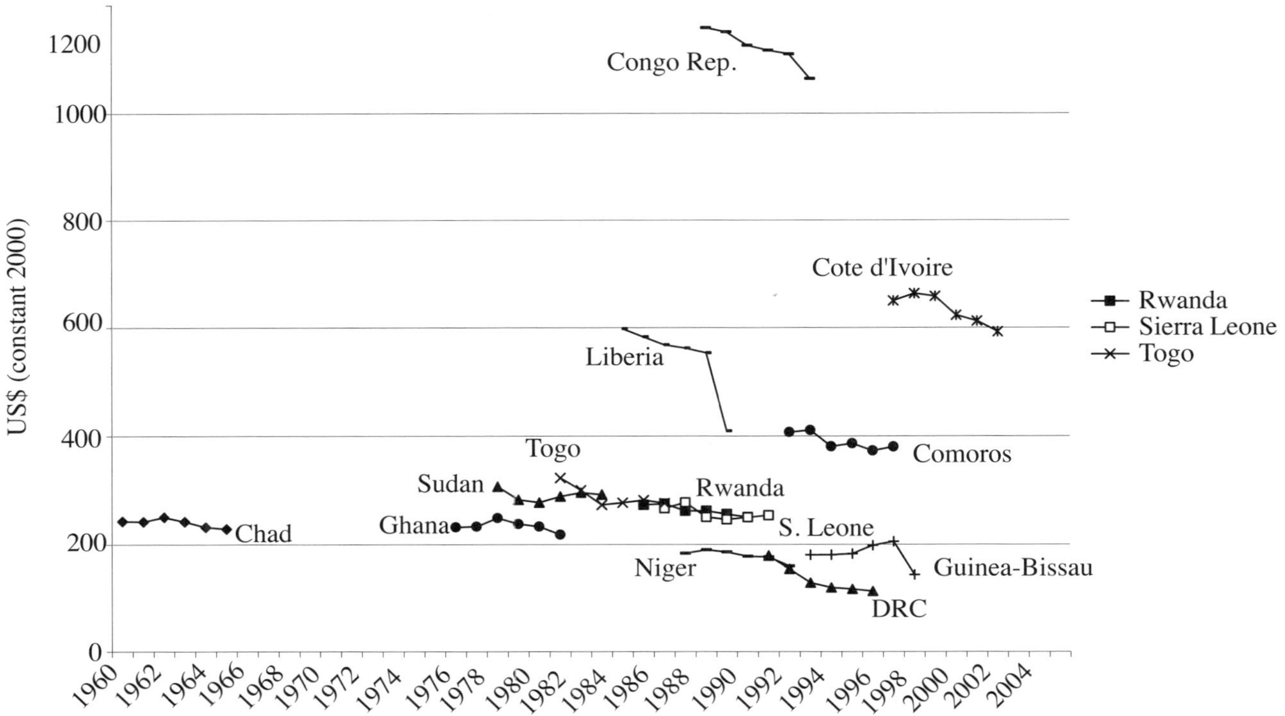

Figure 5.5   Per Capita GDP Increases during Fifth Years Prior to Onset of Armed Conflict

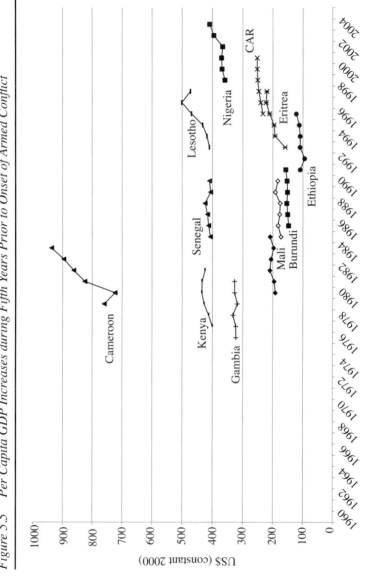

Note: South Africa also had an increase from $2,222 to $2749 (off chart).

Horizontal Inequalities

While the idea that stark inequality would lead to resentment and uprising is intuitively appealing, research has not found empirical evidence of armed war occurring more frequently where vertical inequalities are high. On the other hand, there is more evidence associating horizontal inequality – inequality between groups with ethnic, religious or linguistic ties – with conflict (Stewart 2003). Grievance over historical exclusion from economic, social and political opportunities and power provides incentives to insurgency, and the use of group loyalty and identity can be powerful means to mobilization. These disparities provide explanations for ethnic wars that go beyond historic enmity between groups.

The countries of Sub-Saharan Africa are characterized by the multiplicity of identity groups that compose their populations and a historical legacy of unequal political and economic power between them (UNDP 2004). It is widely held that horizontal inequalities are widespread in African countries where ethnicity became politically and economically salient in colonial and post-colonial times. Available data consistently show sharp inequalities when data disaggregated by ethnicity are available for economic and social indicators such as income, educational attainment, and access to high-level employment positions, as well as in political indicators, such as representation in the government, legislature, military and other institutions of the state. For example, in Namibia, HDI was estimated for six linguistic groups and ranged from a high of 0.960 for German speakers to a low of 0.326 for San speakers (UNDP 2004). Disparities are sharp not only between racial groups but also among Namibia's African populations; HDI for Oshiwambo speakers is 0.641, twice the index for the San speakers (UNDP 2004).

However, such data are not consistently available. This survey reviewed two databases that assess the extent of horizontal inequalities that are politically salient in the context of their potential for armed conflict. First, the Minorities at Risk Project's Aggregate Differential Index (ADI) is a composite of 18 cultural, political and economic indicators that rate differential treatment based on group identity (Minorities at Risk 2005a, 5). Scores are available for 26 of the 32 countries. Burundi, Cote d'Ivoire, Sudan, Liberia, Mali, Ethiopia, Djibouti and Uganda score particularly high, above 10 on a scale where the maximum possible score is 18 (Minorities at Risk Project 2007).

Second, the Failed State Index uses a composite of 12 sub-indicators, including a measure of horizontal inequality: Uneven Economic Development along Group Lines; and two others that indicate the level of political mobilization based on group disparity: Uneven Legacy of Vengeance-Seeking Group Grievance or Group Paranoia; and Rise of Factionalized Elites. Most of the 32 countries score high on uneven economic development; 22 of them are at the 'warning' level, while nine others (Comoros, Angola, Djibouti, Eritrea, Gambia, Ghana, Guinea-Bissau, Mozambique and Senegal) fall just below the cutoff. Three of these countries (Ghana, Mali and Senegal) show low scores in political mobilization (rise of factionalized elites), but the political salience of group inequalities is evident in all the countries, according to this index (Fund for Peace 2007).

While these databases confirm the presence of group exclusion and their political activation, they do not show whether this was a factor that drove past wars. Academic and policy literature that examine the causes of wars in 32 countries identify horizontal inequality or group exclusion as a factor in several.

The war in the southern Casamance region of Senegal is an example of horizontal inequalities becoming a factor in mobilizing violence. Home to the Diola ethnic group, a distinct cultural group, the Casamance region also has the highest poverty and infant mortality rates in the country. Other examples of grievance over horizontal inequalities being a factor include the northerners in the Central African Republic, southern Christians in Chad, northern ethnic groups in Congo (Brazzaville), northern Muslims and immigrants in Cote d'Ivoire, the Afars in Djibouti, the Afar and Somali liberation movements of Ethiopia, Americo-Liberians in Liberia, the Tuareg people of Northern Mali, Hutus and Tutsis in Rwanda and Burundi, Darfur Black Muslims and southern Christian/Animists of Sudan, the Ewe in Togo and northerners in Uganda (Minorities at Risk Project 2007). However, it is important to note that group exclusion does not appear to have been a major factor in many other countries, such as Mozambique, Sierra Leone, Guinea, Somalia, Cameroon and Guinea Bissau.

Neighborhood Spillovers

Wars take on sub-regional dimensions as neighboring countries become embroiled in supporting various warring parties. Neighboring countries serve as safe havens for rebel groups or receive an influx of refugees, incite support among ethnic groups that inhabit more than one state and provide opportunities for profiteers to engage in highly lucrative weapons or natural resource smuggling. States and other groups support warring parties through direct material and political support. For example, Chad provided refuge for thousands of people displaced from violence in Central African Republic and Sudan; the governments of Eritrea and Somalia supported opposing sides in the war in Ethiopia; the governments of Senegal and Guinea sent troops to Guinea-Bissau, while Ethiopia, Eritrea, Yemen, Djibouti, Egypt and Sudan have sent arms to varying warring groups in Somalia (International Crisis Group 2007; Webersik 2004). Finally, in Sudan and Uganda, the respective wars in each have mutually and negatively affected the other.

Environmental Pressure Related to Migration

Although the African continent is relatively sparsely populated when compared with other regions of the world, environmental stress and demographic pressures are present in a number of countries. Mounting demographic pressures is one of the indicators of the Failed State Index – all of the 32 countries score above six and several above nine (Chad, DRC, Ethiopia, Lesotho, Niger, Somalia, Sudan).

Several conflicts have been triggered by rival claims to scarce land or natural resources. Although the conflict in Sudan has been commonly attributed to historical enmity on religious or racial grounds, in fact, resource scarcity lies at the root of the conflict. Drought and desertification have increased pressure on water and land resources, forcing group migration into areas historically settled by others. This encroachment has created stress and led to violence (Youngs 2004, 8). According to the Minorities at Risk database, the Azawad conflict in Mali (1990–96) was driven by socioeconomic exclusion of the Tuaregs, but environmental stress also played a role (2007). The desertification of the Sahel in the late 1960s to early 1970s, as well as frequent droughts in the 1980s, caused a mass migration of Tuaregs from Northern Mali to neighboring countries.

Demographic Youth Bulge

Cincotta (2003) demonstrates a strong statistical relationship between demographic patterns and the incidence of armed conflict. His study identifies countries in which young adults comprise more than 40 per cent of the adult population as more than twice as likely as countries with lower proportions to experience an outbreak of civil conflict. In the absence of employment, opportunity or constructive activities, youth, especially young men, are known to congregate in cohesive groups or gangs that may evolve into politically mobilized insurgencies (Cincotta 2003). This risk factor is present in almost all countries of Sub-Saharan Africa, including those that have experienced major wars, minor wars and no wars. Reviews of data show that each of the 32 conflict countries surveyed here has a youth bulge with a population aged 15–29 years comprising over 44 per cent of the total (UN Population Division 2007).

History of War

Statistical analysis has shown a high risk that conflict will reemerge after an end to violence (Collier and Hoeffler 2002). This has indeed been the history of Sub-Saharan Africa, where formal peace agreements have failed to achieve long-lasting peace. Of the 126 conflicts being surveyed here, there were 154 cessations in fighting but only nine of these lasted 10 years, and another 10 ceased less than 10 years ago and continue to hold. Of the 32 conflict-affected countries only eight have experienced peace of least ten years' duration. In several countries violent state repression or conflict between identity groups has continued unabated (Gleditsch et al. 2002; Harbom et al. 2006).

POLICY RESPONSES TO ADDRESSING RISK FACTORS

The preceding sections have shown the ways in which armed conflict has affected the trajectory of development and vice versa. The destructive impact of wars is a source of current poverty and development challenges. But development patterns such as a history of ethnic exclusion and environmental pressure have been among the drivers of past conflicts and continue to raise political tensions. These linkages have important policy implications for development strategy, as economic, social and governance reform policies have important bearing on these structural factors. For example, budgetary allocations can deepen horizontal inequalities and group grievance; health and education policies such as measures to increase schooling of girls are central aspects of demographic change; inappropriate agricultural and rural policies can aggravate environmental pressures and competition over land. In these and many other ways, development policy can either alleviate or worsen group grievances, the youth bulge and unemployment, environmental pressure and poor governance of natural resources and thus help prevent or exacerbate the risks of armed conflict recurring.

To assess how development policies and priorities address these links between armed conflict and development, Poverty Reduction Strategy Papers (PRSPs) were reviewed where they were available. PRSPs reflect both national priorities and a degree of endorsement by the official donor community. Several of the PRSPs, notably for countries that are emerging from war following a peace settlement, such as Liberia, Guinea Bissau, Congo Republic, Angola and Djibouti, or following a decisive victory such as Rwanda, identify conflict as a major source of their development and poverty challenges. All of the PRSPs emphasize the importance of governance, but mostly not in relation to preventing recurrence of violent conflict.

However, overall, there is scant treatment of armed conflict and its links to development challenges in the 18 PRSPs reviewed. Four made no mention of armed conflict that had taken place or was continuing at the time, and while others mentioned the issue, only Liberia's Interim-PRSP 2007 had a section devoted to an analysis of the root causes of conflict. The lack of attention to armed conflict is particularly surprising where wars were being actively fought at the time that the document was prepared and adopted: The Ethiopia PRSP of 2002 refers only to the border war with Eritrea and in the historical context of pre-1991 wars, not to the ongoing conflicts within the country; the Senegal PRSP of 2002 makes no mention of the persistent fighting in the South that was continuing at the time; and the Chad PRSP of 2003 refers to conflict only twice in the 142-page document, referring only to a 'climate of insecurity and impunity' in a 'conflict-ridden environment' and to 'decades of armed conflict' and its impact on armed forces. These findings are consistent with a recent study (Scharf et al. 2008) that analyzed 20 PRSP and similar documents and more than 80 UN Development Assistance Frameworks and found less than half referred to armed violence.

Regarding structural risk factors, issues such as horizontal inequality, youth employment, demographic pressures, migration, neighborhood spillover effects and the governance of natural resources were not given priority attention. Issues of unequal development along group lines and ethnic exclusion are rarely addressed. Inclusive development approaches, such as equitable growth and greater sharing of power and opportunities are not the explicit stated goals, even in countries where ethnic grievance and exclusion are politically live issues. The term 'equity' most often appears in relation to gender equality. Even the I-PRSP of Liberia, which fully recognizes the pattern of elite rule as a source of the war that lasted over a decade, is weak when it comes to reflecting inclusion as a policy priority. The document says little about setting priorities across regions and activities to ensure distributional balance. While social and physical infrastructure development had been concentrated in Monrovia and the coast and the interior neglected, this strategy makes no provisions to reverse these historic imbalances, and where poverty is concentrated in rural areas, the economic growth strategy does not give high priority to agriculture other than the export-oriented plantation sector (Fukuda-Parr et al. 2007).

Thus PRSPs do not systematically include analysis of conflict's impact on development or analysis of root causes of conflict and grievances over issues of political, economic and social exclusion. Armed conflict that is ongoing in a country is systematically ignored as a source of poverty. Indeed, that both a country's governments and the donors who endorse them turn a blind eye to recent or ongoing fighting in the country inevitably has repercussions for development and poverty.

CONCLUSIONS

In surveying the nexus of development and armed conflicts in Sub-Saharan Africa since 1980, several findings emerge that challenge widely-held assumptions and suggest directions for reconsidering policy priorities, launching new research directions and designing more effective policies for human security.

First, the state as a unit of analysis and focus of policy action does not match the reality of contemporary wars in Africa, where the actors are both state and non-state, involve local and external allies and are motivated by political and private economic ends. Yet data collection, analytical frameworks and policy interventions remain state-centric. New research directions are needed that focus on non-state actors and transnational conflict networks, destructive impacts of conflicts at sub-national levels, and on cross-border alliances and impacts. Some key gaps include: data and analysis of non-state conflicts, and the distributional consequences of conflicts. Current policy research and policy agendas for conflict prevention, peace-building and economic recovery continue to focus on 'post-conflict' settings.

Second, the survey found surprisingly that economic decline did not uniformly result from war. Some economies grew and human outcomes improved even during conflict, as impacts were contained to specific locations or as the economy was buoyed by such exogenous factors as commodity exports. More research is needed to understand how the expected consequences of conflict are contained, and their political implications. More policy attention is needed on the distributional impact of wars, for when development indicators are positive, both national governments and the international community can turn a blind eye to the violence that continues. Not only does this imply neglect of human suffering but also neglect of the growing risk from worsening horizontal inequality.

Third, the survey shows the prevalence of long-term, 'low-intensity' conflicts. They constitute a human security priority because their violence imposes huge human and developmental costs and has the potential to escalate and spread further. They are also a priority for conflict-prevention policy. Yet low-intensity conflicts receive little policy attention, especially as a development challenge. As the conflict in Northern Uganda illustrates, development disparities are both cause and consequence of such conflicts yet they are considered to be a domestic political/security issue and kept out of development policy priority setting. New policy approaches need to be developed in the international community to address these cases.

Fourth, structural conditions identified by recent research as risk factors are present to varying extents in most African countries and particularly in the

32 that have experienced war. Horizontal inequality and the youth bulge are relevant more consistently than others. While all countries are 'poor', in many cases economic decline did not precede conflict. Environmental pressure and natural resource dependence have been factors in few of the 32 countries. The relationship between these underlying risk factors and emergence of armed conflict is neither automatic nor uniform, and their presence should not be considered predictive but rather as relevant risk factors requiring attention. Since they relate to development structures, such conflicts are highly relevant to development policy, including economic and social policies to reduce horizontal inequality, governance reforms to promote political inclusion, as well as economic and social policies to generate employment-creating growth and promote youth employment and manage the demographic transition. Economic growth alone will not remove these structural risks.

Fifth, neither national governments nor the international community have developed and applied systematic approaches to integrating conflict consequences and risks into development policy priorities. Major development policy instruments, starting with the PRSP, need to become more consistent in addressing conflict impacts and risks.

Finally, this survey documents and confirms the high risks of armed conflict in Sub-Saharan African countries as political tensions remain unresolved and structural risk factors prevalent. Perhaps most important, one of the most striking characteristics of armed conflict in Africa has been the fragility of peace; even where there has been an end to violence, there has been almost invariably a resumption. These patterns point to a need for a more proactive approach to preventing conflict by addressing the structural risk factors.

NOTE

This chapter was originally published in the *Journal of Peacebuilding and Development* (2008) and was included here with the kind permission of the authors and the Journal.

1. While governments do not collect data on war, over 60 datasets have been created by academics and NGOs to monitor regional and global trends. The armed conflict dataset maintained by the Uppsala Conflict Data Program (UCDP) and International Peace Research Institute, Oslo (PRIO), is increasingly used in research and policy work because it is comprehensive, is updated annually, and its methodology is considered rigorous.

REFERENCES

African Development Bank/African Development Fund (2006), 'Sudan: Country Dialogue Paper 2006', Country Operations Department, ADF North, East and South Region.

Black, R. (1994), 'Forced Migration and Environmental Change: The Impact of Refugees on Host Environments', *Journal of Economic Management*, **42** (3), 261–77.

Black, R. and M. Sessay (1997), 'Forced Migration, Land-use Change and Political Economy in the Forest Region of Guinea', *African Affairs*, **96** (385), 587–605.

Cincotta, R., R. Engelman and D. Anastasion (2003), *The Security Demographic: Population and Civil Conflict after the Cold War*, Washington, DC: Population Action International.

Coghlan B., R.J. Brennan, P. Ngoy et al. (2006), 'Mortality in the Democratic Republic of Congo: A Nationwide Survey', *Lancet*, **367** (January), 44–51.

Collier, P. and A. Hoeffler (2002), 'Greed and Grievance in Civil Wars', Oxford, UK, Centre for the Study of African Economies Working Paper Series No. 2002-01.

Collier, P., A. Hoeffler and D. Rohner (2008), 'Greed and Grievance: Feasibility and Civil War', *Oxford Economic Papers*, **56** (4), 563–95.

Collier, P., and V.L. Elliot, H. Hegre, A. Hoeffler, M. Reynal-Querol and N Sambanis (2003), *Breaking the Conflict Trap: Civil War and Development Policy*, Washington, DC, World Bank and New York: Oxford University Press.

Eschenbächer, J.H. (ed.) (2006), 'Internal Displacement: Overview of Trends and Developments in 2005', Geneva, Switzerland: Internal Displacement Monitoring Centre/Norwegian Refugee Council.

Fukuda-Parr, S. (2007), 'Rethinking the Policy Objectives of Development Aid: From Economic Growth to Conflict Prevention', Helsinki, United Nations University, World Institute for Development Economics Research (WIDER) Working Paper No. 2007/32.

Fukuda-Parr, S., J.A. Fuentes, A. Parakrama, B. Ruane and V.T. Tran. (2007), 'Integrating Human Rights into National Poverty Reduction Strategies: The Challenge of Development with Equity and the Liberia iPRS', UN/OHCHR Liberia Field Assessment Mission Report, 8–20 January.

Fund for Peace (2007), *Failed States Index, 2007*, at http://www.fundforpeace.org.

Gamba, V. and R. Cornwell (2000), 'Arms, Elites and Resources in the Angolan Civil War', in M.R. Berdal and D.M. Malone (eds), *Greed and Grievance: Economic Agendas in Civil Wars*, Boulder and London: Lynne Reinner, pp. 157–72.

Gleditsch, N.P., P. Wallensteen, M. Eriksson, M. Sollenberg and H. Strand (2002), 'Armed Conflict 1946–2001: A New Dataset' *Journal of Peace Research*, **39** (5), 615–37. Dataset at http://www.prio.no/CSCW/Datasets/Armed-Conflict/.

Harbom, L. and S. Högbladh (2006), 'UCDP/PRIO Armed Conflict Dataset Codebook Version 4–2006'. Dataset at http://www.prio.no/CSCW/Datasets/Armed-Conflict/.

Harbom, L., S. Högbladh and P. Wallensteen (2006), 'Armed Conflict and Peace Agreements', *Journal of Peace Research*, **43** (5), 617–31. Dataset at http://www.prio.no/CSCW/Datasets/Armed-Conflict/.

Harbom, L. and P. Wallensteen (2007), 'Armed Conflicts 1989–2006', *Journal of Peace Research*, **44** (5), 623–34. Dataset at http://www.prio.no/CSCW/Datasets/Armed-Conflict/.

Henderson, E.A. and J.D. Singer (2000), 'Civil War in the Post-Colonial World, 1946–92', *Journal of Peace Research*, **17** (3): 275–99.

Homer-Dixon, T. (1991), 'On the Threshold: Environmental Changes as Causes of Acute Conflict', *International Security*, **16** (2), 76 –116.

Human Rights Watch (2004), 'Ten Years Later', in *Leave None to Tell the Story: Genocide in Rwanda*, at http://www.hrw.org/reports/1999/rwanda/10years.htm.

Human Security Report Project (2005), *Human Security Report 2005: War and Peace in the 21st Century*, New York: Oxford University Press, at http://www. humansecurityreport.info/content/view/28/63/.

—— (2006), *Human Security Brief 2006*, Vancouver, BC: Human Security Centre, Simon Fraser University, at http://www.humansecurityreport.info/index.php?optio n=content&task=view&id=114.

International Crisis Group (2007), 'Somalia: The Tough Part is Ahead', Africa Briefing No. 45.

—— (2003), 'Angola's Choice: Reform or Progress', Africa Report No. 61.

Internal Displacement Monitoring Centre (2007), 'Overview: Internal Displacement in Africa'.

International Institute of Strategic Studies (2007), Armed Conflict Database, at http:// www.iiss.org/publications/armed-conflict-database.

Integrated Regional Information Networks (IRIN) News Online (2005), 'TOGO: UN Report Says at least 400 People Died in Political Violence', 26 September.

Jacobsen, K. (1997), 'Refugees' Environmental Impact: the Effect of Patterns of Settlement', *Journal of Refugee Studies*, **10** (1), 19–36.

—— (2002), 'Livelihoods in Conflict: The Pursuit of Livelihoods by Refugees and the Impact on the Human Security of Host Communities', *International Migration*, **40** (5), 95–121.

Jönsson, J. (2007), 'The Overwhelming Minority: Traditional Leadership and Ethnic Conflict in Ghana's Northern Region', Oxford, UK, Center for Research on Inequality, Human Security and Ethnicity (CRISE) Working Paper No. 30.

Kean, D. (2006), *Conflict and Collusion in Sierra Leone*, New York: Palgrave.

Kaldor, M. (2007), *New and Old Wars*, 2nd ed., Stanford, CA: Stanford University Press.

Lacina, B. (2006), 'Battle Deaths Dataset 1946–2005: Codebook for Version 2.0', Oslo, International Peace Research Institute, Center for the Study of Civil War at http:// www.prio.no/sptrans/-1384481917/Code_Book_2.pdf.

Lacina, B. and N.P. Gelditsch (2005), 'Monitoring Trends in Global Combat: A New Dataset of Battle Deaths', *European Journal of Population*, **21** (2–3), 145–65.

Le Billon, P. (2001), 'Angola's Political Economy of War: The Role of Oil and Diamonds, 1975–2000', *African Affairs*, **100** (398), 55–80.

Marshall, M., T.R. Gurr and B. Harff (2001), 'PITF Problem Set Codebook', *Internal Wars and Failures of Governance, 1955–2004*, Arlington, VA: George Mason University School of Public Policy, Political Instability Task Force at http:// globalpolicy.gmu.edu/pitf/pitfcode.htm#20.

Minorities at Risk Project (2005), 'Minorities at Risk Dataset Users Manual 030703', available at http://www.cidcm.umd.edu/mar.

—— (2007), *MAR Data*, College Park, MD: University of Maryland Center for International Development and Conflict Management at http://www.cidcm.umd. edu/mar/.

Murshed, S.M. (2007), 'The Conflict–Growth Nexus and the Poverty of Nations', New York, United Nations, Department of Economic and Social Affairs Working Paper

No. 43.

Nawaguna, E. (2007), 'Primary School: Girls Beat Boys in Literacy', United Nations Girls' Education Initiative at http://www.ungei.com/infobycountry/uganda_1420.html.

Poverty Net (various), 'Country Papers and JSANs/JSAs', [collection of Poverty Reduction Strategy Papers] at http://go.worldbank.org/SIKR9UVMY0.

Reno, W. (2005), 'The Politics of Violent Opposition in Collapsing States', *Government and Opposition*, **40** (2), 127–51.

Scharf, R., T. Patterson and R. Muggah (2008), 'Reviewing Armed Violence in National Development Planning Instruments – PRSPs and UNDAFs', Background Paper for OECD Guidance on Armed Violence Reduction.

Schraeder, P.J. (1993), 'Ethnic Politics in Djibouti: From the Eye of the Hurricane to the Boiling Cauldron', *African Affairs*, **92** (367), 203–21.

Shahim, K. and J. Searing (1980), Djibouti and the Question of Afar Nationalism', *African Affairs*, **79** (315), 209–26.

Sherman, J.H. (2000), 'Profit vs. Peace: The Clandestine Diamond Economy of Angola', *Journal of International Affairs*, **53** (2), 699–719.

Stewart, F., V. FitzGerald and Associates (2001), *War and Underdevelopment*, 2 vol. New York: Oxford University Press.

Stewart, F. (2003), 'Horizontal Inequalities: A Neglected Dimension of Development', Oxford, UK, Center for Research on Inequality, Human Security and Ethnicity (CRISE) Working Paper No. 1.

Uganda Bureau of Statistics (2006), 'Uganda National Household Survey 2005/06', ID Number UGA-UBOS-UNHS-2005-v1.0.

UNDP (2001), 'Somalia: Human Development Report', United Nations Development Programme, Somalia Country Office, Nairobi, Kenya.

—— (2004), *Human Development Report 2004:Cultural Liberty in Today's Diverse World*, New York: Oxford University Press.

—— (2007), 'Uganda Human Development Report 2007', United Nations Deveopment Programme, Uganda Country Office, Kampala, Uganda.

UNCTAD (2003), *Commodity Yearbook*, Geneva: United Nations Committee on Trade and Development.

UNHCR (2007), 'UNHCR Statistical Online Population Database', United Nations High Commissioner for Refugees at (UNHCR), at http://www.unhcr.org/statistics/populationdatabase, accessed January 8, 2007.

UN Millennium Project (2005), 'Investing in Development: A Practical Plan to Achieve the MDGs', at http://www.unmillenniumproject.org/reports/index_overview.htm.

UNPD (2007), *World Population Prospects: The 2007 Revision*, United Nations Population Division, available at http://esa.un.org/unpp

Van Damme, W. (1995), 'Do Refugees Belong in Camps? Experiences from Goma and Guinea', *Lancet*, **346** (5 August), 360–62.

Webersik, C. (2004), 'Differences Matter: The Struggle of the Marginalized in Somalia', *Africa*, **74** (4), 515–33.

World Bank (2002), 'Memorandum of the President of the International Development Association to the Executive Directors on a Country Assistance Strategy for the Republic of Rwanda', Report No. 24501-RW.

—— (2003), 'Country Assistance Strategy Paper for the Republic of Guinea', Report No. 25925 GUI.

—— (2005), 'Country Assistance Strategy for the Republic of Djibouti', Report No.

3161.

WHO (2002), *World Report on Violence and Health: Summary*, Geneva: World Health Organization, at http://www.who.int/violence_injury_prevention/violence/world_report/en/summary_en.pdf.

——— (2005), 'Health and Mortality Survey among Internally Displaced Persons in Gulu, Kitgum and Pader Districts, Northern Uganda', at http://www.who.int/hac/crises/uga/sitreps/Ugandamortsurvey.pdf.

Youngs, Tim (2004), 'Sudan: Conflict in Darfur,' United Kingdom House of Commons Library, International Affairs and Defense Section, Report No. 04/51.

6. National Security: Deterring and Surviving Civil Conflicts

Marta Reynal-Querol

The Copenhagen Consensus project identified civil conflicts as one of the basic challenges to global development. The experts on the panel noted, 'Measures to reduce the number, duration or severity of civil war would stand very high in the ranking of priorities for development, if they could be expected with any confidence to succeed'.

Why should the international community worry about conflict? Since World War II, more than 80 million people have been killed in internal conflicts. As a matter of comparison, there were 71 million tobacco-related deaths between 1930 and 1999. If we could find measures to prevent internal conflicts, we would have a serious impact on reducing the number of human losses. Moreover, conflict also generates mass displacements of people, which helps spread infectious diseases like malaria and AIDS. Therefore, finding measures to prevent conflict should, without a doubt, be a priority for development.

But, what are the fundamental causes of civil wars, and how can conflicts be prevented? Although there is little consensus to answer these questions, differences in per capita income have received considerable attention. The UN Millennium Project, 'Investing in Development: Practical Plans to Achieve the Millennium Development Goals' notes:

> Poor and hungry societies are much more likely than high-income societies to fall into conflict over scarce vital resources, such as watering holes and arable land.... Poverty increases the risks of conflict through multiple paths.... The implications are twofold: Investing in development is especially important to reduce the probability of conflict. (2005, 6, 8)

Many world leaders agree on this point. And they have stressed the idea that the fight against war, internal war and violence requires a reduction in poverty. Chancellor Gerhard Schröder of Germany, 2001, in Program Action 2015, said

Extreme poverty, growing inequality between countries, but also within countries themselves, are great challenges of our times, because they are a breeding ground for instability and conflict. So reducing worldwide poverty is, not least, essential to safeguarding peace and security.

Also, the idea that economic development is central to reducing the global incidence of civil war is the main message of the World Bank report *Breaking the Conflict Trap: Civil War and Development Policy* (Collier et al. 2003). That poverty is the main cause of conflict is the dominant theory in the empirical literature that studies civil wars, and the worldwide impact of this theory is not under discussion.

However, the idea that poverty is the main determinant of conflict is based on weak empirical grounds. In this study we show how fragile the results that support the idea that poverty is the main cause of conflict are. The basic objective of this study, therefore, is to analyze the effect of alternative institutional designs for the prevention of conflicts vis-à-vis poverty. In particular, we believe that institutional development plays a critical role in the incidence of civil wars. This line of research, if successful, can lead to a new approach to finding measures that could be expected to succeed in reducing the number, duration and severity of conflicts, challenging the traditional hypothesis that poverty is the main cause of conflict.

There is also the issue of how to apply these measures in potentially conflictive countries. The general consensus in the economic literature indicates that external development assistance does not improve the economic development of countries. Therefore, even if poverty were the main determinant of the incidence of conflict, it would be very difficult to act on this determinant. Examining institutional development in potentially conflictive countries opens up new possibilities for action.

We believe that the study of institutions is fundamental to understanding how to prevent or reduce conflict in potentially conflictive societies. Therefore, one goal of this study is to provide evidence on the role of these important institutional dimensions in preventing conflict. We find evidence that measures of the quality and strength of institutions seems to have a significant effect in understanding conflict. This provides some light on the idea that there is something about institutions that matters – and probably matter more than poverty, per se. Djankov and Reynal-Querol (2007, 2008) provide a deep analysis into this.

The literature is still debating democracy's ability – or inability – to reduce the incidence of civil wars. The current consensus seems to indicate that both autocracies and full democracies are less prone to conflicts. The form of democracy is another institutional dimension that seems to matter in preventing conflict. Reynal-Querol (2002a, 2002b, 2005) has studied which types of political systems are more appropriate to prevent social conflict. The basic contribution of this literature is the finding that the level of inclusiveness of the political system captures quite accurately the political aspects that matter to prevent social conflicts.

These findings undermine the emphasis on poverty as a determinant of civil war and indicate that research should concentrate more on institutions than on economic development if we wish to understand the causes of civil war. The evidence provided in this study is supported by some background papers that provide a more quantitative evidence and that address different econometric concerns, for example Djankov and Reynal-Querol (2007, 2008), Reynal-Querol (2002, 2005).

After summarizing two recent studies that try to quantify the costs of conflict and other studies that analyze the reconstruction process, we provide evidence of the limited effect of poverty in explaining conflict. The focus then turns to providing an analytical framework on how to study conflict, followed by an analysis of the role institutional development could lay to prevent conflict, vis-à-vis poverty. Finally, we analyze the role of political institutions in preventing civil wars.

QUANTIFYING THE COSTS OF CIVIL WARS, THE POST-CONFLICT PERIOD AND RECONSTRUCTION

Trying to quantify the costs of conflicts is not an easy task. Obviously, the most direct and terrible cost of civil wars is the loss of human lives, either civilians or combatants, due to direct fighting. War has devastating consequences for a country, including death, displacement of people and destruction of public infrastructure as well as physical and social capital. The World Bank report *Breaking the Conflict Trap* (Collier et al. 2003), one of the most comprehensive analyses, concludes that the economic and social costs of civil wars are not only deep, but also persistent, lasting years after the end of the conflict. However, when the end of war represents the beginning of lasting peace, there are good reasons to believe that recovery, albeit gradual, is possible. This is what neoclassical models of economic growth and convergence would predict and what the evidence of recovery in Europe (after World War II), Korea and Vietnam, among others, would seem to indicate.

The scarce literature that studies the consequences of civil wars has usually focused on the costs *during* conflict. A few studies, for example Chen, Loayza and Reyna-Querol (2008), analyze the costs of civil war after peace agreements are signed. They contribute some stylized facts on the evidence regarding the economic, social, and political aftermath of civil wars. Despite the difficulties in evaluating the impact of conflict, some studies have attempted to do so.

Costs of Conflict: What the Literature Says

There is little controversy as to the direct effects of civil and international wars. They kill people, destroy infrastructure, weaken institutions and erode social trust. Moreover, the destruction of infrastructure and institutions leaves the population under conditions that increase the risk of disease, crime, political instability and further conflict. Collier et al. (2003) provide a review of the literature on the costs of civil war. Collier (1999) finds that during civil war, countries tend to grow at a rate of 2.2 percentage points less than when at peace. Using World Health Organization data on 23 major diseases in populations distinguished by gender and age groups, Ghobarah, Huth and Russett (2003) find that civil war substantially increases the incidence of death and disability produced by contagious diseases. Soares (2006) estimates the welfare cost of violence in a sample of countries by applying a willingness-to-pay approach to account for the health consequences of war. For instance, Soares estimates that the civil conflict in Colombia, by reducing life expectancy at birth by 2.2 years, produces a 9.7 per cent loss in GDP. Other studies focus on the neighboring effects of civil war. Murdoch and Sandler (2002 and 2004) show that civil wars reduce growth over an entire region of neighboring countries. Montalvo and Reynal-Querol (2007) explore the influence of civil war refugees on the incidence of malaria in the refugee-receiving countries. They show that for each 1,000 refugees, between 2,000 and 2,700 cases of malaria occur in the refugee-receiving country.

Chen, Loayza and Reynal-Querol (2007) use an 'event-study' methodology to analyze the aftermath of civil war in a cross-section of countries. Since the objective is to provide a comprehensive evaluation of the aftermath of war, they examine a host of social areas. These are represented by basic indicators of economic performance, health and education, political development, demographic trends and conflict and security issues. For each of these indicators they compare the post- and pre-war situations, aiming to determine the existence and extent of a 'peace dividend'. They find that the average level of GDP per capita is significantly lower after the war, particularly in relation to the control groups. This is undoubtedly a direct reflection of the cost of war. On the other hand, the average growth rate of GDP per capita in conflict countries appears to be significantly higher after the war (by about 2.4 percentage points). The increase is even more pronounced when compared with the change experienced by the control groups. These two results are in line with those in Przeworski et al. (2000) and Barro and Sala-i-Martin (1995) after the destruction of the war, recovery is achieved through faster-than-usual growth. The increase in economic growth occurs with the support of an increase in the investment rate. The contribution by capital accumulation, however, seems to be somewhat weak and is significant only when compared to the control groups. This suggests than the increase in growth is also due to a recovery in capacity utilization and, possibly, improved factor productivity. Finally, the inflation rate is significantly higher after the war, whether compared with the control groups or not. For the few experiences where reliable war-time inflation data is available, the pattern is that the inflation rate increases sharply during the war as government revenue sources dwindle, and then decreases at the onset of peace. The health and education indicators share some patterns. When conflict countries are considered by themselves (that is, without reference to the control groups) there is a marked improvement in health and education in the post-war period as compared to the pre-war period. (Naturally, improvement means a decrease in mortality rates and an increase in school enrollment rates.) When compared with the control groups, however, the improvements are less clearcut. The fact that these health and education indicators improved in absolute terms signals the important influence of world trends (for instance reflecting international educational and health campaigns) even for conflict-ridden countries; however, the fact that the improvements fell below international standards reflects the unquestionable cost of war. Regarding the political variables, there is also evidence of absolute improvement in the post-war period in comparison with the pre-war period. The improvement falls short of what was achieved by the control groups. Again, the cost of the war is reflected in the failure of conflict countries to achieve international standards.

The Post-Conflict Period and Recovery

The empirical literature on the *aftermath* of civil and international war is scarcer. It seems to indicate that countries do recover in the post-conflict period to at least their pre-war situations. In a cross-country empirical analysis, Przeworski et al. (2000) find that post-war economic recovery is rapid. Their results indicate that the average rate of growth during the five years following a war is 5.98 per cent. They also find that wars cause more damage under dictatorships than under democracies; however, recoveries are faster under dictatorships than under democracies. Barro and Sala-i-Martin (1995) explain post-war recoveries – considering the examples of Japan and Germany following World War II – arguing that whenever a war destroys a given production factor relatively more than other factors, the rate of return of the latter increases, thus creating the forces of convergence that spur rapid growth. Collier and Hoeffler (2004a) provide a systematic empirical analysis of aid and policy reform in the post-conflict growth process using a comprehensive dataset of large civil wars and covering 17 societies during their first decade of post-conflict economic recovery. They find that during the first three post-conflict years, absorptive capacity is no greater than normal, but that in the rest of the first decade it is approximately double its normal level. They also find that growth is more sensitive to policy in post-conflict societies.

Some researchers analyze the consequences of intra wars. Organski and Kugler (1977, 1980) analyze the economic effects of the two World Wars on a sample of mainly European countries. They find that in the 'long run' – 15 to 20 years – the effects of war are dissipated in both losers and winners, with a return to pre-war growth trends typically occurring. Miguel and Roland (2005) analyze the impact that the U.S. bombing of Vietnam had on the country's subsequent economic development. They compare the heavily bombed districts with the rest and find that U.S bombing did not have a lasting negative impact on poverty rates, consumption levels, infrastructure, literacy or population density, as measured around 2002. Inferring in regard to other cases, they conclude that local recovery from the damage of war can be achieved if 'certain conditions' are met. Davis and Weinstein (2002) consider the Allied bombing of Japanese cities in World War II as a shock to the relative size of the cities. They find that in the wake of the destruction, there was an extremely powerful recovery. Most cities returned to their relative sizes within about 15 years.

Other studies analyze the effects of terrorist attacks. Montalvo (2006), in a very smart and creative idea, use the electoral consequences of the terrorist attacks of the 11-M in Madrid to analyze the effects of terrorism. This was a particularly relevant case, since the attack took place only three days before the 2004 Congressional Election, which allows the use of credible identification criteria. In particular, he uses the advance voting by Spanish residents abroad, who cast their vote before the terrorist attack, to identify the effect of the bombing. He exploits this macabre natural experiment to run a difference-in-differences estimation using data on three consecutive Congressional elections. The empirical results indicate that a terrorist attack can have a large impact on the outcome of democratic elections. Chen and Siems (2004) examine the effects of terrorism on global capital markets. They examine the response of the U.S capital market to 14 terrorist attacks since 1915, and the response of global capital markets to both Iraq's invasion of Kuwait in 1990 and the 9/11 terrorist attacks in New York and Washington. They find that terrorist attacks and military invasions have great potential to affect capital markets around the world in a short period of time. They also find that U.S capital markets recover sooner than other global capital markets. Abadie and Gardeazabal (2003) use an event-study methodology to analyze the impact of terrorism on firms in the Basque Country. They find that firms with a significant presence in the Basque

Country improved their performance more than other firms when a truce became credible and, correspondingly, their relative performance worsened at the end of the ceasefire.

Chen, Loayza and Reynal-Querol (2007) find that as a result of war, post-conflict countries find themselves behind otherwise similar developing countries in terms of income per capita, some aspects of health and educational achievement as well as key areas of political development. However, when peace is achieved and sustained, recovery is indeed possible. Virtually all aspects of economic, social and political development experience gradual improvement in the aftermath of civil war. Progress in social areas is accompanied by a continuous reallocation of public resources away from military expenditure and, above all, a steady rise in average income per capita.

One crucial issue in post-conflict reconstruction is the overall fiscal framework. The distribution of resources after war could be used as an instrument to solve historical grievances among groups by distributing resources equally between groups and providing services and infrastructure to all regions, without favoring one group in detriment to the other. But this requires some level of funding that must be obtained by raising public revenues. Efforts to raise public revenues and to stabilize the public finances must be designed to ensure that recovery is broad based, so that the majority of people benefit, not just a narrow elite. Addison et al. (2001) discuss some of the principal issues relating to the reconstruction of the financial sector in conflict-affected countries. The study focuses on the reconstruction of the domestic financial sector, together with financial reform, in post-conflict countries. It highlights the choices that must be made and the tensions that exist in financial policy. They argue that 'different types of conflict have different effects on the financial system, and country reconstruction-programmes will reflect this'. Addison and Murshed (2001) also argue, 'Successful Reconstruction after war must rebuild the social contract. The chances of success increase if the economy can achieve broad-based growth.... If Grievances is the main source of conflict the broad-based reconstruction is necessary to recreate a sustainable social conflict'.

Another important controversial issue is the role of aid in conflict-affected countries. It is not clear whether and how aid might contribute to post-conflict reconstruction. In *From Conflict to Recovery in Africa* (Addison 2003b), a group of Africa experts looks at how to achieve broad-based recovery from war, using Angola, Eritrea, Ethiopia, Guinea-Bissau and Mozambique to explain the importance of broad-based recovery in post-conflict reconstruction. To explore how societies go from conflict to recovery, the authors analyze the role played by communities, the private sector and the state. They conclude, 'Unless communities rebuild and strengthen their livelihoods, neither reconstruction nor subsequent growth will be broad based. But communities cannot prosper unless private investment recreates markets and generates more employment. And neither communities nor the private sector can realize their potential without a development state'. They also explain that international actors such as aid donor agencies can help by assisting better peacekeeping, and NGOs can assist by rapidly addressing emergency needs. 'Strengthening the capacities of national actors is therefore essential for international assistance to work well'. Governments need to encourage private investment and protect property rights, and at the same time need to protect the public interest and defend the poor. For this is crucial to ensure democratic institutions that do not favor the elites to the detriment of the poor or ethnic minorities. This book provides a very detailed sequence of action in the reconstruction process. A timetable for multiparty elections is a crucial element. There are some discussions on the timing of the economic reform. A standard view supports the idea that while aid and humanitarian assistance should take place immediately, economic reform should wait until reconstruction is well under way. However, they maintain, 'The argument that economic reform is best keep for a second phase after reconstruction is often taken too far ... well-designed economic reforms raise the chances that recovery will be broad based in its benefits'. Following this line, they also emphasize that strength of property rights should be addressed in the immediate years after war. 'These policies can create employment, which can absorb demobilized combatants. Economic growth also raises the tax base and therefore creates the necessary revenues rebuild necessary for public services and infrastructure'. They paid special attention to emphasize a fairer allocation of public spending across regions and ethnic groups to eliminate the potential grievances that are at the roots of conflict. They strengthen the idea that 'transformation, rather than reconstruction, is the watchword for broad based recovery'. The following paragraph captures this idea very well:

If resources are available, then rebuilding shattered infrastructure is a reasonably straightforward task. Reassembling pre-war institutions may not be too difficult either. But it is a lot harder to transform institutions and policies, especially, when these favor one social group over another. Yet, unless this is done, recovery will be narrow rather than broad in its benefits, poverty will remain high, and conflict will almost certainly return.

Due to the high costs of conflicts, ex-post measures to deal with them have limitations, and ex-ante measures are critical.

THE LIMITED ROLE OF POVERTY IN EXPLAINING THE PROBABILITY OF CIVIL WARS

The idea that poverty is the main cause of conflict is the dominant hypothesis in the empirical literature of civil war, and the worldwide impact of this idea is huge. Many world leaders have stressed the idea that the fight against civil war and conflict requires a reduction in poverty. These ideas have been basically driven by two empirical studies: Collier and Hoeffler (2004b), and Fearon and Laitin (2003). Collier and Hoeffler (2004b) find that political and social variables that are most obviously related to grievances have little explanatory power. In contrast, economic variables, which could proxy some grievances but are perhaps more related to the viability of rebellion, provide considerable explanatory power. Fearon and Laitin (2003) also find that lower per capita GDP has a significant and negative effect on the onset of civil war. Furthermore, the factors that explain which countries have been at risk of civil war are also conditions that favor insurgency: poverty, political instability, rough terrain and large populations. They argue that income per capita is a proxy for the 'state's overall financial, administrative, police and military capabilities'. Once a government is weak, rebels can expect a higher probability of success.

The use of simple linear regressions, or a probit/logit specification, imposes very strong identification conditions that are likely to be violated. The current consensus, which emerges from those analyses, is that poverty is the single, most important determinant of civil wars. This result could be an artifact of simultaneity problems: the incidence of civil wars and poverty may be driven by the same determinants, some of which are probably missing in the typical econometric specifications. The following sections suggest that the empirical evidence on the effect of poverty on civil war is very fragile and based on weak empirical grounds.

Preliminary Findings

Before showing any econometric analysis, I will provide some stylized facts that will cast some doubts on the role of poverty in explaining civil wars. Data on civil wars comes from the Armed Conflict Dataset, a joint project between the Department of Peace and Conflict Studies, Uppsala University and the Center for the Study of Civil War at the Peace Research Institute, Oslo (PRIO). An armed conflict is defined as a contested incompatibility that concerns government and/or territory where the use of armed force between two parties, of which at least one is the government of a state, results in at least 25 battle-related deaths. We call this variable 'civil war'. We use types 3 and 4, which correspond to civil wars. PRIO offers also series to construct armed conflicts

Table 6.1   Civil Wars in OECD and Non-OECD Countries

	OECD	Non-OECD
Civil wars	2	92
No-conflict	26	91
All countries	28	183
Major conflict	2	53
No-conflict	26	130
All countries	28	183

that generate more than 25 deaths per year and a minimum of 1,000 deaths during the course of the civil war, which we call major civil wars.

It is well known that all contemporaneous civil wars are concentrated in non-OECD countries (of course the United Kingdom and Spain are the exceptions due to terrorism). However, not all non-OECD countries suffer civil wars. Taking a sample of 211 countries, which includes 28 OECD countries and 183 non-OECD countries, 92 of the non-OECD countries suffered a civil war during the period 1960–2005. Of these 92 civil wars, 53 turned into a major civil war at some point. Table 6.1 summarizes these statistics.

One reasonable question we should ask is whether the empirical evidence on the relationship between poverty and civil war is driven by the fact that OECD countries are rich and do not suffer conflicts. This is very important, because in the end we want to ascertain whether the relationship between poverty and civil war might explain the different probabilities of conflict among the 183 non-OECD countries. If we want to ascertain good policies to prevent conflict, these policies should also explain the different probabilities of conflict among the 183 non-OECD countries. Because in fact, the question we are trying to answer is why countries like Botswana did well but countries like Sierra Leone did not. Looking at OECD countries does not help much in answering this question.

In order to start checking the role of poverty in explaining the different probabilities of conflict among non-OECD countries, Table 6.2 ranks countries by their level of per capita income in 1960. The first column lists the 15 poorest non-OECD countries in 1960. Column 2 indicates which type of conflict they suffered during the period 1960–2006. Eleven of the fifteen poorest non-OECD countries in 1960 suffered a civil war during the period 1960–2006, and five of them a major civil war. Column 3 ranks the 15 richest non-OECD countries in 1960. Column 4 indicates which type of conflict they suffered

Table 6.2   *Ranking of the 15 Poorest and the 15 Richest Non-OECD Countries in 1960*

15 Poorest	Conflict	15 Richest	Conflict
Ethiopia	Major	Bahamas	
Lesotho	Minor	Venezuela	Minor
Myanmar	**Major**	Bermuda	
Tanzania		Trinidad & Tobago	Minor
Togo	Minor	Argentina	**Major**
Malawi		Uruguay	Minor
Romania	Minor	Saudi Arabia	Minor
Burkina Faso	Minor	Israel	**Major**
Cape Verde		Iraq	**Major**
Congo, Dem. Rep.	**Major**	Puerto Rico	
Guinea-Bissau	**Major**	Iran	**Major**
Niger	Minor	Chile	Minor
Mali	Minor	Mauritius	
Botswana		Barbados	
Rwanda	**Major**	Hong-Kong	

during the period 1960–2006. Surprisingly, we find similar experiences of civil war. Among the 15 richest in 1960, nine suffer some kind of civil war between 1960 and 2006, including four major civil wars.[1]

With these numbers in mind, it would not be a surprise to find in the econometric analysis that once we control for other country-specific variables, no relationship can be found between poverty and civil war using the whole sample of countries.

Many of the poorest non-OECD countries are Sub-Saharan African countries. These countries also have a huge number of civil wars. It is reasonable, therefore, to do the same exercises as in Table 6.2 but using only the sample of Sub-Saharan African countries. Table 6.3 shows the rankings. Column 1 ranks the 15 poorest Sub-Saharan African countries in 1960, while column 3 ranks the 15 richest Sub-Saharan African countries in 1960.

Among the 15 poorest Sub-Saharan African countries in 1960, 11 suffered some kind of civil war, four of which were major civil wars, between 1960 and 2006. However, similar things happened among the 15 richest Sub-Saharan African countries. Ten of the 15 richest suffered some kind of civil war between 1960 and 2006, six of which were major civil wars. These preliminary numbers indicate that if OECD countries are not included in the sample, poverty and conflict seem not to be correlated.

Table 6.3   *Ranking of the 15 Poorest and the 15 Richest Sub-Saharan African Countries in 1960*

15 Poorest	Conflict	15 Richest	Conflict
Ethiopia	**Major**	Mauritius	
Lesotho	Minor	South Africa	**Major**
Tanzania		Namibia	
Togo	Minor	Gabon	Minor
Malawi		Algeria	**Major**
Burkina Faso	Minor	Seychelles	
Cape Verde		Swaziland	
Congo, Dem. Rep.	**Major**	Madagascar	Minor
Guinea-Bissau	**Major**	Mozambique	**Major**
Niger	Minor	Congo, Rep.	**Major**
Mali	Minor	Cote d'Ivoire	Minor
Botswana		Somalia	**Major**
Rwanda	**Major**	Tunisia	Minor
Comoros	Minor	Benin	
Guinea	Minor	Senegal	**Major**

More evidence on this can be provided from Table 6.2 and Table 6.3, and comparing the average income level of the poorest countries that suffered civil war with the poorest countries that did not suffer civil war and also comparing the average income level of the richest countries that suffered civil war with the richest that did not suffer civil war. Figures 6.1 and 6.2 show the average of the per capita income of the poorest countries that suffer civil war and the average of the per capita income of the poorest countries that did not suffer civil war. The average per capita income in 1960 among the poorest non-OECD countries in Table 6.2 that had a civil war is $430 (constant dollars, 1985 base year international prices), and $425 for the ones that did not have any kind of civil war. The average per capita income in 1960 among the richest non-OECD countries in Table 6.2 that had a civil war is $4,112, and $4,013 for the ones that did not have any kind of civil war. These numbers indicate that neither among the poorest nor among the richest countries does per capita income seem to be correlated with civil conflict.

We do the same exercise with the sample of Sub-Saharan African countries in Table 6.3. The numbers again show that the average per capita income of the poorest African countries that suffered civil war, and the average per capita income of the poorest ones that did not suffer civil war is the same. And, as before, the average per capita income of the richest Sub-Saharan African

Figure 6.1   Average GDP among the 15 Poorest Countries (1960)

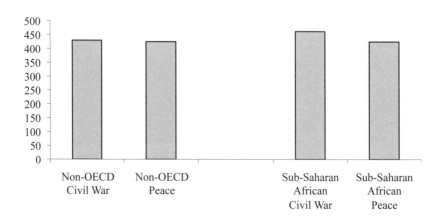

Figure 6.2   Average GDP among the 15 Richest Countries (1960)

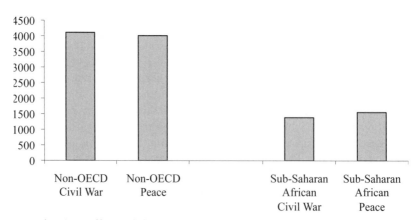

countries that suffered civil war is very similar to the average per capita income of the ones that did not suffer civil war.

These numbers are highly descriptive, but they cast some doubts as to the idea that poverty is the main cause of civil wars. But then, why does the cross-country literature find this effect of poverty on civil wars?

Table 6.4   *Logit Analysis on the Causes of Civil Wars*
              (all Sample and Non-OECD Sample)

	PRIOCW major	PRIOCW major/ minor	PRIOCW major	PRIOCW Major/ minor	PRIOCW Major	PRIOCW Major/ minor
	All sample	All sample	Non-OECD	Non-OECD	All sample	All sample
	(1)	(2)	(3)	(4)	(5)	(6)
Lngdp60	−1.13	−0.78	−0.29	−0.06	−0.42	−0.12
	(−4.05)	(−3.20)	(−0.89)	(−0.19)	(−1.25)	(−0.36)
Lpop60	0.33	0.52	0.61	0.75	0.40	0.59
	(2.17)	(3.28)	(2.56)	(2.14)	(2.13)	(3.19)
Euro1900					−0.02	−0.025
					(−2.94)	(−2.55)
Constant	3.63	−3.07	−6.18	−11.48	−1.92	−8.39
	(1.46)	(−1.16)	(−1.47)	(−2.48)	(−0.54)	(−2.18)
N	128	128	101	101	123	123
R^2	0.1691	0.1540	0.1530	0.1855	0.2065	0.1947

Note: z–statistics in parentheses.

A plausible explanation is that some determinants exist that favor the condition for economic development that at the same time favor the condition for peaceful negotiations, and that are missing in the traditional specification. If this is the case, then OECD countries are peaceful not because they are rich, but because historically they suffer some circumstances that favor negotiation settlements, and economic development at the same time. In the next section we provide some simple econometric evidence that supports this hypothesis. A deep analysis is provided in Djankov and Reynal-Querol (2007).

Simple Econometrics

Table 6.4 shows the results of a simple logit regression on the determinants of civil wars. The dependent variable is a dummy that has value 1 if the country suffers a civil war during the period 1960–2005, and zero otherwise. In order to reduce the endogeneity problems between per capita income and civil war to as great an extent as possible, our specification is a cross-section of countries where the independent variables are taken at the beginning of the period.

Other important advantages that favor the use of a cross-section in this type of analysis are detailed in Djankov and Reynal-Querol (2007, 2008).

   The explanatory variables follow the basic specifications of the literature on civil war (Montalvo and Reynal-Querol 2005; Fearon and Laitin 2003; Collier and Hoeffler 2002; Doyle and Sambanis 2000). Fearon and Laitin argue that income per capita is a proxy for the 'state's overall financial, administrative, police and military capabilities' (2003, 80). Once a government is weak, rebels can expect a higher probability of success. In addition, a low level of income per capita reduces the opportunity cost of engaging in conflict. Miguel and Roland (2005) have argued that the measurement of the impact of GDP growth on civil wars is complicated since there are endogeneity issues. Their set-up is very different from ours. They use annual data and GDP growth. In this situation, the potential endogeneity problem of GDP growth with respect to conflict is very high. For this reason they use rainfall as an instrument for GDP growth. We use a cross-section for civil wars and the GDP per capita at the beginning of the period. This set-up reduces the potential endogeneity problem. The size of the population is another usual suspect in the explanation of conflict. Collier and Hoeffler (2002) consider that the size of the population is an additional proxy for the benefits of a rebellion since it measures potential labor income taxation. Fearon and Laitin (2003) indicate that a large population implies difficulties in controlling what goes on at the local level and increases the number of potential rebels that can be recruited by the insurgents.

   Population and per capita income are the only two variables that researchers have agreed to as being potential causes of civil war and, their effect on civil war is probably one of the most robust (see Hegre and Sambanis 2006). Therefore the explanatory variables for the core specification of the probability of civil wars include the log of real GDP per capita in 1960 (lgdp60) and the log of the population in 1960 (lpop60).

   We present the estimation of a logit model for the probability of civil wars. In columns 1 and 2 we use a sample of 211 countries. In columns 3 and 4 we show the results using the sample of non-OECD countries. In columns 1 and 3, the dependent variable is major civil wars, while in columns 2 and 4 the dependent variable is civil wars. The logit equation is the following:

$$\Pr obq\left(conf \ lict_{i60-05} = 1\right) = \Lambda\left(\alpha + \beta_1 \lg dp_{i60} + \beta_2 lpop_{i60}\right) \qquad (6.1)$$

Where *conflict* is a dummy variable that has value 1 if the country had a civil war during the period 1960–2005 and zero otherwise, α is a constant, *lgdp* is the log of real per capita income in 1960, *lpop* is the log of the population of the country in 1960. In line with the previous literature, when we use the whole sample of countries, we find that poor, large-populated countries have a higher risk of conflict in comparison with rich, small countries. However, results in columns 3 and 4 indicate that the effect of per capita income on civil war is insignificant once we drop OECD countries, in line with our preliminary findings.

These results are not casual. As explained before, the empirical findings on the effect of per capita income on conflict are supported by very weak empirical ground. The results using the whole sample of countries could be an artifact of simultaneity problems: the incidence of civil wars and poverty may be driven by the same determinants, some of which are probably missing in the typical econometric specifications. If this is the case, the results on the relationship between poverty and civil war are driven because there are some historical factors that favor the conditions for development, but at the same time favor the conditions for negotiation and peaceful behavior, which could reasonably explain why OECD countries do not have conflict and are also rich. Thus, this would indicate that increases in income per capita would not be translated into a reduction in the risk of civil war. Therefore, if we could disentangle these effects, it would have important policy implications for the prevention of civil war. Djankov and Reynal-Querol (2007) fully explore this issue, and they find that once historical variables like the log of European settlement mortality rates or the population density in 1500 are included in the civil war regression, per capita income does not have any effect on civil wars. We perform here a similar analysis to show this idea.

In the last two columns of Table 6.4, we perform a very simple analysis controlling for some of these potential determinants that could affect poverty and the existence of conflict at the same time. In particular, we choose one historical variable that captures the historical influence of Europeans during colonization. In particular the variable we use is the percentage of European settlement in 1900, from Acemoglu et al. (2002). In some sense, this variable captures the level of influence of European institutions on colonies. For European countries this variable is 100. We use the whole sample of countries. In columns 5 and 6, we include European settlement 1900, using both definitions of civil wars. We observe that once this variable is included in the civil war regression, per capita income does not have any significant effect on the probability of civil wars.

Since the variable 'European settlement in 1900' was originally constructed for the sample of ex-colonies, we perform the same analysis of Table 6.4, using the ex-colonies sample in Table 6.5. Among the sample of ex-colonies, we find the same results as when using the whole sample. Poor countries have a higher risk of conflict, as well as large-populated countries in comparison with rich, small countries. However, once we drop OECD countries among the ex-colonies, in this case Australia, Canada, New Zealand and the United States,

Table 6.5   *Logit Analysis on the Causes of Civil Wars*
                (Ex-colonies Sample and Ex-colonies Non-OECD Sample)

	PRIOCW major	PRIOCW Major/minor	PRIOCW Major	PRIOCW Major/minor	PRIOCW Major	PRIOCW Major/minor
	Ex-colonies	Ex-colonies	Ex-colonies Non-OECD	Ex-colonies Non-OECD	Ex-colonies	Ex-colonies
	(1)	(2)	(3)	(4)	(5)	(6)
Lngdp60	−0.919	−0.68	−0.27	−0.15	−0.14	0.07
	(−2.28)	(−2.13)	(−0.67)	(−0.41)	(−0.32)	(0.16)
Lpop60	0.66	0.78	0.93	1.04	0.74	0.92
	(2.89)	(4.00)	(3.30)	(3.90)	(3.46)	(4.36)
Euro1900					−0.37	−0.04
					(−2.62)	(−2.32)
Constant	−2.49	−7.54	−10.87	−15.16	−8.67	−14.59
	(−0.60)	(−1.93)	(−2.11)	(−2.75)	(−2.12)	(−2.94)
N	95	95	91	91	93	93
R^2	0.1887	0.2030	0.2245	0.2505	0.2209	0.2410

Note: z–statistics in parentheses.

the effect of per capita income turns out to be insignificant.

In columns 5 and 6 of Table 6.5, we include 'European settlement in 1900' as an independent variable. Once European Settlement is included in the regression, per capita income does not have any significant effect in explaining civil wars.

UNDERSTANDING HOW TO ANALYZE THE CAUSES OF CIVIL WARS

If poverty is not the cause of conflict, then which factors drive civil wars and can be affected by policymakers?

To answer this question it is essential to understand how to study the process of conflict. In the scientific analysis of the causes of civil war, we can create an analogy with the analysis of macroeconomic cycles. Researchers in that field distinguish between shocks and their propagation mechanism as two different and independently interesting issues. For instance, a cycle could be caused by a productivity shock that is propagated through many alternative mechanisms. In the case of civil wars, the situation is similar, although identification is more difficult. In principle, some factors that may affect the onset of a civil war could have no impact on its duration. For instance, in many situations civil wars start by random acts that trigger, given a particular propagation mechanism, full-fledged conflicts. Conflict onset is a very unpredictable event. In many conflicts the onset is related to unpredictable shocks like, for instance, the original trigger of the genocide in Rwanda. Therefore, when trying to find measures to prevent conflict, we should try to identify the propagation mechanisms for conflict. In order for a conflict to exist, we need not only an origin that brings conflict about, but also a propagation mechanism that allows conflict to exist and propagate. All countries receive unexpected shocks, however not all of them enter into conflict. The countries that do not have potential conflict, that is, that do not have the propagation mechanism for conflict, are the ones that are safe. Since onset of conflict is usually produced by unexpected shocks, trying to find measures to prevent them is an impossible task. It is some change that makes conflict start, and that may explain why there was no conflict before. However, in order for conflict to take place, you need some elements of propagation, like social cleavages, economic poverty or repression. Our argument is that in order to reduce the probability of conflict, we need to apply measures that reduce the propagation mechanism for conflict. We believe that institutions are an important instrument that can help on this issue.

Many scholars have stressed the idea that the appropriation of natural resources could be a potential cause of conflict. Collier and Hoeffler (2004b) find that countries with a higher percentage of primary exports over GDP have a larger probability of conflict. Fearon and Laitin (2003) find no effect of primary commodity export dependence on civil war. Fearon (2005) shows that the relationship between primary commodity export and conflict found in Collier and Hoeffler is not robust to minor changes in the sample framing, and recovery of missing data undermine it. Fearon argues that oil is driving these results. Oil predicts civil war risk not because it provides an easy source of rebel finance, but because oil producers have low state capabilities.

Does the existence of natural resources work as a propagator of conflict? What role do natural resources play in the whole process of conflict? The discovery of a natural resource, or a shock in the price of a natural resource (becoming rich or becoming poor in a short period of time), could definitely be conducive to conflict as long as the country has a propagation mechanism. Also, natural resources seem to have played an important role as a source of financing conflict. In order for conflict to exist, we need some kind of financing. Without financing there is no conflict. We believe that natural resources have played an important role as a source of financing the process of conflict, especially, during the 1990s. However, the existence of natural resources per se does not seem to work as a propagation mechanism for conflict.

Therefore, given the process of conflict (shocks, propagation and financing), there are three types of policies that could be applied in order to reduce the probability of conflict: policies that try to avoid shocks, for example diversification policies; policies that try to reduce the propagation mechanism, like institutions that try to reduce the intensity of social cleavages; and policies that try to cut the source of financing, like the Kimberly process. Trying to find policies that protect countries from shocks is simply an impossible task. While diversification can protect countries against shocks concerning the price of some products, it is not possible to predict and avoid unexpected shocks, such as 9/11. Also, policies that address financing are policies with a very short-term effect, because rebel groups look for other, alternative sources of financing. Some of this evidence is explained in the work of Michael Ross who draws upon case studies of Angola to describe this phenomenon:

> Before the end of the Cold War, successful rebel groups in the developing world were typically financed by one of the great powers. Since the Cold War ended, insurgent groups have been forced to find other ways to bankroll themselves; many have turned to the natural resources sector. (Keen 1998)

> In Angola, for example, UNITA (National Union for the Total Independence of Angola) was backed by the United States and South Africa for most of the 1970s and 1980s. But the end of the Cold War, and the end of the apartheid in South Africa, left UNITA with no outside sponsors; as a consequence, it began to rely much more heavily on diamond revenue to support itself. (Le Billon 2001)

This indicates that policies that try to avoid conflict by cutting the sources of financing are policies with a short-term effect. Therefore, if we want to find measures to prevent conflict in the long term, we need to look for policies that address the propagation mechanism for conflict. While the role of poverty as a propagation mechanism for conflict has already been challenged, we believe that institutions could be a key instrument in reducing the potential conflict of countries.

Therefore next section is devoted to analyzing whether there is any robust relationship between the quality of institutions and the existence of conflict, and also to analyze which are the institutional mechanisms that may help to reduce latent conflict.

STRENGTH OF INSTITUTIONS AND CIVIL WARS

To date, institutional development has not been linked to the study of civil wars, from an empirical point of view. An exception is Djankov and Reynal-Querol (2008). Following North (1990), secure property rights and the rule of law have played an important role in the development of Western societies. We believe that the *quality* of institutions could also play an important role in the development of peaceful societies. Although the empirical literature on conflict does not pay much attention to the role of institutional development on conflict, the theoretical literature of conflict (e.g., Haavelmo 1954; Grossman 1994; Grossman and Kim 1996; Skaperdas 1992, 1996; Garfinkel 1990; Garfinkel and Skaperdas 2001; Hirshleifer 1995) has stressed the importance of allowing for imperfect institutions of governance and a lack of enforcement to model conflictive situations on the appropriation of resources. Following the theoretical literature, an imperfect institutional framework, understood as the lack of enforcement and insecure property rights, is a necessary condition for the existence of conflict. Conflict is more probable when less secure property rights exist and enforcement of the law is scarce.

We analyze empirically whether this quality of institutions helps toward the development of peaceful societies. We therefore approach the data with the idea that when government cannot enforce the law and protect property rights, conflict emerges. The quality of institutions is a proxy for the government's efficiency in defending property rights. Institutions, which in some sense capture the efficiency in managing and distributing resources, could therefore be more important in explaining conflict than the scarcity of resources itself, which is captured by per capita income. The idea that strong governments are what matter to prevent conflict is in fact also exposed by Fearon and Laitin, (2003), who argue that they use per capita income as a measure of the 'state's overall financial, administrative, police and military capabilities'. Institutions could capture better the strength of government in implementing the law than per capita income per se.

Preliminary Findings: A First Look at the Data

The theoretical literature on conflict has stressed the importance of allowing for imperfect institutions of governance and lack of enforcement to model conflictive situations regarding the appropriation of resources. Since we do not observe the exact characteristics of institutions that are related with conflict as described in the theoretical models of conflict, we need to identify the institutional variables that better capture this imperfect institutional framework, understood as the lack of enforcement and insecure property rights. In our

Table 6.6   *Ranking of the 15 Countries with the Lowest Quality of Institutions and the 15 Countries with the Highest Quality of Institutions in 1984–99*

15 Worst	Conflict 85–06	15 Best	Conflict 85–06
Guinea-Bissau	**Major**	United States	**Major** (Sept. 11)
Congo, DR	**Major**	Canada	
Colombia	**Major**	Switzerland	
Liberia	**Major**	Norway	
Haiti	Minor	Australia	
Iraq	**Major**	Sweden	
Suriname	Minor	Luxemburg	
Bolivia	Minor	Denmark	
Sri Lanka	**Major**	Iceland	
Guatemala	**Major**	Finland	
Angola	**Major**	New Zealand	
Bangladesh	**Major**	Netherlands	
El Salvador	**Major**	Austria	
Peru	**Major**	Germany W	
New Caledonia		Belgium	

analysis we use the variables provided by the ICRG (International Country Risk Guide). The 'average protection against expropriation risk' and the 'law and order' variables have been widely used in the literature as proxies of the quality of institutions or the strength of the government. Djankov and Reynal-Querol (2008) use both variables to analyze the effect of institutions on civil war considering institutions as an endogenous variable. We will concentrate our analysis using only one of these two variables, the law and order variable, although results are robust to the use of other measures that capture different dimensions of the quality and strength of the government. The law-and-order index measures the strength and impartiality of the legal system and the popular observance of the law. The ICRG provides information since 1984. This variable can take values from 0 to 6. Higher numbers indicate a stronger legal system. We believe that law and order indices are most appropriate to analyze the role of institutions on conflict, because they capture the ability of the government to implement law and order in the country, and this seems to matter greatly when we think of preventing and avoiding conflict.

Table 6.6 lists the ranking of the 15 countries with the weakest law and order system, and the fifteen countries with the strongest legal system. The

Table 6.7   *Ranking of the 15 Countries with the Lowest Quality of Institutions and the 15 Countries with the Highest Quality of Institutions in 1984–99*

Sample of Non-OECD countries

15 Worst	Conflict 85–06	15 Best	Conflict 85–06
Guinea-Bissau	**Major**	Singapore	
Congo, DR.	**Major**	Moldova	Minor
Colombia	**Major**	Slovenia	
Liberia	**Major**	Croatia	Minor
Haiti	Minor	Hong-Kong	
Iraq	**Major**	Cuba	
Suriname	Minor	Taiwan	
Bolivia		Bulgaria	
Sri Lanka	**Major**	Namibia	
Guatemala	**Major**	Botswana	
Angola	**Major**	Brunei	
Bangladesh	**Major**	Bahrain	
El Salvador	**Major**	Saudi Arabia	
Peru	**Major**	Chile	
New Caledonia		Qatar	

law and order index is the average of the law and order indicator from 1984 to 1999. Thirteen of the 15 countries with the lowest scores suffered a civil war between 1985 and 2006, while only one of the 15 countries with the strongest legal system suffered conflict. This is the case of the United States, which was indexed with conflict in 2001 by PRIO due to the 9/11 terrorist attack. Classifying the 9/11 event as a civil war phenomenon is, of course, highly controversial. However, obviously this does not affect the main descriptive results of these rankings. Also one may be worried by the fact that conflict may affect the overall performance of institutions and this could probably be the reason why we find the correlation between bad institutions and conflict. However, we find the same rankings if we consider only the value of institutions in 1984, instead of the average between 1984 and 1999. The reason for using averages is that since the quality of institutions is a very persistent variable over time, we have more observations considering the averages of the available observations over the period rather than just the value for 1984. In any case Djankov and Reynal-Querol (2008) address the issue of endogeneity.

Table 6.8   Ranking of the 15 Countries with the Lowest Quality of Institutions and the 15 Countries with the Highest Quality of Institutions in 1984–99

Sub-Saharan African countries

15 Worst	Conflict 85–06	15 Best	Conflict 85–06
Guinea-Bissau	**Major**	Namibia	
Congo, DR	**Major**	Botswana	
Liberia	**Major**	Gambia	
Angola	**Major**	Tanzania	
Somalia	**Major**	Morocco	**Major**
Sudan	**Major**	Kenya	
Nigeria	Minor	Burkina Faso	Minor
Congo, Rep.	**Major**	Tunisia	
Algeria	**Major**	Cote d'Ivoire	Minor
Uganda	**Major**	Madagascar	
Togo	Minor	Ethiopia	**Major**
Senegal	**Major**	Egypt	Minor
Ghana		Libya	
Mali	Minor	Guinea	Minor
Mozambique	**Major**	Zimbabwe	

After looking at these rankings, the obvious question that arises, as in the case of the per capita income, is whether this relationship is driven by the fact that many OECD countries have good institutions but no contemporaneous civil wars. In order to address descriptively this concern, we perform the same ranking but without considering OECD countries. Table 6.7 shows these results. Surprisingly, and contrary to the case of per capita income, we continue to observe different patterns between countries with good institutions and countries with bad institutions. In this case, 13 of the 15 countries with bad institutions experienced conflict between 1985 and 2006 (in fact we have the same list as before) and only two of the 15 countries with good institutions suffer conflicted, in this case minor conflict. As before, the same results apply if we us the value of institutions for 1984.

However, we still wonder whether this evidence is driven because Sub-Saharan African countries have the worst institutions and concentrate one-third of the contemporaneous civil wars. To address this issue we perform the same analysis but considering only sub-Saharan African countries, in Table 6.8, and

Table 6.9   *Ranking of the 15 Countries with the Lowest Quality of Institutions and the 15 Countries with the Highest Quality of Institutions in 1984–99*

Non-Sub-Saharan African countries, Non-OECD countries

15 Worst	Conflict 85–06	15 Best	Conflict 85–06
Colombia	**Major**	Singapore	
Haiti	Minor	Slovenia	
Iraq	**Major**	Moldova	Minor
Suriname	Minor	Croatia	Minor
Bolivia		Hong-Kong	
Sri Lanka	**Major**	Cuba	
Guatemala	**Major**	Taiwan	
Bangladesh	**Major**	Bulgaria	
El Salvador	**Major**	Brunei	
Peru	**Major**	Bahrain	
New Caledonia		Saudi Arabia	
Guyana		Chile	
Pakistan	**Major**	Qatar	
Honduras		Malta	
Philippines	**Major**	Malaysia	

non-Sub-Saharan African non-OECD countries in Table 6.9. The results are striking and reinforce the evidence we observe before, which is that countries with strong institutions seem to be associated with lower probability of civil wars than countries with weak institutions.

Finally, the results might be driven by the fact that former colonies tend to have worse institutions due to the imposition of the legal system by colonial powers. At the same time, these ex-colonies concentrate more than two-thirds of contemporaneous civil wars. To be sure that these factors are not driving the correlations, we perform the same rankings considering the sample of former colonies. The results in Table 6.10, although descriptive, confirm that there is some evidence that a correlation exists between having bad institutions and the existence of conflict.

These rankings have been performed using the average institutional quality between 1984 and 1999. All of them are robust using the value of institutions in 1984 and also considering the probability of civil war between 1960 and 2006.

Table 6.10   Ranking of the 15 Countries with the Lowest Quality of Institutions and the 15 Countries with the Highest Quality of Institutions in 1984–99

Former Colonies

15 Worst	Conflict 85–06	15 Best	Conflict 85–06
Guinea-Bissau	**Major**	United States	**Major** (Sept. 11)
Congo, DR	**Major**	Canada	
Colombia	**Major**	Australia	
Haiti	Minor	New Zealand	
Iraq	**Major**	Singapore	
Bolivia		Hong Kong	
Sri Lanka	**Major**	Namibia	
Guatemala	**Major**	Botswana	
Angola	**Major**	Bahrain	
Bangladesh	**Major**	Saudi Arabia	
El Salvador	**Major**	Chile	
Peru	**Major**	Qatar	
Somalia	**Major**	Malta	
Sudan	**Major**	Malaysia	
Nigeria	Minor	Oman	

All of this preliminary analysis suggests that the correlation between bad institutions and the existence of conflict is probably not driven by the inclusion of OECD countries that have good institutions and non-contemporaneous civil wars; or by the inclusion of Sub-Saharan African countries, which have the worst institutions and many civil wars; or by the inclusion of former colonies. In the next section we provide some simple econometrics that confirm these preliminary findings.

Some Empirical Results

In this section we present the estimation of a logit model for the probability of civil wars. As before, the dependent variable is a dummy that has value 1 if the country suffers a civil war during the period 1960–2005, and zero otherwise. In columns 1 and 2, and 5 and 6 we use a sample of 211 countries. In columns 3 and 4 we show the results using the sample of non-OECD countries.

In columns 1 and 3 and 5, the dependent variable is major civil wars, while in columns 2 and 4 and 6, the dependent variable is civil wars.

When we use the whole sample of countries, we find that countries with weak institutions have a higher risk of conflict, as well as large populated countries in comparison with countries with strong institutions, and small countries. Moreover, results in columns 3 and 4, indicate that the effect of institutions on civil war keeps its significant effect once we drop OECD countries, in line with our preliminary findings, and in contrast to the effect of per capita income on civil wars that becomes insignificant once OECD countries are dropped from the sample. But still the results using the whole sample of countries could be an artifact of simultaneity problems: the incidence of civil wars and bad institutions may be driven by the same determinants, some of which are probably missing in the typical econometric specifications. If this is the case, it could be that the results on the relationship between institutions and civil war are driven because there are some historical factors that favor the conditions for good institutions, but at the same time favor the conditions for negotiation and peaceful behavior. Therefore, in order to control for historical factors, as in the analysis of per capita income, we control for some of these potential determinants that could affect institutions and the existence of conflict at the same time. In particular, we choose one historical variable that captures the historical influence of Europeans during colonization. The variable we use is the percentage of European settlement in 1900, from Acemoglu et al. (2000). In columns 5 and 6 we include European settlement in 1900, using both definitions of civil wars. We observe that once this variable is included in the civil war regression, institutions keep its significant effect on the probability of civil wars.

Since the variable European settlement in 1900 was originally constructed for the sample of former colonies, in Table 6.12 we perform the same analysis as Table 6.11, using the former colonies sample. Among the sample of former colonies, we find the same results as when using the whole sample. We also obtain the same results if we consider other historical variables such as the log of European settler mortality rates or the density of population in 1500 (Djankov and Reynal-Querol 2008). All these results are robust to consider the value of institutions in 1984 and the probability of conflict between 1985 and 2006.

These results indicate that, although there are historical factors that affect institutions and conflict at the same time, there are still some dimensions of institutional development that affect conflict that are not fully determined by historical phenomena. This means that we could probably affect the probability of conflict by changing institutions. This clearly opens up new possibilities for action to prevent conflict.

Security and Development

Table 6.11   *Logit Analysis on the Causes of Civil Wars*
              (All Sample and Non-OECD Sample)

	PRIOCW major All sample	PRIOCW Major/minor All sample	PRIOCW major Non-OECD	PRIOCW Major/minor Non-OECD	PRIOCW major All sample	PRIOCW Major/minor All sample
	(1)	(2)	(3)	(4)	(5)	(6)
	−1.70	−1.34	−1.78	−1.03	−1.55	−1.23
Institutions	(−5.57)	(−7.04)	(−4.68)	(−4.27)	(−4.67)	(−5.76)
	0.90	0.46	0.93	0.49	0.92	0.41
Lpop60	(3.77)	(2.73)	(3.56)	(2.45)	(3.46)	(2.35)
					−0.01	−0.07
Euro1900					(−0.88)	(−1.06)
	−9.28	−1.89	−9.55	−3.34	−9.91	−1.29
Constant	(−2.73)	(−0.76)	(−2.51)	(−1.05)	(−2.57)	(−0.47)
N	139	139	111	111	130	130
R^2	0.4263	0.3491	0.4011	0.2345	0.4178	0.3586

Note: z–statistics in parentheses.

Institutions Versus Economic Development

The rankings performed in previous sections also show very clearly the idea that per capita income and institutions are not the same phenomena. While poor and richer countries have the same probabilities of conflict, countries with good institutions have a lower probability of conflict than countries with bad institutions. Although this seems an obvious issue after looking at previous rankings, it has not been obvious in the literature that studies the causes of civil wars. Many researchers have assumed that per capita income and the quality of institutions were two proxies of the strength of the government. This thought comes from the fact that OECD countries are rich and have good institutions, compared with non-OECD countries.

Some examples help to clarify that, in fact, poor countries exist with good institutions and no conflict, and at the same time rich countries exist with bad institutions and conflict. The mean of institutional quality among non-OECD countries is 3.18 points of a 0–6 points scale. Botswana in 1984 had a (real) per capita income of $1,947 in constant dollars (International Prices, base year 1985),[1] the per capita income of Tanzania was $463 and that of Gambia

Table 6.12   *Logit Analysis on the Causes of Civil Wars*
            (Ex-Colonies Sample and Ex-Colonies Non-OECD Sample)

	PRIOCW major	PRIOCW Major/minor	PRIOCW major	PRIOCW Major/minor	PRIOCW major	PRIOCW Major/minor
			Ex-colonies	Ex-colonies		
	Ex-colonies	Ex-colonies	Non-OECD	Non-OECD	Ex-colonies	Ex-colonies
	(1)	(2)	(3)	(4)	(5)	(6)
Institutions	−1.77	−1.27	−0.94	−1.77	−1.69	−1.07
	(−4.46)	(−4.81)	(−3.03)	(−3.81)	(−3.93)	(−3.71)
Lpop60	1.05	0.58	0.73	1.23	1.08	0.63
	(3.53)	(2.81)	(2.58)	(3.49)	(3.77)	(2.98)
Euro1900					−0.02	−0.02
					(−0.76)	(−1.38)
Constant	−11.47	−3.57	−6.95	−14.2	−12.09	−4.81
	(−2.69)	(−1.11)	(−1.51)	(2.75)	(−2.86)	(−1.42)
N	88	88	83	83	87	87
R^2	0.4289	0.3444	0.3079	0.4411	0.4323	0.3458

Note: z–statistics in parentheses.

was $801. All these countries had a value for the quality of institutions that was above the sample average, and none of them suffered civil war between 1984 and 2006. By contrast, Colombia, with a per capita income in 1984 of $2,949, Iraq ($4,927), Suriname ($3,277) and Algeria ($2,962), had very bad institutions, and all of them suffered conflict between 1984 and 2006.

Finally we present the estimation of a logit model for the probability of civil wars, including per capita income and institutions at the same time. We reproduce the same analysis as done before but including both variables. Tables 6.13 and 6.14 show the results and confirm the lack of importance of poverty in explaining the existence of conflict, and the importance of institutions in explaining the probability of conflict. All the results are maintained when we control for the inclusion of other variables that have been used in different studies of civil wars, such as mountains, non-contiguous state, primary exports or ethnic polarization.

Up to now we have shown that the effect of per capita income on civil wars is very fragile and based on very weak empirical grounds. At the same time we have shown that institutions seem to have a robust effect on conflict. However, there is a serious issue of potential endogeneity between institutions and conflict. Djankov and Reynal-Querol (2008) address these issues in depth

Security and Development

Table 6.13   *Logit Analysis on the Causes of Civil Wars*
(Sample of All Countries and Non-OECD Countries)

	PRIOCW major All sample	PRIOCW Major/minor All sample	PRIOCW major Non-OECD	PRIOCW Major/minor Non-OECD	PRIOCW major All sample	PRIOCW Major/minor All sample
	(1)	(2)	(3)	(4)	(5)	(6)
Lngdp60	0.65	0.32	0.77	0.40	0.81	0.44
	(3.50)	(1.60)	(3.28)	(1.28)	(3.39)	(1.53)
Institutions	−1.93	−1.67	−1.99	−1.27	−1.85	−1.53
	(−5.29)	(−5.12)	(−4.37)	(−3.66)	(−4.89)	(−4.67)
Lpop60	0.93	0.33	1.01	0.36	0.95	0.34
	(3.50)	(1.60)	(3.28)	(1.28)	(3.39)	(1.53)
Euro1900					−0.01	−0.01
					(−0.86)	(−1.13)
Constant	−13.83	−0.79	−15.60	−3.07	−15.33	−2.03
	(−2.93)	(−0.19)	(−2.90)	(−0.51)	(−2.97)	(−0.46)
N	110	110	84	84	108	108
R^2	0.4330	0.4263	0.3964	0.2257	0.4312	0.4230

Note: z–statistics in parentheses.

and analyze the effect of institutions on civil war, controlling for income per capita. In their set up, institutions are endogenous and colonial origins affect civil wars through their legacy on institutions. Their results indicate that institutions, proxied by the protection of property rights, rule of law and the efficiency of the legal system, are a fundamental cause of civil war. In particular, an improvement in institutions from the median value in the sample to the 75th percentile is associated with a 38-percentage point reduction in the incidence of civil wars.

The measures used in these studies are general proxies of the quality of institutions. The main idea that should arise from them is that increases in income capita will not reduce the probability of conflict. However there is something with the overall quality of institutions that can help in reducing the probability of conflict. We do not mean that law and order measures are the key variable to address in policy actions; however, we claim that institutions matter and that we can make a change in the probability of conflict by addressing changes in the institutional design. Countries in which institutions do not protect citizens from discrimination or abuse, whether by the government

Table 6.14   *Logit Analysis on the Causes of Civil Wars*
             (Ex-Colonies Sample and Ex-Colonies Non-OECD Sample)

| | PRIOCW major | PRIOCW Major/minor | PRIOCW major | PRIOCW Major/minor | PRIOCW major | PRIOCW Major/minor |
| | | | Ex-colonies Non-OECD | Ex-colonies Non-OECD | | |
	Ex-colonies	Ex-colonies	Non-OECD	Non-OECD	Ex-colonies	Ex-colonies
	(1)	(2)	(3)	(4)	(5)	(6)
Lgdp60	0.36	0.13	0.66	0.36	0.96	0.60
	(0.78)	(0.32)	(1.47)	(0.75)	(1.37)	(1.19)
Institutions	−1.95	−1.30	−2.02	−1.04	−1.94	−1.16
	(−4.43)	(−3.71)	(−3.98)	(−2.85)	(−4.14)	(−3.31)
Lpop60	0.99	0.43	1.22	0.62	1.12	0.53
	(3.38)	(0.23)	(3.35)	(1.79)	(3.35)	(2.11)
Euro1900					−0.04	−0.03
					(−1.17)	(−2.04)
Constant	−12.73	−2.15	−18.0	−7.33	−18.46	−7.09
	(−2.34)	(−0.49)	(−2.75)	(−1.01)	(−2.40)	(−1.30)
N	81	81	76	76	80	80
R^2	0.4245	0.3004	0.4418	0.2418	0.4401	0.3154

Note: z–statistics in parentheses.

or other groups, may easily end up in a conflict situation. The measures of quality of institutions, for example the law and order variable that in some sense captures the popular observance of the law, could be a general proxy of whether the legal system protects citizens from such abuse. However, this is just a general proxy that may be well correlated with other measures of institutions that capture other dimensions that matter more to prevent conflict, for example, political institutions. The following section explores different dimensions of political institutions that have been considered in the literature as potential factors to explain conflict and that could be very important when trying to design the political institution that could help to avoid conflict.

POLITICAL INSTITUTIONS AND CIVIL WARS

When looking for the institutional arrangements that can prevent social conflict and civil war, democracy seems to be the first candidate. One should expect that democratic regimes experience less civil war than any other regime. However, the empirical evidence on the effect of these devices as vaccines against civil wars is not clear since democracies, in fact, also experience civil wars. Sambanis (2001), Hegre et al. (2001) and Reynal-Querol (2002a, 2002b, 2005) find that democratic and autocratic states have fewer civil wars, and intermediate regimes are more prone to conflict. The evidence suggests that implementing democratic regimes is not enough to prevent civil wars. Some examples of democracies that suffer civil war are Mali in 1990, Nigeria in 1960 and 1980, Sudan in 1963, Uganda in 1978, the Dominican Republic in 1965, the Philippines in 1972, Sri Lanka in 1971 and 1983 and Papua New Guinea in 1988, among others. Indeed, democracy seems not to be a sufficiently effective vaccine against violence, even it is necessary.

But why do some democratic regimes experience civil war? Probably, freedom is not the only institutional dimension that plays a role in preventing conflicts. Repression is one of the motivations for starting a rebellion; however, for starting a civil war some level of freedom is needed to allow people to get organized. This may be an explanation as to why partially free countries are more prone to civil war than full democracies and full autocracies. In democracies there is no repression and therefore, in principle, no political motivation for rebellion. However, in some democratic regimes, it could be that a majority group is in power, leaving minority groups outside the decision-making process. We could then include political exclusion as a possible motivation for rebellion. Moreover, it could also be the case that groups are regionally concentrated. In that case – even if they are not excluded from central government – since the preferences are regionally concentrated, they would prefer to organize their own resources by themselves. Here decentralization may be a better option for these groups, and then centralization even without having political exclusion can also become a motivation for rebellion among democracies.

Therefore, the question of which regime is more appropriate to prevent violence cannot be reduced to the democratic status of the country. Not all democratic regimes represent voters in the same way, and this can explain why some democracies suffer civil war. Among democratic states, the level of political inclusion of social and political groups varies depending on many factors. Of course the right to vote is crucial, and this institutional dimension would probably be reflected in the level of freedom of the state. Apart from that, one of the main institutional characteristics that influence the level of political and social inclusiveness of the democratic regime is the political system: presidential, parliamentary-majoritarian or parliamentary-proportional.

Around half of the civil wars that have taken place after World War II have occurred in autocratic countries, one-fourth in partially free countries and one-fourth in democracies. We are concerned with democratic states that suffer conflict and civil war. If we divide the period after World War II into short periods of five years and we analyze what happened in each short period, we find that the proportion of countries that start the period with autocracy and experience a civil war is around 11 per cent. The most interesting result is obtained if we compare these percentages with that of free countries in which civil war started. As we expected, the proportion of cases that started the period with democracy and experienced civil war is lower, 4 per cent. If we look at the characteristics of democratic countries that suffered a civil war, and we distinguish these countries with respect to the different political system, we find that there are more countries that start the period with majoritarian and presidential systems and suffer a conflict or civil war rather than countries that have a proportional system and suffer civil war. There are only three countries with a proportional system and conflict: Israel from 1948 until 1996, Lebanon from 1943 until 1976, which ended up in a civil war, and Spain that suffers ETA terrorism. All these countries had a low level of inclusiveness, except Spain, which more recently had a high level of inclusiveness and yet violence persists.

The empirical analysis on the role of political systems and actual inclusiveness in explaining the probability of civil war supports the idea that high inclusive systems have a lower probability of suffering a civil war. Proportional systems are more correlated with high inclusiveness than majoritarian systems (Reynal-Querol 2002a, 2002b and 2005).

CONCLUSION

What are the fundamental causes of civil wars, and how can conflicts be prevented? Although there is little consensus to answer these questions, differences in per capita income have received considerable attention. The scientific analysis of conflict, however, is still in its infancy. Our study, based on background papers on the analysis of the causes of civil wars, provides strong evidence of how weak and fragile is the relationship between poverty and conflict. Instead, institutional design seems to be a key factor in preventing conflict. Since the general consensus in the economic literature indicates that external development assistance does not improve the economic development of countries, even if poverty was the main determinant of conflict, it would be very difficult to act on this determinant. Instead, institutional development in potentially conflictive countries, although is not a trivial issue, opens up new possibilities for action.

The design of institutions that do not discriminate is crucial in this endeavor: Legal systems that ensure transparency in the law process, political systems that ensure inclusiveness in the government, decentralization and allowing the creation of new autonomous states are key elements to ensure peaceful heterogeneous countries and regions.

NOTE

1.   Global Development Growth Database. PennWorld Table 5.6.

BIBLIOGRAPHY

Abadie, A. and J. Gardeazabal (2003), 'The Economic Costs of Conflict: A Case Study of the Basque Country', *American Economic Review*, **93** (1), 113–32.
Acemoglu, D., S. Johnson and J.A. Robinson (2002), 'Reversal of Fortune: Geography and Institutions in the Making of the Modern World Income Distribution', *Quarterly Journal of Economics*, **117** (4), 1231–94.
Addison, T. (2003a),'Africa's Recovery from Conflict: Making Peace Work for the Poor – A Policy Brief', Helsinki, United Nations University, World Institute for Development Economics Research (WIDER) Working Paper No. 6.
Addison, T. (ed.) (2003b), *From Conflict to Recovery in Africa*, New York: Oxford University Press.
Addison, T., G. Alemayehu, P. Le Billon and S.M. Murshed (2001), 'Financial Reconstruction in Conflict and "Post-Conflict" Economies', Helsinki, United Nations University, World Institute for Development Economics Research (WIDER) Working Paper No. 2001/90.
Addison, T. and S.M. Murshed (2001), 'From Conflict to Reconstruction: Reviving the Social Contract', Helsinki, United Nations University, World Institute for Development Economics Research (WIDER) Working Paper No. 2001/48.
Barro, R., and X. Sala-i-Martin (1995), *Economic Growth*, New York: McGraw Hill.
Beck, T., G. Clarke, A. Groff, P. Keefer and P. Walsh (2001), 'New Tools and New Tests in Comparative Political Economy: The Database of Political Institutions', Washington DC: World Bank.
Chen, S., N. Loayza and M. Reynal-Querol (2007), 'The Aftermath of Civil War', *World Bank Economic Review*, **22** (1), 63–85.
Chen, A. and T. Siems (2004), 'The Effects of Terrorism on Global Capital Markets', *European Journal of Political Economy*, **20** (2), 349–66.
Collier, P. (1999), 'On the Economic Consequences of Civil War', *Oxford Economic Papers*, **51** (1), 168–83.
Collier, P. and A. Hoeffler (2002), 'Military Expenditure: Threats, Aids and Arms Races', Washington, DC, World Bank, Policy Research Working Paper No. 2927.
—— (2004a), 'Aid, Policy and Growth in Post-Conflict Countries', *European Economic Review*, **48** (5), 1125–45.
—— (2004b), 'Greed and Grievances in Civil Wars', *Oxford Economic Papers*, **56** (4), 563–95.
Collier, P., L. Elliot, H. Hegre, A. Hoeffler, N. Sambanis and M. Reynal-Querol (2003), *Breaking the Conflict Trap: Civil War and Development Policy*, Washington, DC: World Bank.

Colomer, J.M. (2000), *Political Institutions Democracy and Social Choice*, New York: Oxford University Press.

Davis, D. and D. Weinstein (2002), 'Bones, Bombs, and Break Points: The Geography of Economic Activity', *American Economic Review*, **92** (5), 1269–89.

Djankov, S. and M. Reynal-Querol (2007), 'The Colonial Origins of Civil War', Barcelona University Pompeu Fabra, Department of Economics and Business Economic Working Paper No. 1038.

—— (2008), 'Institutions and Conflict', mimeo.

Doyle, M. and N. Sambanis (2000), 'International Peacebuilding: A Theoretical and Quantitative Analysis', *American Political Science Review*, **94** (4), 779–801.

Fearon, J. (2005), 'Primary Commodity Exports and Civil War', *Journal of Conflict Resolution*, **49** (4), 483–507.

Fearon, J. and D. Laitin (2003), 'Ethnicity, Insurgency and Civil War,' *American Political Science Review*, **97** (1), 75–90.

Garfinkel, M.R. (1990), 'Arming as a Strategic Investment in a Cooperative Equilibrium', *American Economic Review*, **80** (1), 50–68.

Garfinkel, M.R. and S. Skaperdas (2001), 'Conflict Without Misperceptions or Incomplete Information: How the Future Matters', Levine's Working Paper Archive.

Ghobarah, H., P. Huth and B. Russett (2003), 'Civil Wars Kill and Maim People Long after the Shooting Stops', *American Political Science Review*, **97** (2), 189–202.

Grossman, H.I. (1994), 'Production, Appropriation and Land Reform', *American Economic Review*, **84** (3), 705–12.

Grossman, H.I. and M. Kim (1996), 'Predation and Accumulation', *Journal of Economic Growth*, **1** (3), 333–51.

Haavelmo, T. (1954), *A Study in the Theory of Economic Evolution*, Amsterdam: North-Holland.

Hegre, H., T. Ellingsen, S. Gates and N.P. Gleditsch (2001), 'Toward a Democratic Civil Peace? Democracy, Political Change and Civil War, 1816–1992', *American Political Science Review*, **95** (1), 33–48.

Hegre, H. and N. Sambanis (2006), 'Sensitivity Analysis of Empirical Results on Civil War Onset', *Journal of Conflict Resolution*, **50** (4), 508–35.

Hirshleifer, J. (1995), 'Anarchy and its Breakdown', *Journal of Political Economy*, **103** (1), 26–52.

Horowitz, D. (1985), *Ethnic Groups in Conflict*, Berkeley: University of California Press.

Keen, D. (1998), 'The Economic Functions of Violence in Civil Wars', London, International Institute of Strategic Studies, Adelphia Paper No. 320. Quoted in M. Ross (2003), 'Natural Resources and Civil War: an Overview with Some Policy Options', Los Angeles, CA: University of California, Department of Political Science, unpublished paper.

Le Billon, P. (2001), 'The Political Ecology of War: Natural Resources and Armed Conflicts', *Political Geography*, **20** (5), 561–84. Quoted in M. Ross (2003), 'Natural Resources and Civil War: An Overview with Some Policy Options', Los Angeles, CA: University of California, Department of Political Science, unpublished paper.

Lijphart, A. (1977), *Democracy in Plural Societies: A Comparative Exploration*, New Haven, CT: Yale University Press.

Miguel, E. and G. Roland (2005), 'The Long-Run Impact of Bombing Vietnam', Press release, Berkeley: University of California Press.

Montalvo, J.G (2006), 'Voting After the Bombing: Can Terrorist Attacks Change the Outcome of Democratic Elections?', Barcelona, Universitat Pompeu Fabra

Department of Economics and Business Working Paper No. 1000.

Montalvo, J.G. and M. Reynal-Querol (2005), 'Ethnic Polarization, Potential Conflict, and Civil Wars', *American Economic Review*, **95** (3), 796–816.

—— (2007), 'Fighting Against Malaria: Prevent Wars While Waiting for the "Miraculous' Vaccine", *Review of Economics and Statistics*, **89** (1), 165–77.

—— (2008), 'Discrete Polarization with an Application to the Determinants of Genocides', *Economic Journal*, **118** (533), 1835–65.

Murdoch J., and T. Sandler (2002), 'Civil Wars and Economic Growth: A Regional Comparison', *Defense and Peace Economics*, **13** (6), 451–64.

—— (2004), 'Civil Wars and Economic Growth: Spatial Dispersion', *American Journal of Political Science*, **48** (1), 138–51.

North, D. (1990), *Institutions, Institutional Change and Economic Performance*, New York: Cambridge University Press.

Organski, A.F.K. and J. Kugler (1977), 'The Costs of Major Wars: The Phoenix Factor', *American Political Science Review*, **71** (14), 1347–66.

—— (1980), *The War Ledger*, Chicago, IL: University of Chicago Press.

Przeworski, A., M. Alvarez, J. Cheibub and F. Limongi (2000), *Democracy and Development: Political Institutions and Wellbeing in the World 1950–1990*, New York: Cambridge University Press.

Reynal-Querol, M. (2002a), 'Ethnicity, Political Systems, and Civil Wars', *Journal of Conflict Resolution*, **46** (1), 29–54.

—— (2002b), 'Political Systems, Stability and Civil Wars', *Defense and Peace Economics*, **13** (6), 465–83.

—— (2005), 'Does Democracy Preempt Civil Wars?', *European Journal of Political Economy*, **21** (2), 445–65.

Ross, M. (2003), 'Natural Resources and Civil War: An Overview with Some Policy Options', Los Angeles, CA: University of California, Department of Political Science, unpublished paper.

Sambanis, N. (2001), 'Do Ethnic and Nonethnic Civil Wars Have the Same Causes? A Theoretical and Empirical Enquiry (part 1)', *Journal of Conflict Resolution*, **45** (3), 259–82.

Skaperdas, S. (1992), 'Cooperation, Conflict and Power in the Absence of Property Rights', *American Economic Review*, **82** (4), 720–39.

—— (1996), 'Contest Success Functions', *Economic Theory*, **7** (2), 283–90.

Soares, R. (2006), 'The Welfare Cost of Violence across Countries', *Journal of Health Economics*, **25** (5), 821–46.

United Nations Millennium Project (2005), 'A Linchpin to Global Security', http://www.unmillenniumproject.org.

7. Violence, Development and the Rule of Law

Martin Krygier and Whit Mason

Our world affords no starker contrast than that between societies where peace generally prevails and those where violence is commonplace. The former are generally blessed with the rule of law; the latter, cursed by its absence. The strength of the rule of law in a given society is reflected in virtually every aspect of how people live and go about their daily affairs.

Of course, the rule of law is not something you either completely have or lack, like a unique work of art. Rather, one has more or less of it. Its presence, strength and salience differ greatly from one society to another and within different spheres of society as well. These differences matter.

Where the rule of law is strong, people can go about their business without constant fear of predatory behavior, either from the state or their neighbors. Thus it makes sense to contemplate cooperating, even with strangers, on a routine and productive basis, and that commonly happens. To the extent that the rule of law counts in a society, citizens can obtain clear and shared understandings of their own and others' legal rights and obligations and can have reasonable faith that the law will help to constrain and inform other citizens and officials in ways both can rely on and predict in common. Both these aspects – prevention and facilitation – make possible many activities that are difficult and/or dangerous without them. But even if they didn't lead to further specifiable political, economic and other consequences, they are important goals in themselves. Lives are better for them. So the rule of law is an important goal for all modern, modernizing and would-be modernizing societies. It is indeed an ingredient in a civil society properly understood – that is, a society in which it makes sense to be civil rather than predatory or in constant fear of predation (Krygier 2005).

Societies where the rule of law prevails offer an open field for the pursuit of dreams, while those where the law-of-the jungle rules are crowded with continual nightmares. Anyone who has spent time in both kinds of places can describe her own feelings in a way that will capture much of what is important about the differences between them. And yet, when it comes to accounting for these differences – or doing something about them – our ignorance is quite astounding.

Our topic, therefore, could hardly be a more harrowing one, both intellectually and practically. If we make progress toward understanding what makes relatively peaceful societies run as they do, we will be that much closer to ending the brutality that haunts millions of people every day. Yet to do so will require us to extract from our knowledge of healthy societies and their histories lessons that were secret even to those who lived and still live them. Central among these secrets is how to generate the rule of law and what it is that makes its various attributes – institutional, political and normative – cohere as something that limits interpersonal violence within a given society to relatively rare criminal aberrations.

While history is an important guide, we would not advocate trying to replicate most stable nations' histories even if that were possible. Besides lasting centuries, most have been extremely bloody. Our challenge is to try to reproduce the finer fruits of long, often sanguinary histories in a compressed period of time and with minimal violence. Two features of our globalized era give us some hope of being able to shorten and pacify the process – the existence of models in widely varying cultural contexts and the array of technologies that have collapsed distances and time in all areas of modern life. Combined with these, today's reformers approach their task with a more focused sense of mission than virtually any of their professional forebears. That is potentially a blessing, though often a mixed one in practice.

We begin with a sketch of how the rule of law is viewed by those currently attempting to generate it, typically where it has been conspicuous by its absence. Partly in light of the hollowness of many of the institution-focused efforts that have predominated in the field of rule-of-law reform over the past 20 years or so, and partly on theoretical grounds, we will advance two underlying principles of an alternative approach. We will then attempt to describe some of the features essential to rule-of-law societies and the conditions that foster or at least allow them to evolve. Finally, we discuss some of the considerations basic to any attempt to move from circumstances pervaded by internal violence to a political and social order characterized by the rule of law, civility and peace – a precondition for most other desirable features of life.

RULE OF LAW BY THE NUMBERS

The rule of law is so popular these days that there is little it is not called upon to do or to fix. The list is long and can be indefinitely extended, for it has become fashionable to believe, on arguable but not insubstantial grounds, that it is a necessary means to achieve various ends beyond the rule of law itself (Peerenboom 2005; Trubek and Santos 2006; Golub 2006). As Charles T. Call observes:

> Among a plethora of development and security agencies, a new 'rule of law consensus' has emerged. This consensus consists of two elements: (1) the belief that the rule of law is essential to virtually every Western liberal foreign policy goal – human rights, democracy, economic and political stability, international security from terrorist and other transnational threats, and transnational free trade and investment; and (2) the belief that international interventions, be they through money, people, or ideas, must include a rule-of-law component. (2007, 4)

This has two consequences: on the one hand, rule of law reformers try to develop the rule of law because these external ends are thought valuable; on the other hand, they do not consider those ends to be within their province. *We* do rule of law, that is, build the institutions that comprise the formal justice sector; economists, sociologists and politologists do the other stuff, dependent on what we have built. And specialized narrowing does not stop there. Even within the rule of law field, some people focus on judges, others do police and security services. This balkanization has doomed many otherwise thoughtful and well-supported efforts to superficiality.

First, and especially in the early years of deliberate attempts to build the rule of law 'from the ground up' (though in fact more commonly from the top down), rule of law reformers have tended to take what Carothers has called a 'breathtakingly mechanistic approach' based on the notion that 'a country achieves the rule of law by reshaping its key institutions to match those of countries that are considered to have the rule of law' (2006, 21). Remarkably, despite some notable exceptions (e.g., Carothers 2006; Jensen and Heller 2003; Samuels 2006), many bureaucracies and the academics who service them continue to promote precisely the shallow, imitative agenda that Carothers derides (Dobbins et al. 2007).

We believe that the 'build them and they will come' approach to legal institutions is misguided (Hendley, Holmes, Åslund and Sajó 1999; Holmes 1998; Cashu and Orenstein 2001; Hendley 2001). It confuses an abiding, precious, state of affairs, the rule of law, with particular and contingent means thought appropriate to achieve it, and then it elevates the latter as though they were the former. Nothing could be further from the truth. Law-constrained social relations are general, perhaps even universal, goods; particular institutions are merely attempts to attain them. They are worth trying if they work, but should be abandoned if they don't. And what works will vary with time, place, circumstance, history, and current resources and particular challenges, all of which ideally would be known by those who design instruments to secure the rule of law. Not to distinguish means and ends is one of the deepest follies of institutional craftsmanship in general (well known in organizational theory as 'goal displacement'). It is no less so in attempts to craft the rule of law (Krygier 2001, 2002, 2004, 2006, 2009; Stromseth, Wippman and Brooks 2006, 329).

A second problem in rule of law promotion is that it is common for the left hand to be unaware of what the right hand is doing, and the consequences can be costly. For example, 14 years after the collapse of the Soviet Union, the U.S. Agency for International Development (USAID) supported a rule of law program in Georgia that focused on the education and credentialing of lawyers. Though the project created a rigorous bar exam meant to weed out law graduates unqualified to practice, the project's criterion of success was the number of lawyers produced – a single input into the institutional dimension of the rule of law in Georgia. Meanwhile, the U.S.-backed government of President Mikheil Saakashvili employed an array of extra-legal means to crack down on organized crime, earning gratitude from the crime-weary population but immeasurably distorting their embryonic notion of what it meant for the law to rule (Mason 2005a, 2005b).

In another instance of substantial effort yielding superficial results, in 1998 the Asian Development Bank committed $350 million to fund the 'Access to Justice' program in Pakistan, then the largest justice-sector reform program ever supported by a development organization. An assessment of the project noted that Pakistan's judicial sector had been chronically under-funded, resulting in crippling backlogs and the widespread perception that the judiciary was corrupt and lacked independence. The project's first phase provided on-the-job training for judges, study tours to Britain, Canada, Australia, the United States and Singapore, consulting and software to improve courts' efficiency, organizational reform and computers. These efforts yielded a number of technical improvements visible only to those working in the courts. On the negative side, the courts remained under-funded, reflecting the ruling powers' lack of interest in improving judicial capacity, and 'the lack of visible linkage of the reform agenda to poverty alleviation and benefits for the ordinary person' (Armytage 2003). Nine years after the program was launched, President Pervez Musharraf dismissed the chief justice of Pakistan's high court for what were widely believed to be self-interested political reasons.

UNKNOWN UNKNOWNS

It is hard to do justice, so to speak, to the inadequacy of such approaches. Even if they were based on sound understanding of the bases of the rule of law, they run up against the economists' 'theory of the second best'. This holds that if in an ideal theoretical model a combination of factors and circumstances would produce a particular optimal result, but some of these factors are missing, you won't necessarily achieve the next-best result by simply seeking to maximize those of the stipulated factors that remain, in the circumstances that you have. The problem further compounds when we have such a poor idea of what the relevant factors actually are. 'Aid providers know what endpoint they would like to help countries achieve', writes Carothers, 'the Western-style, rule-oriented systems they know from their own countries. Yet they do not really know how countries that do not have such systems attain them' (2006, 21). That is certainly a problem, and we will return to it. But it reflects a deeper ignorance: we do not really know how countries that do have such systems attained them.

One reason for this is that the strength and salience of the rule of law in any particular society are usually overdetermined: so many things seem to have gone right in societies where the rule of law is strong, and so many things wrong in societies where it is weak, that it is hard to separate causes from effects.

It is fairly uncontroversial, for example, that the rule of law is comparatively strong in England, a rich country with ancient legal institutions and traditions, a legal profession of lineage and power, law-related practices that have developed over long periods and a strong culture of legality that has seeped into the workings of most people's everyday lives (Thompson 1975, 258–69), all interwoven and with little deliberate design to produce the results they have. To pluck out of this dense thicket of institutions, cultures, traditions, mores and practices, merely the formal rules or architecture of legal institutions is simply to pick at leaves.

This appears to be true of legal transplants too. We have rather thin answers, for example, for why the rule of law was so readily transplanted to Australia, along with the criminals who were transported there in the eighteenth and nineteenth centuries (Neal 1991; Krygier 2002a; Hendley et al. 1999). Few experts were on the job, after all, and most had other things on their minds. Moscow and many other places since the late twentieth century, beneficiaries of advice from vast teams of rule-of-law specialists who appear to think about nothing else, have exhibited somewhat less success (Holmes 1999). Neither the reasons for success nor for failure are self-evident.

It must be somewhat disconcerting to professional rule-of-law promoters that most of the greatest success stories of the rule of law owed nothing to them. No one designed such successes from the ground up; typically they were inherited, occasionally tinkered with and at least once, in the United States, tinkered with greatly and to great effect. Their rule of law was not a grand rationalist program of institutional design, but what the philosopher Michael Oakeshott has called the 'pursuit of intimations' (1991, 57) of existing, sometimes very old, traditions. That is far from the only way that institutions can develop, but a society is very lucky indeed when it has good institutional intimations to pursue. Most societies in which interpersonal violence is endemic have not been so lucky.

HOW TO RECOGNIZE THE RULE OF LAW

We begin with two general propositions that we believe hold true wherever and whenever the rule of law is found. They frame all we say, and they should be stressed, since discussions about the export and import of the rule of law too often proceed without any general framing principles or context. This lack of foundation has often accounted for the fruitlessness of well-intentioned efforts and the disappointment now readily apparent and growing in the literature of rule-of-law promotion (Carothers 2006; Jensen and Heller 2003; Samuels 2006).

First, the rule of law is better understood *as a state of affairs*, with complex, multi-layered elements of various provenances, rather than any particular set of institutions. It is 'a contingent reality, real *insofar as* certain things go on', to borrow a phrase from Gianfranco Poggi (2000, 85). You have it assuming that some things, such as legally constrained and channeled social relations, routinely occur more, and others, such as lawless and violent behaviors, routinely occur less.

This is a point to keep in mind – for restraint upon interpersonal violence was a goal much closer to the core of traditional conceptions of what the state of affairs known as the rule of law *includes* than those, such as democracy and economic development, more commonly emphasized today as what the rule of law is hoped to *deliver*.

Second, while it is an oft-repeated and often empty banality to say that the rule of law can only be understood 'in context', this is true in a deep and textured sense that is far from banal, but too seldom understood. Legal sociology tells us some relatively simple things about the contexts of state law that are as important as they are almost willfully neglected by rule-of-law promoters, and indeed most lawyers. And not only the sociology, but also the politics, of the rule of law matter.

The nexus between interpersonal violence and the rule of law in the context of development encompasses a number of fields – redrafting legal codes, judicial reform, security sector reform, human security/protection – that in practice are virtually always pursued separately ('stovepiped' or 'siloed') and all too often thoroughly estranged from one another. The lack of congruence between this chapter and any one of these areas of practice, far from undermining its practical applicability, stems from our argument that most aspects of a society – its balance of power, economic structure, family patterns, education, media, as well as legal institutions – are relevant to the degree the rule of law prevails within it. Since these interconnections are unseverable, anyone interested in introducing the rule of law should take them more seriously than many rule-of-law reformers have hitherto (Krygier 2001, 2002, 2004, 2006, 2008; Stromseth, Wippman and Brooks 2006).

A State of Affairs

We want to argue that what Carothers calls 'the elusive essence' of the rule of law is not simply a set of institutions, regardless of how wisely they incorporate customary law or otherwise take account of contextual factors. It is, rather, a set of relationships of which the essence lies as much in the balance among the elements as in the elements themselves. Rule-of-law societies, those characterized by the mother of all other social virtues – freedom from the violence of anarchy or despotism – depend neither on virtuous institutions nor on virtuous people per se, but on virtuous relationships among people. These, in turn, depend upon a lot more than just the law.

The idea of the rule of law long predates its current evangelists, and what its many generations of proponents have thought important about it differs from contemporary packages or menus in two significant respects. The first is that, until recently, it has been much easier to glean overlapping understandings of the state of affairs that the rule of law represents than it is to find a specific and agreed upon recipe for producing it. When Aristotle spoke of it being better to be ruled by laws than by men, he was saying something important and enduring, but the details of whatever particular model or formula he may have had in mind have ceased to interest us. And whatever institutional arrangements were thought to represent the rule of law over the long English rule-of-law tradition, they have varied greatly over time and many bear little resemblance to anything we would identify with the rule of law today. Yet to speak of such a tradition is to point to something of deep social, indeed civilizational, significance. As a matter of public ideology *and* practice, law *counted* as a restraint on ways to exercise power, much more than it has in many other societies with a less robust commitment to the rule of law or, as often happens in violent societies, a commitment to the absence of the rule of law. In all three sorts of societies, however, there were usually plenty of institutions having to do with law, broadly defined.

Second, and of particular importance for our theme, the alleged virtues of the rule of law, though greatly prized by its partisans, were once less promiscuously strewn about than they are today. Or, to put the point another way, seen as a state of affairs, the concept of the rule of law included a particular end state: restraint on the possibilities of unruly – arbitrary, capricious, despotic, willful and unrestrained – exercises of power. What *further* goals that end state might serve has been disputed and varied over time and in different societies. But whether or not one thought that the rule of law was good for the economy or democracy or human rights, no one doubted that you didn't have it unless law was able to serve as an effective constraint on the possible ways in which power could be exercised.

As many thinkers have realized, the stakes are high. Thus, as the philosopher Judith Shklar glosses the thought of Montesquieu on this subject, his

> whole scheme is ultimately based on a very basic dichotomy. The ultimate spiritual and political struggle is always between war and law.... The institutions of judicial citizen protection may create rights, but they exist in order to avoid what Montesquieu took to be the greatest of human evils, constant fear created by the threats of violence and the actual cruelties of the holders of military power in society. (1998, 24–25)

What most classical accounts of the rule of law have in common, then, is less a particular enumeration of institutional measures than something like this: the rule of law exists insofar as law can and does make an effective contribution to restraining the possibility of unruly exercise of power, whether by the mob or the state. The rule of law or its parallel (though not equivalent, see Palombella 2009) concepts in various languages – *Rechtsstaat, état de droit, stato diritto, państwo prawa*, and so on – has been a central element in the solution proposed, again and again, to two questions – what to do about unruly peoples (Thomas Hobbes's question) and what about unruly states (John Locke's question). Insofar as a given society has successfully answered those questions, there we have the rule of law.

That is what we have in mind, too, when we note the extent to which a country is blessed with the rule of law or cursed by its absence. An escapee from Haiti to the United States, or from Timor Leste to Australia, may know little about the destination's institutions, but she is likely to understand that there is more of the rule of law in her place of arrival than that of departure –

enough to risk life and limb to leave her homeland for a strange new country. In this sense, the rule of law is to be valued not merely for what else it might deliver (which it might or might not), but for itself.

It is also connected to other goods, not merely, to use Amartya Sen's distinction (2000), *causally* – meaning that it might or might not lead to other good sorts of development, but *conceptually*, in that, like a 'typical summer's day', a well developed and civil society properly understood includes the rule of law among its many constitutive and inextricably interconnected elements. As Sen puts it

> We cannot very well say that the development process has gone beautifully even though people are being arbitrarily hanged, criminals go free while law-abiding citizens end up in jail, and so on. ... Legal development is constitutively involved in the development process ... even if legal development were not to contribute one iota to economic development ... even then legal and judicial reform would be a critical part of the development process. (2000, 9–10)

Given the concern with reliable constraint and channeling of the exercise of power, an overarching concern of writers on the rule of law and allied concepts over centuries of discussion has been how to institutionalize these things. The answers have been many. The notion of constitutional restraints, for example, existed for centuries before anyone thought up a binding and written constitution in the eighteenth century (McIlwain 1958). Now almost everyone has a constitution, and it is typically taken as a necessary condition for the rule of law (with the small embarrassment that the United Kingdom, scarcely an also-ran in the rule-of-law stakes, has never had one). Roughly similar comments may be made of a bill of rights: Australia, which also does not do especially poorly in protecting rights, still has no such documents. Enshrining separation of powers, and generally the principle that powers need to be balanced by other powers, has also been popular. And, as we shall see, many other stratagems have been tried. Our only point here is to stress that those stratagems are merely means to a valuable state of affairs – the rule of law – and they are means of a special, complex sort. The means of the rule of law cannot be manufactured, pre-wrapped and exported. They must be assessed in terms of their proven ability to serve its ends in concrete social and historical circumstances, with the understanding that methods that worked well in some societies might fail or have unanticipated consequences in others, and that many methods may not travel well without considerable adaptation.

Law in Society

Answers to what the rule of law requires in particular circumstances, then, will be far more particular, contingent and variable than answers to why anyone might want it. History, existing social, political and legal institutions, culture and structures will affect what aids achievement of even a universal goal in a particular time and place (Krygier 2004). Moreover – and this is our second principle – these answers will need to look well beyond legal institutions, since many of the conditions of effective, restraint on unruly power lie embedded within extra-legal, social and political structures and cultures, as indeed do the institutions of law themselves.

This is not merely to repeat the common mantra – context matters. We can say more about legal contexts than that. The bottom line, even when all institutions have been imported and officials trained, retrained and equipped, is that to be more than purely decorative, the rule of law requires the law to *count*, which in turn requires that it be widely expected and assumed to count, both by those who exercise it (which, where citizens make use of the law, should be far more than just officials) and by those affected by its exercise. What is involved when the law counts is a complex sociological question on which the law bears. It is not in itself a legal question, for it depends as much on characteristics of the society and polity as of the law, and on their interactions.

What does it mean for 'law to count' in a society in such a way that we feel confident in saying that the rule of law is strong there? All the questions asked in this chapter have a sociological dimension, this one above all. It asks about the social reach and weight of law, and the answers, whatever they are, will have to attend to questions of sociology and politics as much as of law. Indeed, social and political questions are central to the place of law in a society, and they will be answered differently in different societies, whatever the written laws say or have in common. This is not because the law has no significance, but because the nature and extent of that significance cannot be inferred from the law itself.

Where the law really does seriously count, when the law is socially and politically significant, the legal position will bear closely on the factual position and the hour of the lawyer is at hand. But that is only because what lawyers don't know, the conditions of legal effectiveness, gives significance to what they do, the law. When those conditions are lacking, lawyers' talk is beside the point. For if no one is listening, it doesn't matter too much what the law is saying.

Legal philosophers usually mention that the law must be effective, but that merely hints at the complexity of what the rule of law depends on: far greater complexity than is needed for a merely effective legal order. Guides for rule-of-law practitioners talk of the need for a culture of legality (Dobbins et al. 2007). However, effectiveness is a rather black box, whose contents are not obvious. Moreover, as we shall see, culture is only a part of the extra-institutional infrastructure that a society depends upon for the rule of law to be in good order. It depends on many things beyond culture to be in good shape, even while those things themselves are affected by the cultures in which they develop.

The rule of law is manifest in the extent to which legal institutions, concepts, options and resources frame, inform and support the choices of citizens. This can occur and vary in several ways. Though direct recourse to legal institutions is the most obvious route, it is not the most important, since in no society does more than a very small fraction of law-related behavior, even of law-related and law-affected disputes, ever reach those institutions (Felstiner, Abel and Sarat 1980–81; Galanter 1983). In fact, 'Courts resolve only a small fraction of all disputes that are brought to their attention. These are only a small fraction of the disputes that might conceivably be brought to court and an even smaller fraction of the whole universe of disputes' (Galanter 1981, 3). It is a socio-legal truism, which still escapes many lawyers, that the importance of legal institutions is poorly indicated by the number of people who make direct use of them.

While citizens rarely invoke official channels, a more socially significant indicator is the extent to which they have utilized – and are able and willing to use – legal resources. Legal sociologists identify such usage – often labeled as cues, standards, models, 'bargaining chips', 'regulatory endowments', authorizations, immunities – in relations with each other and with the state as realistic (if necessarily imperfect) indicators of what they and others can and are likely to do. These endowments, in turn, are not merely gifts from the institutions; they depend upon 'the capabilities of actors to receive, store and use them, capabilities that reflect their skills, resources and opportunities' (Galanter 1981, 16). These capabilities in turn

> Are not immutable qualities intrinsic to the actors [but] derive from, and are relative to, structures of communication and structures for organising action. Capabilities depend, for example, on location in a network that carries information about rights and remedies and on proximity to remedy institutions or 'exit' alternatives. The process of distributing and extracting endowments is framed by the larger structures of social life. As these structures undergo change, the character of the centrifugal flow of effects from the courts will change too. (Galanter 1981, 16)

The primary impact of such institutions is not, then, as magnets for the very small proportion of disputes that ever come to them in even the most legalistic society, but as beacons sending signals about law, rights, costs, delays, advantages, disadvantages and other possibilities into the community. In some societies these signals don't work or are dim, while in others, citizens see no reason to heed them. In many societies citizens have no reason to heed them. But even when these signals are bright and visible, and people take them seriously, they are not the only ones that are sent out or received in a society. They compete with other signals, some of them brighter and much closer to home, sent by social networks in which people are embedded. In turn, the receivers are not a single entity or homogeneous group but plural, different, self- and other-directed, within numerous, often distinct or overlapping, 'semi-autonomous' groups that affect them, often deeply (Moore 1978).

Moreover, these groups are not merely mediators of signals from the central justice institutions; they do a lot of 'law jobs' themselves. This is true even in the most modern societies with highly developed and effective legal orders. In them, and *a fortiori* in societies less well endowed with effective official law, 'Just as health is not found primarily in hospitals or knowledge in schools, so justice is not primarily to be found in official justice-dispensing institutions' (Galanter 1981, 17).

In all societies, then, even the most highly law-abiding, the significance of law for those who receive it is commonly very different from the imaginings of those who send it. This is all the more likely to be the case where law is sent, as it so often is in societies beset by interpersonal violence, into disputed and hostile territory.

In 2003, while attending a workshop on 'Rethinking the Role of Law After Communism', Stephen Holmes remarked that a production technology is easier to transplant than an interaction technology, a pithy summary of the core of our argument here. And even with this caution, the metaphor of technology simplifies the problem. For as Frank Upham has observed of those professing the 'new rule-of-law orthodoxy': 'Law is seen as technology when it should be seen as sociology or politics' (2006, 76). Our previous remarks in this section have been sociological in the main, but – particularly in countries where interpersonal violence is pervasive – politics are key. While it is true that law is always and everywhere mediated, refracted, transformed and often resisted and rejected by the semi-autonomous fields it must penetrate to affect, it is also true that not every group has the same power as every other. Holmes' observation about Russia has resonance in this connection everywhere, but particularly in the context of countries in the throes of internecine strife, where governments are often weak:

> Foreign legal consultants and experts report the greatest rate of success (that is, their advice is swallowed whole and the laws they draft are actually passed by parliaments) in societies where law is virtually unenforced. This is natural. In any relatively free

society, powerful domestic forces will be indifferent to the content of unenforced legislation. Where laws are not enforced, legislative drafting can be donated as an amusement park for foreign lawyers. (I once met a lawyer sitting in the lobby of the IMF who boasted: 'I wrote the Civil Code of Afghanistan'.) By contrast, as soon as laws begin to be reliably enforced, powerful social forces have an incentive to put their stamp on legislation and to make sure that the regulatory framework functions to their advantage. This partiality of the supposedly neutral law to well-organised social forces makes Western legal development managers nervous. But it is a part of the legal-reform landscape that they ignore at their peril. (1999, 73)

The rule of law as a state of affairs, then, prevails insofar as private individuals and state officials generally behave in ways that law affects, constrains and successfully contributes to keep within civil bounds and without civil war. This behavior reflects the largely unconscious attitude and expectation among ordinary people and state officials that they will be better off behaving in these ways than not. This attitude, in turn, reflects, though imperfectly, empirical realities – in particular the balance of power in their society as embodied by its norms and mediated by its social structures, networks and institutions.

All this depends on much beyond the official law, and so the rule of law is too important to leave to lawyers alone. Again, Sen gets it right: 'Even when we consider development in a particular sphere, such as economic development or legal development, the instruments that are needed to enhance development in that circumscribed sphere may not be confined only to institutions and policies in that sphere' (2000, 10). And, as he reminds us, 'If this sounds a little complex, I must point out that the complication relates, ultimately, to the interdependences of the world in which we live. I did not create that world, and any blame for it has to be addressed elsewhere' (2000, 27).

CONTEXTS AND ELEMENTS

What, then, are some of the features of a society in which the rule of law can be effective and interpersonal violence is typically and routinely, restrained? The following six elements are crucial, though the enumeration is not intended to be exhaustive, merely suggestive.

Civil Society

The phrase 'civil society' has become remarkably popular in recent years (see, e.g., Krygier 1997, 2002, 2005). No one will be heard to denounce civil society; instead, people compete to find ways to praise it. But the torrent of praise has both multiplied and obscured the term's meanings. Without quibbling over alternative definitions, for our purposes a civil society is simply a society that is civil. The significance of the qualification 'civil' might be grasped by reflecting for a moment on societies where incivilities are rampant.

Uncivil societies generate and crucially depend upon the maintenance of a double moral standard, with sharp boundaries and an unbridgeable gulf in between: one standard for intimates and another for strangers. Such a rigorously maintained double standard cannot be a happy solution when a society contains more than a few non-intimates. One can of course try to kill them or drive them away – as in much of the former Yugoslavia, Rwanda, East Timor and too many other places.

If such draconian options are unavailable, one can still be rude, hostile, suspicious and uncooperative. In many societies this is a reasonable option – even the only reasonable option – since in these societies there are few reasons to cooperate with strangers, many good reasons to be suspicious of anyone they don't know well, and no good reason not to be. For obvious reasons, such hostility tends to be self-perpetuating.

This option was widely practiced under despotically, if not fruitfully, powerful communist states, and it also occurs when states fail or where they never succeeded. A weak state, too, favors bullies and encourages pre-emptive hostility toward – and distrust of – others. In such conditions a market develops for entrepreneurs of violence and protection. That market is serviced by the original Mafia in southern Italy, and what are derivatively and appropriately called mafias in post-communist Russia. Similar markets boomed – though they were the only ones that flourished – among the warlords who roamed and terrorized much of the former Yugoslavia during the Balkan wars. As Michael Ignatieff observed of the war zone of Vukovar: 'Every man goes armed. No one ventures beyond the village. No one trusts anyone they have not known all their lives' (1995, 48). And, tragically but wisely, people distrust many people they *have* known all their lives.

Another social option altogether, somewhat rare, is for non-intimates to be civil to each other. No one will do this if the costs are prohibitive or the benefits illusory. A civil society is one that contrives to keep down the costs and spread the benefits, so that it is reasonable to be nice or at least not nasty.

In civil societies, routine non-predatory social relations can occur among non-intimates that neither depend upon love or deep connection nor – as is common in uncivil conditions – are fractured by their absence and replaced by suspicion, hostility, hatred or simple fear. Cool, civil connections are not the only ones that occur – nor should they be – but in the public realm the possibility of such connections is key to most of the more positive attributes associated with developed countries. People have familial, ethnic, religious and linguistic attachments which often matter to them greatly and which differ; but they don't kill for them. Nor is it a realistic expectation that they might. Civil relationships are not especially close, and they are not hot like love and hatred. They are the character of relationships among members of healthy voluntary associations, not of close families on the one hand, nor of opposed troops on the other. They are ones in which the opposite of my friend is not my enemy but, say, my acquaintance or colleague or neighbor. I can do business with him, and I do not necessarily betray anyone by doing so.

Merely civil relationships are not worth dying for, but a society pervaded by civil relationships may well be. A civil platform is a secure place to stand. It is immeasurably preferable to its historically conjoined 'other' – fanaticism (Colas 1997; Oz 2006) – as it is to routine hatred, suspicion, hostility and vengefulness. Indeed, it seems to be the only situation that marries security and freedom.

In the political life of a civil society, even opponents inhabit a common, or at least overlapping, moral universe: competitors within some common frames of reference, however unspoken and superficially denied; they are not mortal foes. In civil polities, power is disciplined by institutions, among them law. As we will see, it is a mistake to think this necessarily weakens power. On the contrary, it can strengthen it in important and fruitful ways, while at the same time it channels, restrains, disciplines and limits the ways in which it can be exercised. In such circumstances, law too is a significant ingredient in the psychological economy of individuals' lives. It can effectively communicate public signs of bounds within which politicians and people might with some confidence be expected to act. When they don't, this is this the stuff of scandal, not normal operating procedures.

Elections matter in civil polities; many people are concerned, but no one is especially scared. No one is killed or even worries about being killed, whatever the result. A prime minister in one such society (Australia, as it happens) publicly described his opponents as 'vermin' but they did not worry for a second about being exterminated; nor, when he lost an election to them, did he.

Perceptions

Political scientists and economists often talk about 'collective action problems'; civil society and the rule of law are collective action triumphs. People must be persuaded to forebear from actions that could be advantageous to themselves, at least in the short term.

Individuals' perceptions and expectations of their own societies are central to how they behave; if they believe themselves to be living in a Hobbesian world, they would be foolish to behave in other than Hobbesian fashion.

Since Hobbesian conditions have been remarkably widespread, the existence today of societies that have escaped them testifies to the possibility, however improbable, of surmounting the prisoner's dilemma inherent in being among the first to respect the law where heretofore the law had not been worthy of it. Overcoming this dilemma requires people to place their faith in the law and their fellow citizens' respect for it or its enforcement mechanisms, or, more typically and reliably, in a combination of the two.

Expectations reflect the conditions in which people live, but only imperfectly so. First, expectations are largely self-fulfilling: those who lack trust in their fellows would be foolish to be trustworthy themselves. At the same time, people adapt to past conditions, which may vary considerably from current ones. Together this means that people's level of security will reflect their own behavior based on their memories, perceptions or hearsay about dangers in the past. Kosovo Serbs living in the enclave of Grbavica, for instance, insisted that Albanians would beat them up if they so much as set foot in nearby Pristina. How could they be so sure? Because they hadn't been there for years due to the danger (King and Mason 2006).

Persons seeking to foster the rule of law in a developing society must ask: What is required for people to support and believe in the rule of law and what conditions foster such support? The centrality of these questions cannot be overemphasized. The touchstone for all those working to create the state of affairs known as the rule of law should be the perspectives, expectations and attitudes of the individuals who make up the society.

Culture

Where could civil and lawful perspectives, expectations and attitudes come from? A common answer, in even the most enlightened treatments of this question, is 'culture'. Thus in their excellent book, *Can Might Make Rights?* Stromseth, Wippman and Brooks repeatedly and rightly stress that '"promoting the rule of law" is an issue of norm creation and cultural change as much as an issue of creating new institutions and legal codes' (2006, 75). They devote a chapter to 'creating rule-of-law cultures', in which they emphasize, 'The rule of law is as much a culture as a set of institutions, as much a matter of the habits, commitments, and beliefs of ordinary people as of legal codes. Institutions and codes are important, but without the cultural and political commitment to back them up, they are rarely more than window dressing' (2006, 311).

This is all true and important, and everything the authors say about how to generate a 'rule-of-law culture' is illuminating. The rule of law is bound up with all those fundamental aspects of a state and society that determine the extent to which it is rational for a person to behave civilly and within the law. But the rule of law cannot prevail on the basis of every citizen making a daily calculation of the relative merits of behaving legally and illegally, and almost all of them concluding each time that it makes sense to remain within the law. Norms, routine expectations, common understandings and reactions that are 'second nature', are all of crucial importance, and these are commonly encoded in and transmitted by culture. As Philip Selznick observes, 'The rule of law requires a culture of lawfulness, that is, of routine respect, self-restraint, and deference' (1999, 37).

Where institutions and rules of restraint are strong, a large part of that strength typically flows not directly or solely from the institutions and rules themselves, but from the traditions in which they were formed and from the culture that they themselves generated and that grows around and encrusts them, shaping the routine expectations of participants and observers. Moreover, the wider social efficacy of official law requires not merely that elites observe and seek to enforce it, but also that it enter into the normative structures that nourish, guide, inform and coordinate the actions of ordinary people: people who do not merely comply resentfully when they feel they might otherwise be punished, but who comply happily (enough) even when they are confident they will not be.

If institutions and rules are to endure and take on strength, then they owe their solidity to understandings and expectations – many of them borne by and grounded in cultural traditions within which the institutions and rules take on meaning and significance. These understandings, expectations and traditions, in turn, gain strength from their often-invisible pervasiveness. Where thickly institutionalized constraints do exist – indeed, typically where they do their best work – they are often not noticed, for they are internalized by both the powerful and those with less power, as the normal ways to behave. Limits are not tested because people cannot *imagine* that they should be. The absence of such a predisposition makes the burden on those things within the control of the institutions and/or interveners dauntingly heavy.

However, notions of culture can mislead. This is particularly the case when, as often, culture is taken to be homogeneous, organic, slow-moving and inescapable. In a great deal of talk about the rule of law, 'culture' operates as a residual category, the bag into which everything apart from rule-of-law recipes is thrown, and to which cursory and usually ritual deference is given before the important 'hard' stuff is taken up. This simultaneously diminishes the significance of the specific items in the culture bag while exaggerating their imperviousness to change. For not everything that we assume to be 'cultural' is so, and, it should be observed, culture can change and be changed by forces and pressures that are not elements of culture.

Were culture as impervious to change as is often imagined, we all may as well hang up our boots and watch events take their preordained course. But as Krygier wrote earlier

> Cultural sensitivity is not the same thing as cultural determinism. The former might encourage 'piecemeal social engineering' which – in the face of some institutionalist enthusiasms – would be salutary. The latter is likelier merely to encourage despair. And when, as often in recent debates, culture is invoked as a kind of prime 'unmoved mover' of the social world, there are reasons to share Hermann Goering's reaction[1] to the term, though they are not his reasons. (Krygier 1999, 90)

Fortunately, culture is not so stubbornly autochthonous or so determining. Much that we call culture – willingness to trust in the law, or its absence; expectations that the law will matter – flows from many other than cultural sources. It is embedded in social structures, networks, institutions and the ways all of these operate and interconnect and, when they do, change. Sometimes people fail to rely on the state because of deeply embedded cultural distrust of, hostility to and alienation from the state. Sometimes they distrust it because it is untrustworthy, whether because it works in crooked ways or just fails to work. To categorize all this as 'cultural' is to homogenize it in unuseful ways, and to forget that often a lot more than culture is involved and needs to be addressed (Holmes 1995).

For example, observers typicaliy attribute deference to heads of family to deeply engrained cultural values. In fact, in societies where such norms prevail, the heads of family normally control all resources, and those acting deferentially are heavily dependent on their seniors' goodwill. When this economic dependency changes, the deference often changes as well. In the mid-1990s, the government of Singapore realized that many newly prosperous citizens were no longer taking care of their retired parents, as had been traditional among the state's various ethnic communities. Singapore responded by passing a 'filial piety' law to compel its citizens to show their parents the regard that had previously been assumed to be automatic (Low 2002).

Institutions

From the emphasis on civil society, perceptions and culture, a reader might infer that the current argument diminishes the importance of legal institutions. This is not at all the case. No society has such a perfect balance of power and such well-developed norms that it can dispense altogether with institutions that provide facilities for orderly and cooperative forms of social engagement and punish violations of its legal order. Particularly where violence threatens, effective sanctions on violations are essential to preserve the credibility of a legal order. Without credibility, the law can play no meaningful part in the life of a community. With it, institutions can positively affect civil society, perceptions and culture.

For the rule of law to prevail, it must resonate with people's actual experience, the most important aspect of which is the shape of encounters between more and less powerful individuals and groups. If a group has demonstrated its impunity, no one in their right mind will ever use the law to try to challenge it. Similarly, if those who break the law can continue profiting from doing so, it would be foolish to try to compete with them while acting within the law. This was dramatically demonstrated when a man widely believed to be Kosovo's leading smuggler approached Whit Mason, an official at the UN mission there. His representatives told the UN official that he would be willing to conduct his import business solely on legal lines – if the UN border guards would agree to stop other smugglers, and thereby prevent them from underpricing him.

Civilizing Power

The rule of law depends upon – and contributes to – civilizing power, in both senses of that term. Power is needed to civilize society; anarchy is not a picnic. But power itself needs to be civilized; for tyranny is no picnic either. If states are ineffectual, there will be no rule of law and no civility. Non-state powers will fight or rule, and either way it will not be pretty. Likewise, uncontrolled state power can turn into despotism. States need to be able to constrain powerful non-state actors, but themselves be constrained, in part by the rule of law. States that are so constrained are simultaneously more effective in fostering civil society than unconstrained states and also more limited in their capacity to foment incivilities of their own accord. Michael Mann identified this important distinction. States gain 'the power to coordinate civil society, that is, infrastructural power', just as they lose – and in crucial part because they lose – the ability to wield 'power over civil society, that is, despotism' (1988, 32).

There are many institutional and constitutional devices designed to constrain – but not emasculate – state power. But such an arrangement first requires powers that can balance other powers (Holmes 1995). Where power is so concentrated in a single individual or group that they can act with impunity, they will nearly always behave badly (see, e.g., Chang 1997). The need for balances of power has been recognized since before the advent of modern democracy – in England after Magna Carta, in the estates of the realm in pre-revolutionary France, and so on. Robert Dahl has persuasively argued that 'polyarchy' – the diffusion of power among a number of centers – is an essential basis of a liberal democracy (1998, 88).

The formal separation of powers is not sufficient. Each branch of government is constrained by the resources it controls and its reputation within the society as a whole. The peaceful ascension of the post-Islamist Justice and Development Party in the secular Turkish Republic, for instance, has been possible because of the enormous public support for both of the main contenders for power, the party and the army (Bubalo, Fealey and Mason 2008).

But democracy – much less democratization – in itself does not ensure a balance of power conducive to civility. Where power is concentrated in a large group, even a majority, which defines itself and its prerogatives in exclusivist terms, that group would still tend to impose its will on the rest in such a way that led minorities to live in fear and, potentially, to rebel (Mann 2005; Paris 2004).[2] People must have a basis for believing they can prosper without it necessarily being at another's expense.

Overarching and Overlapping Ties

A crucial condition of civility, according to Max Weber, is the shift to a modern state structure where political power is non-arbitrary and state business is conducted by a bureaucracy whose members derive their authority from the offices they hold rather than the persons they are or those with whom they are connected.

> As a result the officials are appointed to their positions on the basis of contracts, their loyalty is enlisted in order to ensure the faithful execution of their official duties, and their work is rewarded by a regular salary and by the prospects of regular advancement in a lifetime career. Conscious orientation toward abstract norms and the depersonalization of the exercise of authority tend to increase the stability of expectation under the rule of law. (Bendix 1996, 194)

The development of the norms essential to the rule of law requires complex interdependency, which enables plus-sum growth and both reflects and engenders identification with a set of moral obligations to a community that extends well beyond one's own relations and friends.

For civility to make sense, citizens must identify with their political community sufficiently to agree to pool a significant portion of their sovereignty – in particular, the exclusive legitimate use of force – in its collective organs. The writ of a regime across a given territory depends not only on its formal political attributes, but also on its citizens' identification with it. Anderson argues that people's identification with those they will never personally meet depends on an elaborate cultural construction usually sponsored and at least endorsed by the state. Key contributors to the construction of the 'imagined community' include an educational system promulgating a state-centric view of history and geography as well as the national media (Anderson 1991).

Identification with an imagined community also depends on not identifying exclusively with a single constituent part of that community. The perceived exclusion of people from the western side of East Timor from the higher ranks of its fledgling army was at the root of the rebellion that derailed the country's state-building efforts. Many other nation- and state-building efforts around the world have been undone or hampered by regionalism, which often is underpinned by patronage networks.

PROCESSES OF TRANSFORMATION

So far, this chapter has outlined characteristics of the state of affairs known as the 'rule of law' and what factors facilitate that state of affairs. In countries where the rule of law is strong and long-established, people regularly benefit from this state without understanding it. Things are different in countries wracked by interpersonal violence, where the challenge is to establish conditions in which the rule of law might come to count and, in time, help tame the sources of violence. What follows are some considerations relevant to taking up that challenge.

Before discussing the practical implications of the foregoing picture of what the rule of law entails, we must acknowledge the very different contexts in which rule-of-law reform activities are carried out. Building the rule of law while containing interpersonal violence is central to executive post-conflict interventions such as the UN Mission in Kosovo, as well as to non-executive post-conflict interventions, particularly when an armed insurgency continues, as in Afghanistan. It can receive a considerable investment of professional attention and have limited leverage over local institutions, such as the EU's rule-of-law support mission in Georgia, or it can involve a vast financial investment with virtually no influence over the implementation of its recommendations, as with the Asian Development Bank's $350 million 'access to justice' program in Pakistan. What follows seeks to be as practically useful as possible without being specifically adapted to any single type of intervention. While these recommendations inevitably describe an idealized scenario, they derive from general truths about the rule of law and the conditions that influence the degree to which this rather rare state of affairs prevails in a given society. Most examples are from post-conflict interventions because it is in these situations that interveners have the most influence, making them the clearest measures of the consequences of the dominant approaches to reform.

Challenges

Much writing on the best practices in fiercely contested environments such as those in which security and rule of law reform typically take place implies that interveners operate in a vacuum, and the only reason they wouldn't already follow best practice is ignorance. (This attitude is embodied in such common practices as 'human rights training', as if those who lack respect for human rights are merely missing information, rather than holding attitudes that need to be changed through a judicious blend of coercion and persuasion.) For policy advice to be meaningful, both in the society concerned and within the interveners' own institutional environments, it must take into account the factors that militate against the best course being chosen.

Societies where people do not believe it behooves them to behave civilly toward one another are not, contrary to the premises implicit in many reform efforts, blank slates. However much they may vary, certain challenges will be common to virtually all of them. All lawless environments include individuals and groups who benefit from the status quo. Where a conflict has been long running, hardened insurgents may realistically feel that no legal pursuit, regardless of what political settlement might be achieved, could profit them as much as continuing their outlaw activities. Elements of the IRA, the Tamil Tigers and the PKK undoubtedly fall into this category. Such incorrigible spoilers have to be crushed. Many others, however, like the Kosovo smuggler referred to above, may be sufficiently pragmatic and integrated in the non-criminal world to look for opportunities to enjoy their ill-gotten gains in peaceful conditions only possible when the rule of law prevails.

Most people in uncivil societies are intimidated by predatory forces that they perceive as powerful and threatening, and they have learned from experience to place little faith in whatever mechanisms in society are supposed to protect the weak. They have little trust in one another, apart perhaps from very small circles, and no experience asserting their rights or trying to help themselves in confrontations with the more powerful. Police working in areas with low social capital receive little cooperation. Particularly in cases involving organized crime, people will refuse to provide evidence, much less testify in court; the population's lack of faith in the police's ability to protect them thereby becomes a self-fulfilling prophecy.

The fearful majority will likewise be cynical about moralistic rhetoric, which they will have heard used and thereby discredited by even the most repugnant regimes. When interveners ask the population to believe that the rules of their society have changed, they are generally asking for blind trust from people who have been burned for as long as they can remember. People in a society where the law is struggling to become meaningful face a gambler's dilemma: no one wants to be a chump – perhaps even a dead chump – by being among the first to place his faith in a shaky or nascent legal order.

In the face of such daunting hurdles, how can interveners, whether in an executive or purely supportive mode, help to create the conditions for what we call the rule of law? The process must go something like this:

- First, create a balance of power so that any act of brutality would exact a high cost for the perpetrator. Crucial elements in this balancing process are fostering crosscutting identities, so that any given individual identifies herself as a member of more than one group (Sen 2007) and changing the calculations of potential spoilers. Simultaneously, prepare institutions so when they are called upon, they will perform and justify the interveners' own claims about them.
- Next, contrive situations in which to induce a leap of faith in the emerging order and nascent institutions by a critical mass and/or persons of exceptional influence.
- Finally, reward the leap of faith with good institutional performance and overall outcomes. For example, opium farmers in Afghanistan or coca farmers in the Andes will not be filled with confidence in the legal order if the police do a consummately professional job eradicating their crops and protecting them from drug lords, but the government then fails to help them move into equally remunerative livelihoods.

Of course, this is all easier said than done. Undoubtedly, every society that has moved from Hobbesian to civil conditions has gone through some such process, but such processes themselves create instability. Huntington cites a plethora of strong statistical correlations to support his argument that 'modernity breeds stability, but modernization breeds instability' (1968, 41).

Social mobilization contributes far more directly to instability than does economic development. 'Urbanization, increases in literacy, education, and media exposure all give rise to enhanced expectations which, if unsatisfied, galvanize individuals and groups into politics. In the absence of strong and adaptable political institutions, such increases in participation mean instability and violence' (Huntington 1968, 47). The potentially destabilizing mechanisms of social mobilization are also the primary levers for managing expectations and making change coherent. This overlap reinforces the need to harness these mechanisms to a narrative of transformation that resonates with people's experience. While this seems obvious, in practice development efforts all too often generate expectations before creating the institutions necessary to make good on them.

Roland Paris (2004) makes a similar argument about the destabilizing effects of democratization. Instability arises from mobilization outpacing institutional development, creating a gap between expectations and the means even to attempt to satisfy them. Governments are often tempted to invest in education at an early stage of development efforts because this is perhaps the most potent tool for change under the government's direct control. Rapid advances in education, however, are often not matched by available jobs for new graduates. This mismatch creates a pool of frustrated young people who are all the more potentially threatening for being educated. The point is not to short-change education, but to ensure that progress in this sector is accompanied by commensurate expansion of employment opportunities and a narrative that helps people make sense of and navigate their changing landscape.

Marking Change

In many societies undergoing rule-of-law reform, existing legal codes have been discredited by association with authoritarian or predatory regimes. Rather than guarding the continuity of law, which in healthy conditions helps ensure that change is incorporated into people's norms and understandings of their social compact with one another, interventions are often better off drawing a sharp line under the discredited regime by drafting new legal codes (Rose Ackerman 2004). The UN Division of Peacekeeping Operations is exploring the creation of draft uniform criminal and civil codes to be used in all post-conflict environments, a move that will greatly facilitate making clean breaks with discredited law, but it will also increase the challenge of persuading the people affected to regard it as embodying their values and defending their interests (Durch 2007).

Institutional Impediments

The nature of politics in donor countries and within development bureaucracies also militates against implementing best practices. Short electoral cycles and even shorter budgetary cycles drive interventions to focus disproportionately – if not exclusively – on those tasks that might be achieved quickly. This institutional bias in favor of short-term thinking is generally reinforced by the pressure of events on the ground, combined with the bureaucrat's tendency to avoid disaster more assiduously than he pursues achievement. The result, likewise prevalent in other organizations, is that the urgent generally overtakes the important.

Institutions (and often nations) bear an understandable desire to be given credit for their work that often impinges not only on time, but also on operational space. Agencies or offices working in distinct but obviously closely related areas often make only desultory efforts to coordinate their work with their supposed partners, even when they are from the same country. The U.S. Agency for International Development's development strategy for Pakistan's tribal areas, for instance, was developed without any meaningful coordination with the U.S. military, which is supporting the government of Pakistan's counterinsurgency strategy in the same area – largely because of institutional rivalry and conflicting organizational cultures. While largely ignoring the counterinsurgency campaign, the strategy also entirely overlooks the political disenfranchisement at the heart of the region's estrangement from Islamabad. Political issues were excluded from the strategy because the drafters' terms of reference did not include them; political issues were excluded, in turn, because the Musharraf regime had welcomed financial support from the United States and other donors but rejected interference in how it dealt with the tribal area. As a result, USAID was to pour $750 million into building infrastructure and institutions, the Department of Defense intended to spend many millions on counterinsurgency and no one would address the region's very obvious political grievances (Perlez 2007).

The preoccupation with quick achievements and guarding turf can sometimes stymie an activity altogether. The UN Mission in Kosovo, for example, never had a unit devoted to conflict resolution because donors felt its work would take too long for it to show results, and none of the institutions involved wanted to let any of their rivals take charge of such an important activity (King and Mason 2006, 249).

Two massive efforts combining development, limiting interpersonal violence and creating the rule of law – the international interventions in Kosovo and in Afghanistan – both failed to rise to most, if not all, of these challenges. Though one may argue that they are extreme examples, the high level of attention and investment in building the rule of law that both have received make them paradigmatic of conventional efforts.

Kosovo

In 1999, the international community intervened in the Serbian province of Kosovo – first in the form of an aerial bombing campaign by NATO, then through a multidimensional administration with a Security Council mandate to run Kosovo day-to-day, build up the structures for substantial democratic self-governance and prepare to hand over control to local authorities. The trigger for intervention was the Serbian security forces' killing, abuse and subsequent mass displacement of Kosovo's Albanian majority. Implicit in the intervention was the goal of transforming Kosovo from the violent, predatory society it had been into one in which all its people could live in security and dignity.

From its inception, the UN Mission (UNMIK) and its multinational military counterpart (KFOR) failed to establish the credibility essential to suppressing interpersonal violence and fostering the rule of law. Pretensions of even-handedness were discredited from the beginning by KFOR's failure to prevent the pressured exodus of over half the Serbian minority and the persecution of those who remained. Among the Albanian majority, the interveners inadvertently fostered an aura of impunity around those with physical power, both former militants and organized criminals (many belonged to both groups). KFOR soldiers, who for months were the only significant security presence on the ground, were ill-equipped and poorly trained for preventing attacks on individuals or small groups, much less for investigating crime, making arrests or managing prisoners. Police were slow to deploy and for years lacked the forensic resources and investigative prerogatives necessary to combat powerful criminals and militants. Of those who were arrested, Albanian judges were pressured into acquitting well-connected Albanian malefactors while prolonging the incarceration of Serbs on scant evidence. The culture of impunity was exacerbated still further by interference on the part of key donor countries, notably the United States, which directed UNMIK prosecutors not to pursue top militants-cum-criminals – 'thugocrats' – for fear of provoking a popular backlash (King and Mason 2006, especially pp. 59–61, 97–101, 144–46, 194–95). Six months into the intervention, UNMIK further discredited itself in the eyes of locals when it succumbed to pressure from Albanian jurists to reverse its original decision to use Serbian law as of 1999, which locals regarded as tainted by association with Milosevic (Covey et al. 2005). Later, UNMIK antagonized local jurists still further by imposing international prosecutors and judges to try the most sensitive cases. A key lesson from Kosovo is that in a post-conflict environment, locals are not sufficiently insulated from coercion to be able to try sensitive cases effectively. It is better to employ internationals from the beginning and gradually shift authority to local judges and prosecutors than to begin unrealistically and have to demote a judiciary that is already established.

While failing to punish spoilers for flouting the law, UNMIK also failed to use 'soft power' mechanisms to persuade ordinary people to believe in and support the new legal order. The mandate that created the UN Interim Administration in Kosovo, UNSC 1244, left unresolved the underlying cause of the armed conflict – the question of who would rule Kosovo. Given this enormous handicap in building a sustainable peace, one might have expected the mission to use all available means – an intensive public information effort, sensitivity to the effect of various actions on public confidence, education reform, careful regulation of the media and various efforts to facilitate the non-violent resolution of disputes – to change the attitudes that had led to and resulted from the conflict.

In fact, though, efforts to win hearts and minds or to build public confidence in the new order were generally marginal at best. Education was among the first portfolios that UNMIK turned over to Kosovo's provisional authorities. The local media, both Albanian and Serbian, for their part, maintained a steady barrage of non-factual and unconstructive nationalist demagoguery from the very inception of the UN administration there.

More generally, the UN mission adopted a hands-off approach to political culture. In post-war Germany and Japan, educational reforms, control of the media and public symbols and propaganda were all used to foster pacific attitudes. 'From the very beginning, UNMIK engaged the Kosovo Albanians and was particularly keen on establishing a close relationship with the potential "spoilers", mainly including the former KLA leaders', explained Blanca Antonini, who in 1999 and 2000 was deputy head of civil administration in UNMIK. In practice that meant that KFOR and UNMIK were more concerned with placating those who opposed inter-ethnic tolerance than those few who supported it.

Reinforcing this anxiousness to avoid provoking violent elements, most of the occupiers regarded the local Albanian population as the aggrieved party in a one-sided conflict and assumed that they would be well-intentioned partners in the territory's reconstruction. Operating from such assumptions, the international authorities naturally regarded measures to purge the media, educational system and public sphere of noxious influences as inappropriately intrusive. 'The international community – and UNMIK in particular – did not have as a priority the question of culture, and made little or no effort to integrate the experience that both major communities in Kosovo had accumulated prior to the international intervention', said Antonini. 'By failing to do this, it sidelined as irrelevant an issue of enormous sensitivity in the context of a conflict where the symbols of cultural identity were often more powerful than weapons'.[3]

On 4 September 2007, thousands of Kosovo Albanians marched in protest against the murder of a respected police officer, Triumf Riza, by automatic weapon fire in broad daylight in a busy part of Pristina, the provincial capital. Though a young man arrested two days after the murder had confessed, he was widely believed to have been acting on behalf of a much feared mafia boss, Enver Sekiraqa. A commentary on the murder expressed popular disillusionment over the obvious impunity of well-connected criminals:

The police should think hard about why they have not arrested hundreds of other criminals in connection with this – and other – murders, when they were racketeering, bribing and stealing. On the other hand, when the police prepare cases for trial, the courts often release the defendants. This apparent inability of the courts to convict the accused is, one fears, inspiring and encouraging criminals. I can only conclude that the judiciary has failed to deal with many of the 'you-know-whos' in Kosovo. That was exactly the message coming from thousands of protesters who symbolically turned their backs on the Kosovo courthouse. It was an eloquent expression of the loss of their trust in the state of law, order and justice in Kosovo for which ultimate responsibility remains with the UN administration. But now and for the first time in Kosovo's recent history, people are raising their voices against this weak and impotent judiciary. They are arguing that many people would still be alive if certain notorious criminals had been put behind bars.[4]

Afghanistan

The $10 billion international presence in Afghanistan, purportedly to transform it from being a territory hospitable to international terrorists into one governed by the rule of law, has presided over the country's transition from a vicious pseudo-theocracy to a patchwork of fiefdoms run by warlords and disputed by Taliban insurgents.

Powerbrokers and warlords fill the police ranks with their own protégés and use it for their own predatory ends. From the beginning of the international intervention, the Afghan National Police was composed of 'mid- and lower-level commanders who had seized the title of police chief in provinces and districts and incorporated their militias into the police after the Taliban's fall' (ICG 2007, 5). As international attention focused on building a new Afghan national army, 'The interior ministry was left to become "the locus of interactions between state institutions and criminal interests ... Political influence (both from within and outside the Ministry) may be brought to bear to ensure specific appointments or to promote or prevent law enforcement interventions"' (Buddenberg and Byrd 2006, 198). As the ICG commented: 'One of the most disillusioning aspects for the population, and the root of the culture of impunity that has sprung up, is the Kabul centre's propensity simply to transfer police officials when there are complaints. As a civil servant in Kunduz asked, "If food tastes bad in one province why will it taste better in another?"' (ICG 2007, 5).

Different areas of security reform in Afghanistan – police, army, disarmament, counter-narcotics and the justice sector – were divided among five different donor nations. 'Rather than being treated as a whole, SSR [security sector reform] became a series of discrete programs which moved at very different paces, with little coordination between them, including on matters where there was important substantive overlap' (ICG 2007, 6).

In an effort to get 'more boots on the ground' to help fight the insurgency in the south, the Afghan government armed militias and labeled them the 'Afghanistan National Auxiliary Police'. One diplomat characterized the move as trying 'to make a virtue of necessity'. Though wearing the same uniform as actual police, these auxiliaries received only 10 days of training and remained loyal to their local commander. 'Given complaints about police corruption and abuse, putting 11,000 men in police uniform with even less training is not the way to legitimize state institutions in the eyes of Afghans' (ICG 2007, 13–14). Since most of these 'auxiliaries' are Pashtuns, ethnic Tajiks and Uzbeks in the north naturally question why they are being asked to disarm even as their ethnic rivals are re-armed at state expense.

According to the International Crisis Group, 'Internal policing and security strategies in Afghanistan do not stress fighting the crime against average citizens which often has a greater impact on their sense of security than the insurgency. Instead, many communities view the police as predatory' (ICG 2007, 16). In the capital of embattled Helmand province, a mechanic told the ICG that if paid off, the police would let a person go free even if caught red-handed with explosives, but they won't pay their bills for having their vehicles repaired. 'Such behaviour not only alienates people but can also actively drive them to anti-government forces. The 1950 Police Commission to Malaya "viewed police corruption as a major source of the people's dissatisfaction with the government. The many bad policemen served as some of the best recruiting agents for the insurgents"' (Corum 2006, 14).

Themes and Principles

Having railed against mechanistic approaches, we can hardly now promote formulaic 'lessons learned', especially given that we are addressing rule-of-law reform in general. But the nature of the rule of law as a state of affairs in which the balance among the elements is as important as the elements themselves, combined with what we know generally to be true of bludgeoned people and the destabilizing effects of change, allows us to put forward a number of principles that will be important to bear in mind in any conceivable effort to conjure the rule of law.

Understand needs holistically
Efforts to promote the rule of law need to be based on a holistic understanding of the rule of law as a state of affairs, dependent upon the balanced contribution

158 Security and Development

of a multiplicity of disparate elements. Legal institutions contribute to – but also reflect – the balance of power in a given society and the norms operating among its mainstream population. A holistic understanding, therefore, requires far more than attention to the law, security forces and judiciary (Call 2007). Power must be sufficiently diffused so that no individual or group can act with impunity against any other, and norms, institutions and structures must be targeted to generate a worldview that places obligations to intimates and strangers on a moral continuum rather than in sharply differentiated categories. In practice, this means closely coordinating with others who may see little connection between their tasks and the rule of law or, where these areas remain unaddressed, others who may be addressing them.

This does not mean, of course, that interventions must supply all the ingredients that together comprise the rule of law; few societies are entirely lacking in all these ingredients. And even if a society were to lack all of them, the ambition to supply them all is bound to lead to disappointment. Overweening transformative ambitions have their own problems, as the victims of revolutions all over the world have come to recognize. A preference for what Karl Popper called 'piecemeal' over 'utopian social engineering' is typically not evidence of cowardice, but of good sense. Interventions should recognize and build on existing strengths and fill in or correct gaps. They must recognize, however, that even technically perfect judicial institutions will not give rise to the rule of law in the absence of other elements that may be beyond the scope of their mandate, such as a common belief that no one is above the law and a prevailing sense of moral obligations toward strangers.

Put public confidence at the center
It is difficult to overstate this. While many elements conspire to make the law rule in a given society, they are relevant only and precisely to the extent that they shape the attitudes, expectations and behavior of the people in that society.

The response to the Malayan Emergency, in which the term 'hearts and minds' was first coined, remains a paragon of effective counterinsurgency and more broadly of efforts to return stability and the rule of law to a society where violent anarchy threatened. Shortly after his arrival in Malaya, High Commissioner Gerald Templer declared to his staff that the consistent observance of human rights and the rule of law is essential to a mission's moral authority. 'Any idea,' said Templer, 'that the business of normal civil government and the business of the Emergency are two separate entities must be killed for good and all. The two activities are completely and utterly related' (Cloake 1985, 267).

Templer 'grasped immediately that circumstances required the actions of the Government to be broadened and that the population had to be won over, not intimidated, if the guerrilla war was to be successfully prosecuted ... In many ways, Templer acted more like a politician running hard for a second term in office than a general running a colony' (Stubbs 1989, 151). Early in 1952 he wrote to a colleague, saying 'The shooting side of the business is only 25 per cent of the trouble and the other 75 per cent lies in getting the people of this country behind us' (Cloake 1985, 262). In late 1952 the police in Malaya launched 'Operation Service' to portray officers as servants of the people. It was a huge success (Stubbs 1989, 157).

This point derives from the insight – conspicuously absent in Iraq, where putative 'democracy' was expected to compensate for violence, looting, collapsed utilities and general mayhem – that 'however powerful nationalist or religious forces may be, that of material wellbeing is as strong if not stronger' (Thompson 1966, 65). Similarly, 'Without a reasonably efficient government machine, no programs or projects, in the context of counter-insurgency, will produce the desired results'. This 'reasonably efficient government machine' would be conspicuously absent from occupations half a century hence (Mason 2005a, 2005b).

Robert Thompson, who spent 12 years in Malaya and eventually became minister of defense, codified a number of principles, including, 'The government must give priority to defeating the political subversion, not the guerrillas' (1966, 163). The key is establishing the legitimacy of the government in the eyes of the general population. 'If the guerrillas can be isolated from the population, i.e., the "little fishes" removed from "the water", then their eventual destruction becomes automatic' (Thompson 1966, 56). Oliver Lyttelton, secretary of state for colonial affairs, led a delegation to Malaya in December 1951. Lyttelton called for a review of the government's propaganda campaign, starting with the provision of public services on which, to be successful, all propaganda would have to be based. 'We have to see that our philosophy opens up to the people of Malaya the prospect of a finer and freer life than that which our enemies are trying to instil' (Stubbs 1989, 138).

In recent decades, interveners and development professionals working on fostering the rule of law have tended to behave like the old command economies of the communist world, creating whatever they choose and assuming the consumers, bereft of choice, will wear it. Though consulting with stakeholders has often been emphasized rhetorically, in practice, certainly in the area of rule of law and security reform, public input generally has been at best a secondary activity.

As a means of improving police accountability, the ICG report on police reform in Afghanistan suggests that 'provincial police liaison boards, with civil society representatives' could be created. But even in this thoughtful report, engaging the public is an afterthought. As usual, involving those most affected by security problems and efforts to ameliorate them is regarded as belonging to the 'advanced course', both in the sense that only exceptional members of the development community appreciate its importance and in the sense that engaging the people most affected is stressed – if ever – only at a late stage in the reform process.

Consulting widely and deeply with representative members of the community affected by rule of law and security reform is the most efficient way to measure shifts in the power and credibility of institutions, and it is the only way to account for the inevitable gap between objective circumstances and subjective perception. Doing this effectively requires a faculty too little exercised by those driving social change, empathy or what Mills called 'the sociological imagination' (Mills 2000). But even the most brilliant exercises of sociological imagination are no substitute for a far less ambitious activity – listening.

Confront or co-opt spoilers early

Where the law doesn't rule, thugocrats do. Discussions of development, even in the most nakedly predatory societies, often proceed as if extreme underdevelopment is an accident of nature simply waiting for a Good Samaritan to correct it. In fact, every society, even the poorest, has winners as well as losers. Those who have benefited from the status quo constitute potential spoilers in any effort to change it. A criminalized society is the mirror image of a rule-of-law society: the distribution of resources rewards criminals for their activity and favors its continuation.

As in the case of the presumed smuggler in Kosovo who wanted to give up crime, co-optation is sometimes an option for defusing spoilers. However, interveners should only be sanguine about co-optation where, in terms of the spoiler's own values, the appeal of behaving legally clearly outweighs the appeal of continuing his predatory or illegal behavior. Astonishingly often, however, interveners have been willing to accept the word of some of the most degenerate people on earth at face value. Because it is easier in the immediate term, interveners virtually always convince themselves that they can afford to avoid confronting the warlords and others who have flourished in conditions of violence. In Somalia, Liberia and Sierra Leone, interveners effectively enhanced the power of the most dangerous men in those countries, Mohamad Farah Aideed, Charles Taylor and Foday Sankoh, respectively. In Bosnia, political divisions created by ethnic cleansers were sanctified by the constitution drafted by the international community, allowing the amalgam of ethnic militancy and organized crime to thrive within each fiefdom. In Afghanistan, interveners allowed warlords to continue ruling virtually all the country's territory, with crippling results. And in Iraq, spoilers were confronted with a dearth of resources and the absence of a larger transformational narrative that could persuade Iraqis to foreswear ethnic and sectarian violence in favor of national structures. This record of failure reinforces what would appear obvious even without it: a rule-of-law intervention that is not prepared to defeat those who prosper through violence will be defeated by them.

Reform police, judiciary and corrections as parts of a single coherent system
As we have seen, institutional reform conventionally receives the lion's share of attention in rule-of-law reform efforts. Even here, though, a mechanistic, piecemeal approach often yields meager results: 'Developing a reasonably functioning justice system requires astute attention to how the various components relate to one another and to the larger political system and culture in which they are embedded. If reformers miss these larger links and interactions, their reform effort as a whole will be a good deal less than the sum of its parts' (Stromseth, Wippman and Brooks 2006, 179).

The most obvious nemesis of institution-building efforts is the accommodation of warlords and other spoilers who realistically recognize rule-of-law reform efforts as a mortal threat. Those assessing claims that their society's legal order has changed measure that claim against the treatment of powerful thugocrats. Demonstrations of impunity vitiate any number of salutary achievements in other areas of rule-of-law reform. A reformed justice system will likewise fail to win public trust if it fails to serve the needs of ordinary people because, for instance, it is accessible only to the rich. From the point of view of the public, the judicial system is only as strong as its weakest link. Jane Citizen doesn't want a choice between a good police force or competent, fair courts or a prison system that keeps people incarcerated and isolated from society for their full term; she wants a system that effectively deals with criminals, and that environment requires all three elements to be working effectively. If, as in the example from Kosovo, police work effectively but the judicial system fails to convict and sentence guilty suspects, the credibility of the entire system will be fatally undermined.

Subordinate the past to the future
There is no consensus on how much emphasis should be placed on the accountability of those who have committed atrocities in the past. Stromseth, Wippman and Brooks argue that

> The long-term impact of accountability proceedings on the rule of law depends critically on three factors: first, the effective disempowerment of key perpetrators who threaten stability and undermine public confidence in the rule of law; second, the character of the accountability proceedings pursued, particularly whether they

demonstrate credibly that previous patterns of abuse and impunity are rejected and that justice can be fair; and third, the extent to which systematic and meaningful efforts at domestic capacity-building are included as part of the accountability process. (2006, 254)

Again, the key consideration is how various approaches would affect public confidence in the emerging political and legal order. Different societies and individuals process trauma differently, making any generic recommendations in this area futile. Interveners must consult with the people affected by past abuses about how to deal with the past while building a better future and act accordingly. Here, strong leadership can help keep people looking forward; but alas, Mandelas are rare.

Don't allow the urgent to overtake the important

Interveners will always be tempted to put the exigency of the moment ahead of the imperatives of long-term transformation. Often this will entail bending or breaking the law or collaborating with those who do. In Afghanistan, for instance, the need for boots on the ground to combat Taliban insurgents has led the government and its international patrons to push warlords' militiamen through ten-day courses, then deploy them clad in the uniform of ordinary police. With no understanding of – or respect for – the law or of the responsibilities of police work, these militiamen will inevitably tarnish the reputation of Afghanistan's fledgling police force.

In Afghanistan, 'Programs to advance the transparency and democratic accountability of the [security] sector, while situating it within a clear legal framework, have been superseded by a singular focus on training and equipping the country's fledgling security forces' (ICG 2007, 13; Sedra 2006, 95). The 'urgent' – in this case, countering the insurgency – fully displaced the 'important', indeed imperative, need to create the rule of law, which alone will ensure Afghanistan's long-term security and stability.

In Malaya, Thompson's second principle was: 'The government must function in accordance with the law'. He acknowledges the temptation to act outside the law in dealing with terrorism and guerrillas, but argues:

Not only is this morally wrong, but, over a period, it will create more practical difficulties for a government than it solves. A government which does not act in accordance with the law forfeits the right to be called a government and cannot then expect its people to obey the law. Functioning in accordance with the law is a very small price to pay in return for the advantage of being the government. (Thompson 1966, 52–53)

Though it's a price worth paying, it requires forbearance that eludes most politicians and international public servants under pressure.

Foster cross-cutting identities

Individuals with multiple forms of identity may find it easier to find common ground with others. 'A country with "cross-cutting" cleavages is one in which political, ideological, ethnic, racial, religious or linguistic divisions overlap one another, such that individuals on opposite sides of one divisive issue are often allies on another issue. By contrast, when the principal subgroup divisions reinforce one another very closely, the society can be described as having a "cumulative" cleavage structure' (Paris 2004, 171). Where individuals identify with clearly separated communities and do not also identify with groups occupied by members of other communities, the issues that affect them for good or ill will tend to discourage compromise and spawn maximalist positions. Half the soldiers in East Timor's army rebelled in 2007 because they were all from the west of the country and assumed they were discriminated against on that basis. But if half the army felt discriminated against, but not in a way that corresponded to a monolithic group identity, it is hard to imagine the rebellion occurring.

Paris cites the contrast between India, with its cross-cutting identities, and Sri Lanka, where 'prevailing linguistic, regional, religious, ethnic and class cleavages are mutually reinforcing and have "cumulatively" divided the country's Sinhalese and Tamil communities'. In India, class and regional identities transcend the Hindu-Muslim divide, forcing even the Hindu nationalist Bharatiya Janata Party to emphasize non-nationalist issues in the south and east, 'Where the Hindu-Muslim rivalry is of limited appeal' (Paris 2004, 171).

Cross-cutting identities can also be fostered. New institutions can mix people of different backgrounds and create a shared identification with the institution or community of which they are both a part. For this to be effective, the institution has to provide security and benefits that rival those of an individual's organic network. Educational activities can also help individuals realize their membership in groups beyond the one with which they have traditionally identified. A young person from Kosovo might attend a regional camp, for instance, and realize that in addition to being an Albanian, like many new friends in Belgrade and Skopje she's also a feminist, a fan of hip-hop music and an EU hopeful.

The 'democratization industry' has typically subscribed to the view that since civil society is good and in Western societies it often takes the form of voluntary associations, democratization efforts should promote voluntary associations. But whether such associations are conducive or detrimental to a society that is actually civil depends in part on whether their membership corresponds to existing cleavages or cuts across them (Berman 1997; Paris 2004, 160–61). It also depends on the existence of a state strong enough to contain them, rather than be usurped by them.

Reinforce political change and institution-building

Post-conflict occupations since World War II have invested great resources in winning hearts and minds. For a complex combination of reasons, more recent post-conflict interventions have devoted much less attention to this crucial dimension of social and political change.

As noted, the phrase 'winning hearts and minds' was first coined by Gerald Templer during Malaya's communist insurgency. When he took charge, the government stepped up its efforts to provide a modicum of public services and amenities in the New Villages to which thousands of Chinese had been relocated. A paper produced by the Federal Legislative Council in May 1952 noted, 'The New Villages mean in effect a new life for the people who dwell in them and it is important that this new life should, after the initial disturbance of moving, be more attractive than the old'. Henceforth, the government would strive to provide each New Village with a minimal standard of public services. The paper also called for fostering a reasonably friendly feeling towards the government and police and the launching of community activities such as Boy Scouts, Cubs and Girl Guides (Stubbs 1989, 169). Templer himself became Chief Scout, while his wife Peggie spoke on the radio in Malay. The most successful community centers had a café or canteen. The Malayan Chinese Association sponsored sports teams, especially basketball. Most New Villages had Women's Institutes that taught childcare, health, cooking and sewing (Mason 2005a, chap. 6). In Kosovo, by contrast, virtually no international UN staff member spoke local languages, they rarely participated in community activities, and they were very slow in organizing activities that could have an impact on morale. For example, Special Representative of the Secretary-General Michael Steiner once directed that fire trucks in the ethnically divided city of Mitrovica be painted red. After repeating the order for six weeks, in the face of continued bureaucratic resistance and inaction, Steiner finally gave up (King and Mason 2006, 140).

In post-war Germany and Japan, the occupiers took charge of education and transformed schools into transmitters of the attitudes that the Germans and Japanese would need in order to sustain and give substance to the new institutions being built. In Kosovo, however, education was one of the first public services transferred to local control, with the result that it remained a mechanism of partisan political patronage and perpetuated nationalist values inimical to Kosovo's transformation into a society in which all its residents could live in security and dignity.

Similarly, in the immediate aftermath of war in Japan and Germany, the media was tightly controlled to prevent the dissemination of hate speech and conspiracy theories. These continued to flourish in Kosovo under UN administration, which only rarely imposed weak fines for hate speech and then only after the damage was already done.

Ensure that rhetoric matches realities on the ground

However effective an intervention's use of the levers of persuasion and education, messages will not long remain credible if contradicted by actual experience. All interventions and most development projects now include a 'public information' component, but this ordinarily operates quite independently from the rest of the activity. In the area of rule of law, credibility is so fundamental and the stakes so high that interveners must not encourage people to behave differently until the institutions are ready to reward that behavior with positive outcomes.

The importance of this issue is compounded by the widespread practice of despotic or ineffective regimes using the rhetoric of stable democracies. The vast majority of people living in societies targeted by rule-of-law interventions will have strong impressions of 'courts', 'police', 'prosecutors' and other institutions and officials bearing the labels of their rule-of-law society counterparts. If institutions go on using the same names, uniforms, insignia and so forth while they are being reformed, their sub-par performance will perpetuate the public perception that such institutions are eternally doomed to ineffectuality. Reform programs should focus on transforming institutions with no fanfare, and only when they are ready to perform as promised, roll them out in a fashion that dramatically underscores the break with their institutional forebears.

Provide protection to the most vulnerable

The overriding imperative to build up the credibility of newly transformed institutions means they cannot be put in a position of responsibility for public security before they are equal to the task. While transforming all the components of the justice system in a society where interpersonal violence is rife, other forces and instruments, generally international, must be deployed to mitigate interpersonal violence while establishing the long-term basis for a rule-of-law society. Interveners should pay particular attention to conditions for women, for whom 'peacetime, paradoxically, can yield increasing violence, insecurity and economic and political constraints' (Fitzsimmons 2007, 351–52).

CONCLUSION: THE HUMAN FACTOR

Most of the principles we have advocated in this chapter are familiar, at least in general terms, to a significant minority of scholars and practitioners. For these principles to prevail in practice, in the face of the innumerable pressures to subordinate them to considerations of expediency, practitioners must understand them deeply and believe in them passionately.

Many rule-of-law reform efforts have proceeded on the implicit assumption that where there's a way (in the form of institutions), the will to use them will emerge spontaneously. With regard to a society's inclination to be ruled by law or by raw might, the old adage is right: where there's the will, the way will be found; the opposite, however, does not hold.

Interveners must focus on creating the will to behave civilly and in support of the legal order. This will, in turn, arise where people see that by supporting the law and behaving civilly, they will survive, and ideally not merely survive but flourish. Many things have gone right in societies that today enjoy that state of affairs, characterized by sets of institutions appropriately empowered and so balanced as to prevent predatory behavior by any one centre of power, that we call the rule of law. The wisest interveners in the world cannot create all these conditions. But by listening to the people affected and trying to look at changes through their eyes, they can understand what is required for respecting the law and behaving civilly to make sense. That would be a huge improvement on approaches that have regarded people as a passive adjunct to the blueprints imported wholesale from First-World law libraries.

NOTES

We have taken into account the insightful remarks of the commentators on our original paper, Alejandro Gaviria and M. Ann Brown, as well as contributions from the floor in the subsequent discussion.

1. A line commonly attributed to Goering is 'whenever I hear the word "culture" I reach for my revolver'. Another and cleverer version attributed to him is 'whenever I heard the word "culture" I reach for my Browning' (with the pun on a brand of revolver and the English poet).
2. The threat of rebellion, indeed, is one of the limitations on the impunity of a majority or powerful minority.
3. Whit Mason, telephone interview with Blanca Antonini in New York, 11 November 2004.
4. Krenar Gashi, Balkan Investigative Reporting Network, September 2007.

REFERENCES

Anderson, B. (1991), *Imagined Communities*, London: Verso.

Armytage, L. (2003), 'Pakistan's Law and Justice Sector Reform Experience: Some Lessons', paper presented at the 13th Commonwealth Law Conference, Melbourne, Australia, 14 April.

Bendix, R. (1996), *Nation-building and Citizenship*, Edison, NJ: Transaction.

Berman, S. (1997), 'Civil Society and the Collapse of the Weimar Republic', *World Politics*, **49** (3), 401–29.

Bubalo, A., G. Fealey and W. Mason (2008), 'Zealous Democrats: Islam and Democracy in Egypt, Indonesia and Turkey', Sydney, Lowy Institute for International Policy.

Buddenberg, D. and W. Byrd (eds) (2006), *Afghanistan's Drug Industry: Structure, Functioning, Dynamics and Implications for Counter-Narcotics Policy*, New York: UN Office and Drugs and Crime and the World Bank, p. 198. Quoted in ICG (2007), 'Reforming Afghanistan's Police', International Crisis Group, Asia Report No. 138, (30 August).

Call, C.T. (ed.) (2007), *Constructing Justice and Security after War*, Washington, DC: United States Institute of Peace Press.

Carothers, T. (ed.) (2006), *Promoting the Rule of Law Abroad*, Washington, DC: Carnegie Endowment for International Peace.

Cashu, I.G. and M.A. Orenstein (2001), 'The Pensioners' Court Campaign: Making Law Matter in Russia', *East European Constitutional Review*, **10** (4).

Chang, I. (1997), *The Rape of Nanking*, New York: Basic Books.

Cloake, J. (1985), *Templer, Tiger of Malaya: The Life of Field Marshal Sir Gerald Templer*, London: Harrap.

Colas, D. (1997), *Civil Society and Fanaticism*, Stanford, CA: Stanford University Press.

Corum, J.S. (2006), 'Training Indigenous Forces in Counter Insurgency: A Tale of Two Insurgencies', Carlisle, PA: U.S. Army War College Strategic Studies Institute, p. 14. Quoted in ICG (2007), 'Reforming Afghanistan's Police', International Crisis Group, Asia Report No. 138, (30 August).

Covey, J. et al. (eds) (2005), *The Quest for Viable Peace: International Intervention and Strategies for Conflict Transformation*, Washington, DC: United States Institute for Peace.

Dahl, R. (1998), *On Democracy*, New Haven, CT: Yale University Press, New Haven.

Dobbins, J., S.G. Jones, K. Crane and B.C. DeGrasse (eds) (2007), *The Beginner's Guide to Nation-Building*, Santa Monica, CA: RAND.

Durch, W. (2007), *Twenty-First-Century Peace Operations*, Washington, DC: United States Institute for Peace.

Felstiner, W.L.F., R.L. Abel and A. Sarat (1980–81), 'The Emergence and Transformation of Disputes: Naming, Blaming, Claiming ...', *Law and Society Review*, **15** (3/4), 631–54.

Fitzsimmons, T. (2007), 'Engendering Justice and Security after War', in C.T. Call (ed.) *Constructing Justice and Security after War*, pp. 351–52.

Galanter, M. (1981), 'Justice in Many Rooms: Courts, Private Ordering, and Indigenous Law', *19 Journal of Legal Pluralism*, **1** (25), 1–47.

Galanter, M. (1983), 'Reading the Landscape of Disputes: What We Know and Don't Know (and Think We Know) About Our Allegedly Contentious Society', University of Wisconsin-Madison, Disputes Processing Research Program Working Paper No. 1983-1.

Golub, S. (2006), 'A House Without Foundations', in T. Carothers (ed.), *Promoting the Rule of Law Abroad*, Washington, DC: Carnegie Endowment for International Peace, pp. 105–36.

Hendley, K. (2001), '"Demand" for Law: A Mixed Picture', *East European Constitutional Review*, **10** (4).

Hendley, K., S. Holmes, A. Åslund and A. Sajó (1999), 'Debate: Demand for Law', *East European Constitutional Review*, **8** (4), 88–108.

Holmes, S. (1995), 'Cultural Legacies or State Collapse? Probing the Postcommunist Dilemma', presentation to Collegium Budapest/Institute for Advanced Study, Public Lecture No. 13.

Holmes, S. (1995), *Passions and Constraint: On the Theory of Liberal Democracy*, Chicago, IL: University of Chicago Press.

Holmes, S. (1998), 'Citizen and Law after Communism', *East European Constitutional Review,* **7** (1), 70–88.

Holmes, S. (1999), 'Can Foreign Aid Promote the Rule of Law?', (Fall 1999), *East European Constitutional Review*, **8** (4), 68–74.

Huntington, S.P. (1968), *Political Order in Changing Societies*, New Haven, CT: Yale University Press.

ICG (2007), 'Reforming Afghanistan's Police', International Crisis Group, Asia Report No. 138 (30 August).

Ignatieff, M. (1995), *Blood and Belonging: Journeys into the New Nationalism*, New York: Farrar, Strauss and Giroux.

Jensen, E.G. and T.C. Heller, (eds.) (2003), *Beyond Common Knowledge: Empirical Approaches to the Rule of Law*, Stanford, CA: Stanford University Press.

King, I. and W. Mason (2006), *Peace at Any Price: How the World Failed Kosovo*, Ithaca, NY: Cornell University Press.

Krygier, M. (1997), 'Virtuous Circles: Antipodean Reflections on Power, Institutions and Civil Society', *Eastern European Politics and Societies*, **11** (1), 36–88.

—— (1999), 'Institutional Optimism, Cultural Pessimism and the Rule of Law', in M. Krygier and A. Czarnota (eds), *The Rule of Law after Communism*, Aldershot, UK and Brookfield, VT: Ashgate, pp. 77–105.

—— (2001), 'Transitional Questions about the Rule of Law: Why, What and How?', *East Central Europe/L'Europe du Centre-Est*, **28** (1), 1–34.

—— (2002a), 'The Grammar of Colonial Legality: Subjects, Objects and the Rule of Law', in G. Brennan and F.G. Castles (eds), *Australia Reshaped: Essays on 200 Years of Institutional Transformation*, New York, Cambridge University Press, pp. 220–60.

—— (2002b), 'The Quality of Civility: Post-Anti-Communist Thoughts on Civil Society and the Rule of Law', in A. Sajó (ed.), *Out of and Into Authoritarian Law*, Amsterdam: Kluwer, pp. 221–56.

—— (2004), 'False Dichotomies, Real Perplexities, and the Rule of Law', in A. Sajó (ed.), *Human Rights with Modesty. The Problem of Universalism*, Leiden: Martinus Nijhoff, pp. 251–77.

—— (2005), *Civil Passions: Selected Writings*, Melbourne: Black, Inc.

—— (2006), 'The Rule of Law: An Abuser's Guide', in A. Sajó (ed.), *The Dark Side of Fundamental Rights*, Utrecht: Eleven International Publishing, pp. 129–61.

—— (2009), 'The Rule of Law: Legality, Teleology, Sociology', in G. Palombella and N. Walker (eds), *Relocating the Rule of Law*, Portland, OR: Hart Publishers, pp. 17–42.

Low, S. (2002), 'Proposed Filial Piety Law Sparks Debate among Lawmakers', *Taipei Times*, (10 January): 2.

Mann, M. (1986), *Sources of Social Power*, Vol. 1, New York: Cambridge University Press.

—— (1988), 'The Autonomous Power of the State: Its Origins, Mechanisms and Resources', in M. Mann (ed.), *State, War and Capitalism*, New York: Blackwell.

—— (2005), *The Dark Side of Democracy*, New York: Cambridge University Press.

Mason, W. (2005a), 'Contradictions between Ends and Means in Post-Imperial Protectorates', unpublished master's thesis, Cambridge University.

—— (2005b), 'Trouble in Tbilisi', *The National Interest*, (1 March).

McIlwain, C.H. (1958), *Constitutionalism: Ancient and Modern*, rev. ed., Ithaca, NY: Great Seal Books.

Mills, C. Wright (2000), *The Sociological Imagination*, New York: Oxford University Press.

Moore, S.F. (1978), 'Law and Social Change: The Semi-Autonomous Social Field as an Appropriate Subject of Study', in S.F. Moore (ed.), *Law as Process: An Anthropological Approach*, New York: Routledge, pp. 54–81.

Neal, D. (1991), *The Rule of Law in a Penal Colony*, Melbourne, Australia: Cambridge University Press.

Oakeshott, M. (1991), *Rationalism in Politics and Other Essays*, Indianapolis, IN: Liberty Press.

Oz, A. (2006), *How to Cure a Fanatic*, Princeton, NJ: Princeton University Press.

Palombella, G. (2009), 'The Rule of Law and its Core', in G. Palombella and N. Walker (eds), *Relocating the Rule of Law*, Portland, OR: Hart Publishers, pp. 17–42.

Paris, R. (2004), *At War's End: Building Peace After Civil Conflict*, New York: Cambridge University Press.

Peerenboom, R. (2005), 'Human Rights and Rule of Law: What's the Relationship?', *Georgetown Journal of International Law*, **36**, 809–945.

Perlez, J. (2007), 'Aid to Pakistan in Tribal Area Raises Concerns', *New York Times*, (16 July).

Poggi, G. (2000), *Durkheim*, New York: Oxford University Press.

Rose Ackerman, S. (2004), 'Establishing the Rule of Law', in R.I. Rotberg (ed.), *When States Fail: Causes and Consequences*, Princeton, NJ: Princeton University Press.

Samuels, K. (2006), 'Rule of Law Reform in Post-Conflict Countries: Operational Initiatives and Lessons Learnt', Washington, DC, World Bank, Conflict Prevention and Reconstruction Unit Working Paper No. 37.

Sedra, M. (2006), 'Security Sector Reform in Afghanistan: The Slide Toward Expediency', *International Peacekeeping*, **13** (1), 94–110.

Selznick, P. (1999), 'Legal Cultures and the Rule of Law,' in M. Krygier and A. Czarnota (eds), *The Rule of Law after Communism*, Aldershot, UK and Brookfield, VT: Ashgate, pp. 21–38.

Sen, A. (2000), 'What is the Role of Legal and Judicial Reform in the Development Process?', paper presented at the World Bank Legal Conference, Washington DC, 5 June.

Sen, A. (2007), *Identity and Violence: The Illusion of Destiny*, New York: W.W. Norton & Co.

Shklar, J.N. (1998), 'Political Theory and the Rule of Law,' in J.N. Shklar and S.

Hoffman (eds), *Political Thought and Political Thinkers*, Chicago, IL: University of Chicago Press.

Stromseth, J., D. Wippman and R. Brooks (2006), *Can Might Make Rights? Building the Rule of Law After Military Interventions*, New York: Cambridge University Press.

Stubbs, R. (1989), *Hearts and Minds in Guerrilla Warfare: The Malayan Emergency 1948–1960*, New York: Oxford University Press.

Thompson, E.P. (1975), *Whigs and Hunters: The Origins of the Black Acts*, Harmondsworth, UK: Penguin.

Thompson, R. (1966), *Defeating Communist Insurgency: Experiences from Malaya and Vietnam*, London: Chatto & Windus.

Trubek, D. and A. Santos, (eds) (2006), *The New Law and Economic Development: A Critical Approach*, New York: Cambridge University Press.

Upham, F. (2006), 'Mythmaking in the Rule-of-Law Orthodoxy', in T. Carothers (ed.), *Promoting the Rule of Law Abroad*, Washington, DC: Carnegie Endowment for International Peace, pp. 75–104.

8. Securing Against Natural Disasters: Better Preparedness and Better Development

Ajay Chhibber and Rachid Laajaj

Worldwide, the risks linked to natural hazards have increased sharply in recent years, with the number of recorded natural disasters having increased exponentially from around 50 per year in the early 1970s, to almost 400 per year in 2005 (see Figure 8.1). In constant dollars, the costs of natural disasters between 1996 and 2005 reached over US$650 billion in material losses, which is more than 15 times higher than the cost from 1950 to 1959.[1] Over this period some 2 billion people were affected by disasters in one way or another. Natural hazards are an increasing hindrance to the development of the many developing countries and need to be addressed. How much of the growing vulnerability to disasters is due to human actions and how much due to nature has been a subject of some debate. This chapter argues that hazards are created by nature, but disasters are largely man-made. Therefore, development and disasters are closely interlinked. Moreover, while much focus is placed on very visible cataclysmic events such as earthquakes, floods and tsunamis, we must become more aware that disasters often arise from the slow buildup of human pressure on resources, leading to natural resource degradation and increased frequency of disasters such as floods or famines. And while many disasters are considered a product of under-development, many are also the result of choices made on development strategies.

What is striking also is the picture by disaster types, with huge increase in two types of disasters: flood and windstorm (including hurricanes and typhoons). The frequency of natural disasters caused by other categories, earthquakes, volcano, slides, and pest-infestation has not changed markedly, although there is a small but perceptible increase in droughts. How much of this recorded increase is due to better reporting and how much is due to real natural activity is still a subject of debate. The shift of population into more disaster-prone areas could be one reason for more recorded natural disasters. More worrisome is the hypothesis that one manifestation of climate change is an increase in the frequency of natural disasters, especially floods and

Figure 8.1   Hydro-Meterological Disasters Increasing Worldwide

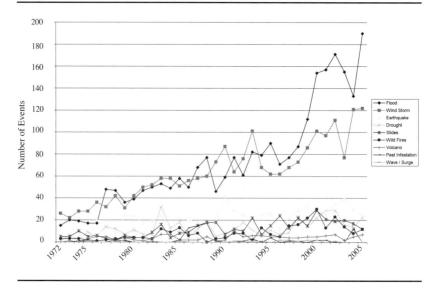

Source: Parker, Little and Hueser (2007).

windstorms, as they are related to temperature changes in the oceans. Broadly, natural disasters are classified into two categories: hydro-metrological and volcanic, with a marked increase in the former category, although news media have focused considerably on earthquakes in Pakistan, Sumatra, Java, Haiti and Japan. But recent floods in Mexico and South Asia, as well as typhoon activity in the Pacific Ocean and South China Sea affecting Vietnam, Cambodia, Laos, Philippines, Taiwan (China) and China all are examples of increased hydro-metrological phenomenon.

Windstorm activity, which shows a marked increase, causes damage from flooding and also from wind activity itself. The marked increase in this type of disaster has been linked to increases in ocean temperature; higher temperatures allegedly increase the intensity of windstorms and thereby increase their destructive power. Category 4 and 5 windstorms have been increasing over the last decade. Their destructive power has also increased because of shifts in the concentration of population to the coastal areas, indiscriminate coastal development and loss of natural protection provided by mangroves. Sea level rise is also a major factor in coastal erosion. Part of the sea level rise is attributed to melting ice caps and part of it is due to an increase in the oceanic temperature itself. The increase in flooding is a hydro-metrological phenomenon, but it is also linked to human developmental actions, such as deforestation. Other causes relate to peri-urban settlement in areas without adequate drainage or in areas that were kept open for normal drainage, but were subsequently taken over for settlement by migrants with nowhere else to live.

There is also growing evidence that there are links among conflict, security and disasters, with the pressure on resources often leading to the increased probability of conflict. While much focus has been on the scramble for natural assets such as oil, diamonds and forests, we have seen conflict and insecurity also arise from the slow build-up of disasters coming from a lack of resources and sometimes from the increased vulnerability created following a disaster. This is evident in some of the conflicts in Central Africa and more recently in the Darfur region of the Sudan, where the rebellion began in the 1970s, right after Africa's greatest famine. This chapter argues that we need to consider a much more comprehensive link among disasters, security and economic development.

This chapter explores the links between economic development and vulnerability to natural hazard in order to better understand the factors that need to be addressed to help countries get better prepared to deal with natural disasters, as well as to better understand how choices made through development policies affect vulnerability to disasters. The second section shows that while it is easier to understand the short-term impact of natural disasters, the long-term economic impact of natural disasters remains uncertain. We present a framework for looking at the long-term impact of disasters and summarize the available theoretical and empirical literature. The third section stresses the reciprocal influence of development and vulnerability, highlighting the possibility of a vicious circle: a highly vulnerable and poor country may suffer frequent disasters that prevent it from development and thus from improving its resilience. The fourth section provides some case studies, providing examples of either poorly or well-managed disasters. The fifth section discusses better ways of coping with natural disasters. The focus here is on better financial mechanisms, and on better measures for preparedness that are currently overlooked. Finally, we end with some ideas for how disaster response can be factored into long-term development.

THE ECONOMIC IMPACT OF NATURAL DISASTERS

Several studies have evaluated the short-term cost of natural disasters. An exhaustive assessment of the short-term costs must include both direct costs (damage to buildings, crops, social infrastructure) and indirect costs (lost output and investment, macroeconomic imbalances, increased indebtedness). The World Bank estimated that from 1990 to 2000, natural disasters have caused damage representing between 2 to 15 per cent of an exposed country's annual GDP (World Bank 2004). With such large costs – in many countries much larger than their aid budgets, and in some cases larger than the country's investment rate – it is important to focus, more than has been the case so far, on the impact of natural disasters, their relationship to economic development priorities and strategy and better coping mechanisms.

There is little doubt that most natural disasters have severe short-term consequences on the economy and cause tremendous human suffering. Over the last several years horrendous loss of life and suffering occurred in Pakistan from the Kashmir earthquakes, in Indonesia, Thailand and parts of South Asia from the Tsunami cause by a quake off Sumatra, from Hurricane Katrina in Louisiana and from repeated stories of flooding in South Asia, Vietnam, Mexico and Central America. The costs of human life, capital and economic losses from large and small disasters are huge and, if avoidable, could lead to large welfare gains. For this reason alone it would be important to study ways in which the short-term impact of natural disasters could be reduced. But it seems even more important if we can demonstrate that natural disasters have long-term impact. Decisions on how to cope with natural disasters can have consequences over long periods and into future generations. But very few studies assess the long term-consequences of natural hazards. This chapter outlines the findings of the past studies, developing theoretical as well as empirical analysis of the long-term economic impact of natural disasters.

A Positive Impact on Growth?

Because natural disasters are frequently succeeded by higher growth rates that seem to compensate for the economic impact of the disaster, one could expect that disasters are just a temporary disruption of the development process that has no impact on the long-term development of the country. Aghion and Howitt (1998) provide a theoretical explanation to this observation with a Schumpeterian model of endogenous growth. In the model, growth is generated by technological change that is embedded in new capital replacement needed after the disaster. As a result, a natural disaster can even lead to a positive overall impact on the economy.

Some authors have tried to model the long-term effects of disasters. Using arguments on economic linkage and substitution effects, Albala-Bertrand (1993a) constructed the first macroeconomic model of the economic impact of a natural disaster. In this model, a first step was to set an upper limit for the impact of a one-time disaster on output, assuming that all losses are to capital stocks, which is homogenous and irreplaceable in the short term. The result is basically that the reduction in the output is proportional to the reduction in the stock of capital. The author then modifies some assumptions, considering for example that loss is split between capital and output, that capital loss is estimated at replacement cost, and that capital is heterogeneous. As a result, Albala-Bertrand finds a much smaller impact on output, and he considers this to be much more realistic than the first result. The implication is that a natural disaster is unlikely to have a long-term impact on growth. It explained why macroeconomic indicators improved during the years following the disaster and quickly returned to their normal level.

Benson and Clay (2004) come to the opposite conclusion by arguing that resources used following a disaster are not necessarily additional and can have a high opportunity cost. They provide a number of channels through which natural hazard can influence the path of growth and development:

- The stock of capital and human resources can be damaged (through migration and death) or their productivity reduced by disruption of infrastructure and markets.
- Increased spending can lead to higher fiscal deficits and cause inflation.
- Reallocation of expenditures draws funds from planned investments.
- Even when funded by aid, this aid may not be entirely additional: Donors tend to advance commitments within existing multiyear country programs and budget envelopes. As a result, the amount of aid provided following the natural disaster is also diverted from development aid flows.
- Consecutive natural disasters create an atmosphere of uncertainty that discourages potential investors.

Other Possible Scenarios

A common problem in preparing an economic assessment following a disaster is the confusion caused by mixing stock losses with changes in flows. A distinction is necessary between the impact of the disaster on stocks and flows. Physical and human capital and public debt are examples of such stocks, which can be affected directly (destruction of infrastructure, livestock) or indirectly (the variation of a flow causes the variation of the corresponding stock). An increase in the public deficit (a flow) would help add to the public debt, while a diversion of investments (a flow) to fund the relief costs would reduce the stock of physical capital. In return, annual flows are dependent on stocks: physical and human capital stocks are determinants of the GDP (a flow). These multiple and complex interactions need to be considered when evaluating the economic impact of a disaster.

Figure 8.2 Possible Long-Run Impact of a Disaster on GDP per Capita

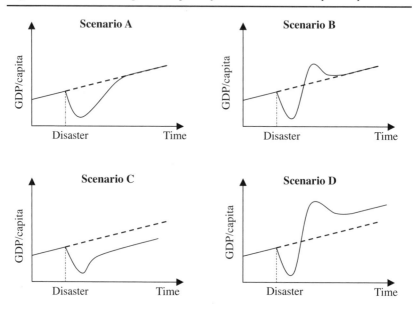

Because of contradictory effects, theory does not provide clear-cut conclusions about the impact of natural disasters on the long-term growth rate. It may be useful to outline different scenarios that would then need to be tested.

Disasters reduce the stock of human and physical capital, which leads to immediate losses in annual production. This short-term reduction of GDP can also be direct, for example, when a drought reduces agricultural production. If a negative impact is commonly observed in the short-term, the medium-term and long-term impact of disasters is still subject to debate. Scenarios A, B, C and D of Figure 8.2 are graphic representations of the possible predicted impact of a disaster on the long-term growth rate. In scenarios A and B, the disaster does not influence the long-run growth path of income: the shock has a negative impact on the GDP, eventually followed by an expansion during the reconstruction (in order to match the initial stock of capital), and the production level returns to its long-run state of equilibrium. In scenario C, because the disaster has permanently reduced the stock of capital, the new long-run equilibrium is established at a lower level of GDP. Finally, in scenario D, the restitution of human capital and physical capital brings with it technological change that enhances the long-run growth rate of the economy.[2] It should be noted that different types of disasters could be associated with different scenarios. For example, an earthquake is more likely to be associated with scenario B or D because it is generally followed by considerable reconstruction that may trigger an expansion and, eventually, technological change. But at the same time, an earthquake may also lead to large loss of human capital, which will reduce the long-run growth rate of the economy. Conversely, Scenario A or C could correspond to a drought because when the loss is generally restricted to the annual production and the household's livelihood, it is unlikely to lead to greater production potential unless it leads to major investments in irrigation or other drought-reducing technologies. Empirical testing of these assertions would be useful.

Empirical Evidence Goes Both Ways

Because of considerable methodological difficulties, different studies have led to different findings and no consensus has emerged about the long-term consequences of natural hazards. One of the first empirical evaluations of the long-term impact of disasters on the economy was provided by Albala-Bertrand (1993b). In a statistical analysis of 28 disasters in 26 countries from 1960 to 1976, he found that the long-run growth rate and some other key variables were not affected by disasters (similar to Illustrative Scenarios A and B). Benson and Clay (1998) have noted the lack of assessment of the non-agricultural or economy-wide macroeconomic impacts of droughts in Sub-Saharan Africa. Even if the direct impacts of droughts are the most easily observable, indirect and secondary impacts on the non-agricultural and macro-economy should not be neglected. They are often not examined as recurrent issues that could potentially affect the rate and pattern of development. Benson and Clay try to fill the gap despite the considerable methodological difficulties to establish a non-drought counterfactual in order to isolate the natural hazard's effect. They found that drought shocks have large economy-wide impact but that the extent of the impact varies tremendously according to a number of factors. According to their results, the level of complexity of the economy and increased intersectoral linkages are among the main factors that increase the risk that a disaster will affect not only the agricultural sector, but the whole economy.

Benson (2003), in a cross-sectional study including 115 countries, found that the average growth rate from 1960 to 1993 was lower in countries that experienced more natural disasters (as in Illustrative Scenario C). Critics have pointed out that the more developed countries have experienced fewer disasters and therefore the results might reflect Quah's (1993) finding of a polarization towards a bimodal distribution. Indeed, Quah observed a long-term divergence of income between developed and developing countries; hence, the lower long-term growth rate in countries with frequent disasters (mostly developing countries) is not sufficient to draw conclusions regarding the direction of causality. It is generally difficult to isolate the impact of natural hazard from other factors that influence the path of growth and development, because countries with stronger institutions have higher growth and also are better able to handle natural hazards and therefore are better able to reduce the probability of huge disasters.

Few studies have examined whether the occurrence of a natural disaster increases the risk of civil war through its economic and social impact. Using a panel of 41 African countries from 1981 to 1999, Miguel et al. (2004) found that a negative growth shock of five percentage points (instrumented by extreme rainfall variations) increases the likelihood of conflict by 50 per cent the following year.

Some models have been developed that focus specifically on one of these transmission channels. For example, the International Institute for Applied Systems Analysis modeled the potential impact of disaster on capital accumulation, while Cochrane (1994) explored the impact of disasters on a country's indebtedness. Using a recursive Keynesian growth model, Cochrane assumes that the recovery costs are entirely funded by external borrowing and hence generate an increase in interest rates. The consequences are an increase in debt stock as well as a reduction of long-term investment and growth.

Nonetheless, all the studies mentioned have been subject to some criticism. Lavell (1999) points out that models such as those presented here should be submitted to an *a posteriori* evaluation in order to compare real with projected performance. Insufficient empirical work has been done on these issues.

Another problem that has received insufficient attention is that different types of natural disasters have different consequences. For example, Benson and Clay (2004) note the need for a distinction between geological and hydro-metrological disasters. While geological events, being less frequent but often more cataclysmic, are more likely to generate Schumpeterian innovation and stimulate a post-disaster growth, hydro-metrological disasters are generally more frequent, creating an atmosphere of uncertainty that hurts the investment climate and requires adaptation costs. Indeed in the Albala-Bertrand study mentioned earlier, most of the countries that were found to have achieved higher growth rates in the two years following a disaster, as compared with the two preceding years, had experienced earthquakes. Other disaster events were mainly succeeded by a lower post-disaster growth rate.

More recent empirical studies have shown that natural disasters can have a positive long-run impact on economic growth. Skidmore and Toya (2002) have shown that higher frequency of climatic disasters (as opposed to geologic disasters) is associated with higher rates of capital accumulation, increases in total factor productivity and economic growth (as in Illustrative Scenario D). Because disaster reduces the expected return to physical capital, and thereby increases the relative return to human capital, it can lead to faster growth. Moreover, as capital is replaced it comes embedded with new technology and thereby helps increase the rate of economic growth. They also argue that natural disasters increase adaptability so that cultures experiencing natural disasters may be able to adopt new technology more readily. But this argument could go in the opposite direction as well because people subject to repeated disasters could adopt more risk-averse behavior and therefore be less willing to adopt new ideas and new technology. In the case of geologic disasters, as opposed to Albala-Bertrand study, Skidmore and Toya (2002) find a negative impact on long-run growth but the coefficients are not statistically significant. Okuyama (2003) and Okuyama, Hewings and Sonis (2004) even put forward the idea that older capital is more likely to be exposed when a disaster hits the capital stock. Therefore the replacement of this capital stock would create a positive productivity shock and may affect positively the permanent growth rate of the economy.

The argument that natural disasters act as a tool for Schumpeterian creative destruction has been criticized. Crespo Cuaresma, Hlouskova and Obersteiner (2008) argue that destruction of capital stock by a natural disaster is quite different from Schumpeter's view of creative destruction, which emphasized competition dynamics as the engine behind technological progress. Using gravity models to study the technology spillovers in imports, they conclude that countries with higher exposure to natural disasters (especially climatic disasters over the medium term and with geologic disasters over the short-run) get fewer technology spillovers. Moreover, the same authors also show that the relatively more developed developing countries benefit more from technology spillovers following a disaster. Therefore, they summarize that catastrophic risk tends to affect technology absorption negatively, and the effect is stronger the less developed a country is. Furthermore, catastrophic risk variables tend to be significant determinants of cross-country differences in the long-run patterns of knowledge spillovers to developing countries.

How does the literature on the effect of disasters on growth fit in with the widespread growth literature, in which policies and institutions are shown to be key determinants on long-run growth? Does a country's ability to cope with disaster risk also depend on the strength of its institutions and, more specifically, on the nature of its disaster response institutions? Do these determine how a country both copes with a natural disaster and how it recovers from that disaster? Popp (2006) argues that this is the most effective direction to pursue in dealing with disasters. Disasters do have long-term consequences on a country's economic development, although we cannot say precisely how much, as it depends on the types of disasters, how large are they relative to the country and how strong are the country's institutions. Popp also distinguishes between risk and uncertainty and the importance of systematic information on disasters, their frequency and impact. Risk arises from being highly prone to disasters, but uncertainty arises from not knowing about it with sufficient precision and therefore adding a premium to the likelihood of a disaster. Insurance companies factor in a risk premium into disaster insurance policies, but where there is lack of adequate information, uncertainty premiums are added on and often make the costs of insurance prohibitively high. But it is not insurance markets alone that matter. The uncertainty premium affects all investment decisions and may in the long run be a bigger hindrance to development than the cost of the actual disaster, as it will affect both the quantity and nature of investment.

Given the difficulties macroeconomic studies face in terms of isolating the impact of natural disasters, microeconomic results can provide valuable insights concerning the long-term consequences of natural disasters. Using a panel dataset from Zimbabwe, Alderman et al. (2006) found that children who were between 12 and 24 months of age during the 1982–84 drought had a higher probability of being stunted[3] during preschool years, which is a manifestation of malnutrition. As a result, the cohort affected by the drought has been found to be 2.3 centimeters shorter and have 0.4 fewer grades of schooling attained 13 to 16 years later. This study highlights the long-term, irreversible consequences of natural disasters on human capital in poor countries.

Carter, Little, Mogues and Negatu (2006) use longitudinal panel data from Ethiopia (for the drought of 1998–2000) and Honduras (following Hurricane Mitch in 1998) to study how different categories of households cope with the disasters. Their study shows the existence of 'poverty traps', which are threshold levels at which households which fall below them are unable to cope and recover to their original level of well-being. Richer households in Honduras were able to recover their assets some three years after the hurricane, but those with incomes below US$250 per year were unable to recover and fell into a low level of equilibrium. In Ethiopia, although the impact of the drought was different from that of a hurricane, the poorer households were able to recover faster than richer households, but to a level of low equilibrium suggesting the existence of poverty traps. Dercon (2007) notes that this situation suggests the existence of poverty traps linked to human capital, resulting in a permanent state of low human capital and earnings.

Using simulation-based econometric methods, in a growth model applied to panel data from rural Zimbabwe, Elbers and Gunning (2003) found that risks associated with disasters reduced the mean capital stock in the observed region by 46 per cent. The most innovative part of their work comes from the distinction between ex-post (observed directly after the shock) and ex-ante effects of risk (the costly behavioral response to risk, such as a discouragement to invest). They show that the ex-ante effect represents two-thirds of the negative effects of risk, stressing the inadequacy of most existing studies, which focus on the ex-post effect of risk. This also explains how frequent disasters can generate significantly different effects than a one-time huge disaster (which would have no ex-ante effect). Moreover, these studies also show the intergenerational effects of a one-time disaster if the response of households to cope with those shocks leads to irreversible decisions, such as increased drop-out rates in schools or inadequate attention to health care, leading to higher disease rates. Disaster-response mechanisms must be designed with such shocks in mind.

When estimating the overall cost of natural hazard, too much attention has been paid to the major events. Lavell (1999) stresses the importance of smaller-scale disasters, which are much more frequent than the larger ones, but not registered in the statistical databases because they are small enough not to involve the central authorities and are typically handled by local governments. According to Lavell, 'The cumulative losses associated with the "smaller disasters" may be as significant as that attributed to large-scale disasters'.

Moreover, many 'smaller but recurring disasters' are observed around the world with little action taken to address the problem. This issue is different from vulnerability to natural disasters, but it is also accentuated by climate change and human behavior. Although different from vulnerability to natural disasters, land degradation and soil erosion are also accentuated by climate change and human behavior, with increasing consequences on the poor. In Uganda, for example, the exposure to natural hazards has led to land degradation and accentuated the impact of climate variability on crop output. In the most affected districts (Kabal, Kisoro, Mbale), which are also the most densely populated with a density of more than 250 inhabitants per square kilometer, 80–90 per cent of the area is estimated to be affected by soil erosion (Uganda National Environment Management Authority 2002). Land degradation is a worldwide issue: the *World Disaster Report* (World Bank 1997) estimated that 80 per cent of the poor in Latin America, 60 per cent of the poor in Asia and 50 per cent of the poor in Africa live on marginal lands characterized by poor productivity and high vulnerability to natural degradation and natural disaster.

Given the methodological difficulties linked to empirical analysis, qualitative studies might be more useful. Benson and Clay (2004) have provided a number of case studies, highlighting the long-term negative effects of disasters. For example, the Bangladesh government has recognized that 'inadequate infrastructure to deal with floods have been a constraint on investment in productive activities as well as on utilization of installed capacity' (Bangladesh 2000). Similarly, leaders in the Philippines have encountered tremendous difficulties when trying to improve the country's transport system and meet the social infrastructure needs of the population because of an extremely high exposure to natural hazard, mainly floods and windstorms. Dominica (1979) and Montserrat (1995–98) are examples of a considerable loss of human capital through emigration linked to natural disasters. Clearly more work both qualitative and quantitative is needed to further explore these issues.

INTERACTIONS BETWEEN DEVELOPMENT AND VULNERABILITY

Before going forward with the analysis, the concept of vulnerability needs to be clarified. Vulnerability to natural hazard can be decomposed into two main components: the exposure to shocks and resilience. The degree of exposure to shocks is a function of the frequency and size of natural hazards affecting the population and the proportion of the population affected by the hazard, which in part is determined by choices made by people in where they live. The degree of exposure is therefore the result of the frequency and intensity of natural hazards, which are mainly exogenous, and where people choose to live. In some cases the choice is voluntary, e.g., people prefer to live in coastal areas or along river beds. In other cases the choices are involuntary, as when population pressure drives people to live in marginal areas. Resilience is the capacity to cope with natural disasters, including both preparedness (land and building codes, better forecasting) and response to disasters (such as financing mechanisms, post-disaster relief), Therefore:

$$V = f(NH, P, R) \tag{8.1}$$

where V is vulnerability, NH is the number and intensity of natural hazards, P is the population exposed to disaster, and R is the level of resilience. It is expected that NH and P increase vulnerability while R reduces it. Note that in this framework, climate change can affect V by increasing the intensity and frequency of NH and by increasing the proportion of population that will be affected by disasters.

Hewitt (1983) and Blaikie et al. (1994) have made major contributions to the study of natural disasters and development. They stress the role of social structures in shaping vulnerability. Besides, Sen (1981) and Drèze and Sen (1989) are among the pioneers in considering famine not just as a natural disaster, but also as an avoidable economic and political catastrophe. They show that famines were caused not so much by lack of food, but by lack of entitlement to resources, based on access to economic, social and political power. These works have strongly influenced the conception of prevention and management of famines in the developing world, as well as the idea that disasters are man-made or policy induced.

To pursue the analysis, it is crucial to understand that a natural disaster is not a completely exogenous event. A natural disaster is used as shorthand for humanitarian disaster with a natural trigger or, as provocatively stated by Wisner, a natural disaster is a failure of human development (Pelling 2003). As we will see, natural disasters are the consequences of natural hazards, but also, to a large extent, the reflection of development flaws. They are quite often not so natural, but are the result of exposing the population to greater vulnerability by lack of preparedness or by the nature of the development process itself. Therefore the risks of natural disaster must no longer be considered as exogenous factors, but as central to development planning itself.

Determinants of Vulnerability to Natural Hazards

Well-managed, sustainable economic development typically reduces the exposure to natural hazard. A reduction of the proportion of the population working in the agricultural sector increases the resilience of the country, since the overall level of production becomes less sensitive to the hydro-meteorological conditions. The inter-sectoral linkages are another determining factor of resilience: countries with a high degree of dualism, with a large capital-intensive extractive sector, are less sensitive to natural hazards. For example, droughts had limited effect on the macro-economy of Botswana, Namibia or Zambia, all of which draw most of their resources from the mining industry. But some types of development can increase exposure. For example, with higher incomes and coastal development there has been a huge migration of people and assets to coastal areas all over the world, which has led to greater exposure to hurricanes, tornadoes and tsunamis. Parker et al. (2007) show that about one-quarter of the world's population now live within 100 kilometers of the coast. Of the 25 mega cities around the world, 14 are on the coast and seven are within a few hours' drive from the coast. Unplanned urban development and lack of effective building codes have made many urban areas in the developed world highly vulnerable to disasters. As more and more people move to live in the peri-urban areas around cities, they pose a growing risk to people living in them. At the same time, migration is also a coping strategy whereby people are forced to move out of harm's way, as in Montserrat due to the volcano, or migrate due to dwindling resources, as in the Darfur region.

The financial system
Development is generally linked to a better financial system, which allows a wider diffusion of the impact of the disaster, especially when it facilitates

small-scale savings and transfers. In Zimbabwe, for example, after the 1991–92 drought, a well-developed financial system facilitated transfers from urban to rural regions. Later we will discuss the role and importance of micro-credit.

Trade openness

More-open economies have fewer exchange constraints. As a consequence, any increase in imports for relief and reconstruction will not displace normal imports. Moreover, local inflation can be contained more easily in a more-open economy following a disaster. But again, more study is needed on how openness to trade helps or hinders recovery from natural disasters.

Institutions

One of the most important factors that determine the resilience of a country is the willingness of the government to consider preparedness for natural hazards a priority. This includes a long-term commitment to mitigation and preparedness, even when no disaster has occurred during the preceding years. Along with this, transparency, better reporting of relevant expenditures, and post-disaster reallocations are essential, as well as the enforcement of appropriate land-use and building codes.

On the other hand, the coincidence of a natural disaster and political instability can have dramatic consequences. Such was the case during the violent independence struggle in Bangladesh during the mid-1970s or the war in Mozambique during the 1990s, which destabilized Malawi's transport system and provoked an arrival of refugees. A more recent example is the case of Zimbabwe in 2002. Angola, Lesotho, Malawi, Mozambique, Swaziland, Zambia and Zimbabwe have all suffered from food shortages after three years of drought combined with flooding in some areas. However, Zimbabwe, which was once considered the 'breadbasket' of southern Africa, became the most vulnerable country of the region. Political violence, fueled by inflation, unemployment, racial tensions, land reform issues and soaring rates of HIV/AIDS have greatly weakened the country's capacity to provide effective relief. The government took control over the distribution of mealie meal to ensure that this basic food is supplied only to supporters of the ruling ZANU-PF party (Osborne 2002). Sen was the first one to observe that famines are the result of human behavior, stressing that they do not happen in democracies, where a free press and free speech create excellent early-warning systems. While Sen provided Zimbabwe as an example of a democracy that has successfully prevented famines despite sharp declines in food output, he recognized himself that Zimbabwe no longer qualified for the exemption he had given it before.

Public awareness and institutional responses

Only a population informed and concerned by risks related to natural hazard can create the appropriate incentives for the government to invest sufficiently in preparedness and mitigation. In Turkey, public awareness was very low despite frequent seismic events. The Marmara earthquake in 1999 created a new level of public awareness not only because of the unprecedented scale of the disaster, but also because it was mainly urban, making it difficult for the politicians, local municipalities, building contractors and civil engineers to shirk their responsibilities (Ozyaprak 1999). Turkey has seen a series of earthquakes, each followed by improvements in disaster response. But when the Marmara earthquake struck, Turkey's disaster response systems had long been neglected, and the main agency for disaster response had been downgraded to a small department under the Ministry of Reconstruction. The agency's role in coordination had become lax, similar to the problems encountered by the U.S. Federal Emergency Management Agency (FEMA) once it became part of the overall U.S. national security apparatus after the 9/11 terrorist attacks. As a result, FEMA, once held up as a model for disaster response, was unable to respond effectively during the Hurricane Katrina disaster in Louisiana. Turkey has since taken steps to become more proactive and less reactive, and the government is trying to strengthen Istanbul's readiness to handle a large earthquake. Sen (1981) has also compared the response to droughts in India and China, arguing that India avoided famines because of its free press, whereas China suffered a major famine in 1984 because the system could withhold information on the drought and was unwilling to admit problems and seek assistance.

Toya and Skidmore (2005) used cross-country econometric analysis to show that countries with higher income, higher educational achievement, greater openness, more complete financial systems and smaller government expenditures experience fewer losses from natural disasters.

Vulnerability due to human factors

In 1972–73, the Sahel experienced a catastrophic drought during which thousands of people and millions of animals died (de Waal 1997; Mortimore 1998). This catastrophe was the result of both natural and human factors. The preceding droughts in the late 1960s and early 1970s had increased people's vulnerability, especially in the rural areas, by depleting their stock of physical capital (savings, grains, animals) as well as human capital through health deterioration or rural-to-urban migration. Indeed, the rural communities were the most vulnerable for a combination of socioeconomic factors: (1) isolation due to poor communication and transport links; (2) an urban bias in policymaking resulting from poor rural representation; (3) a focus on short-term stabilization rather than long-term economic development and (4) an emphasis on industrial investment and the conversion of agriculture to cash crops at the expense of the production of food for local consumption (Baker 1987; Shaw 1987; Rau 1991).

The relevance of those human factors is highlighted by the fact that, subsequently, the Sahel endured many droughts comparable to those of the early 1970s, but none of them led to such a massive, regional-scale famine (Mortimore 2000). If natural hazard increased the vulnerability in the short-term, in the long run the population has developed many strategies to cope with drought, such as agricultural diversification and migration.

In this case, the emphasis on industrialization, cash crops and export earnings in countries that are primarily rural – where most of the population cannot afford or lacks access to imported foodstuffs – has increased the vulnerability of the region. This example illustrates the existence of a local-level adaptive capacity and the danger inherent in a 'top-down' approach to development, especially when it is based on global economic paradigms disconnected from the rural communities' reality (Pelling 2003).

The Complex Relationship Between Vulnerability and Development

Considerable development effort can be wasted when vulnerability is not taken into consideration. In Honduras, after Hurricane Mitch (1998), President Carlos Flores stated that his country's development was set back 30 to 50 years. Indeed 70–80 per cent of the transport infrastructure was destroyed, including almost all bridges and secondary roads. One-fifth of the population was left homeless, crops, animal losses led to food shortages and the lack of sanitation generated outbreaks of malaria, dengue fever and cholera (National Climatic Center 2004).

Dore and Etkin (2003) point out the importance of the adaptive capacity at an institutional level. They define six necessary conditions for adaptation by observing how developed countries respond to current climate issues:

- Developed countries have the technical know-how to understand climate.
- They have resources to devote to research on climate and the related risks.
- They develop the necessary technology to cope with climate.
- They share risks through government disaster-assisted programs and through the insurance market.
- The insurance market mediates moral hazard problems through mechanisms such as a minimum deductible, rebates for minimizing damages or premium reductions for making no claims.
- They invest resources in emergency responses at all levels of government.

Figure 8.3a Possible Long-Run Impact of Successive Disasters on Income

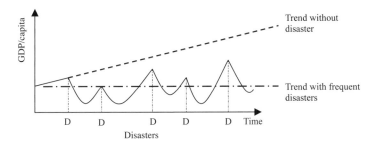

The six conditions are generally costly and require high-quality institutions and human capital. It can be deduced that a country needs to be relatively developed to meet the necessary conditions for a high resilience to natural hazard. At the same time, a vulnerable country is highly exposed to disasters that would be harmful to its development process. Consequently there is a risk that poor countries could become locked in a vicious cycle, whereby they are vulnerable because of their low level of development, and this vulnerability regularly brings them back to their initial level of development through natural disasters. We had earlier summarized the literature on 'poverty traps' for individual households, but we can imagine that a country hit by repeated disaster could fall into a low-level equilibrium trap and be unable to lift its per capita growth rate. As represented in Figure 8.3a, high vulnerability would result in frequent large-scale natural disasters. Even if one disaster would generally not have long-term effects (such as represented in Scenario A of Figure 8.2, for example), the succession of disasters does not allow the country to reconstitute its capital and other productive capacities. The result is high instability, but also an inability to reach the path of growth that would have been expected in the absence of disaster. This could be the story of Ethiopia, for example, which is particularly vulnerable since agriculture accounts for 41 per cent of the GDP, 80 per cent of the working force and 80 per cent of exports. Repeated droughts in Ethiopia lead to a low-level growth equilibrium than would be the case without droughts. Undoubtedly, vulnerability is only one of the numerous factors that can explain the stagnation of a least developed country, but its role should not be neglected, including its role through indirect channels such as discouraging private investments or increasing the risk of political instability. Further work on this vicious link between vulnerability and development would be valuable, although the establishment of a counterfactual would be difficult.

Figure 8.3b   Possible Long-Run Impact of Climate Change on Income

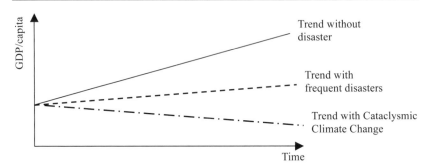

In order to progressively emerge from this situation, highly exposed countries need to consciously incorporate how best to build resilience and reduce vulnerability into their development policy. Some authors, such as Katrina Allen (2003), go even further and argue that the distinction between resilience to natural hazard and development is mainly theoretical and has more meaning for government bodies than for local communities. At a local level, both are strongly related to the lack of livelihood. Similarly, humanitarian crises are extensively linked to the sociopolitical context. According to the author, isolating vulnerability from the wider social background risks treating symptoms rather than cause. The Mozambique case study below illustrates how vulnerability and poverty can be tackled jointly.

If the projections made in Stern (2007), which incorporate the impact of more severe climate change, are correct, then we must also include the possibility of a sharp drop in income and consumption. Figure 8.3b incorporates such a scenario without any prevention or coping action. This grim scenario would lead to a huge increase in poverty, malnutrition and even mass famines, as well as serious disruption to development. Climate change would be the ultimate natural disaster with such large negative impacts that countries would face a sharp drop in GDP/capita.

CASE STUDIES

La Josephina Landslide in Ecuador

In 1993, a huge landslide occurred in La Josefina, located in the mountainous southern region of Ecuador, near the city of Cuenca. The landslide covered the entire valley, and dammed the Rio Paute, impounding it for 33 days, during which 1,000 hectares were flooded. In all, about 200 persons were killed by the flood and 14,000 persons displaced, with extensive damage to land and buildings. The costs to agricultural lands, factories and residential infrastructure reached several million dollars.

This case is a good example of a natural disaster caused by a combination of human and natural factors. The area was exposed to a permanent danger of landslide; below the landslide site, there are about 35 scars of slides from the past. But this geography should not mask the human responsibility. The area has a dense rural population and after the land reforms, lands were divided into excessively small plots and worked by farmers with little experience using overly intensive agriculture. Mono cultivation of maize in rows following the slope was a frequent practice, even though this technique leads to heavy erosion.

During the 33 days of flood, 47 NGOs were criticized for their lack of effective assistance and the provincial government for its passivity. Codevilla (1993) argued that there was an excess of *asistencialismo* (dependence on handouts) from the locals, simply waiting to be helped. No structure in place was able to handle the disaster.

Morris (Pelling 2003) suggested promoting soft engineering (making low-energy adaptations), rather than a hard-engineering approach (trying to match the power of nature). These suggestions spring from Abramovitz's recommendations (2001) advocating greater control over land use, limitations on intensive farming, and the development of forestry in critical zones. This implies recognition of the significant risks linked to natural hazard, which cannot be totally controlled, and the acceptance of a tradeoff between higher short-term productivity due to intensive farming and the long-term benefits resulting from the maintenance of a more resilient ecosystem.

A Successful Recovery in Mozambique

In a vulnerable country, one disaster can set back hard-won development efforts. Mozambique is one of the poorest countries in the world, with 69 per cent of the population below the poverty line. The peace agreement of 1992 put an end to 17 years of civil war. Beginning in 1992, the growth rate of GDP per capita averaged 6 per cent until the flood of 2000. The flood killed 700 people, displaced 650,000 were and affected 4.5 million (a quarter of the population). It devastated 140,000 hectares of crops and their irrigation systems, 350,000 livestock were lost or seriously injured, 6,000 fishermen lost at least 50 per cent of their boats and gear, and about 500 primary schools and seven secondary schools were destroyed.

However, the long-term economic consequences of the disaster largely depend on the capacity of the country to handle the recovery program.

Mozambique's recovery seems to have been generally effective. Recovery programs have provided an opportunity for investments in upgraded services and infrastructure (Cosgrave 2001), many affected people have been assisted, and the rehabilitation and rebuilding of schools and health facilities has encouraged the development of new social structures, such as associations and community committees.

This success can be explained by different factors, among them the creation of the National Disaster Management Institute in 1999, developing a culture of prevention, immediate and massive flows of aid and – above all – the government's determination to establish a recovery program aimed at strengthening national reconstruction and development policies. The objective was not simply to restore the previous level of development, but to generate social and economic improvements that would increase the resilience to future disasters. Responses to the flood in 2001 showed significant improvements and clear signs of progress (UNICEF 2002). Preparedness measures had been taken, including the pre-placement of food, boats and other relief materials. Neighboring countries were contacted to coordinate the displacement of affected populations.

One of the key elements to the success of the reconstruction was the extraordinarily high level of donor response (around \$450 million in May 2000) and a commitment from the government to maintain macroeconomic stability. These aid flows dampened the negative impacts of the disasters, allowing a rapid return to high levels of growth. Therefore, the 2000 and 2001 floods were not considered to have had a lasting negative economic impact. A World Bank report on the case of Mozambique (2005) noted the following reasons for the successful recovery:

- Intensive labor-based infrastructure works for disaster mitigation.
- Where possible, use of local rather than international contractors.
- Increased levels of accountability and transparency through the use of independent reviews and evaluations of recovery works.
- Good practice guidelines to ensure gender issues were addressed, and adequate attention paid to recovery of complex livelihoods, land tenure issues and standards for housing.
- Emphasis on building capacity for disaster management at the district level and sharing information on budget and planning for disasters.

Combining Vulnerability and Poverty Reduction

Instead of thinking of disaster response and development as two separate activities, can we think of programs and projects that inherently combine them? An example of a successful project combining vulnerability and poverty reduction comes from Niger, one of the poorest countries in the world. Implemented by the Small Rural Operation in Niger, the project took 11 years (from 1988 to 1998) and targeted an area with a chronic food deficit for the population. The aim was to reduce drought vulnerability by intensifying off-season crop production through widespread use of existing, simple, low-cost technologies. Around 35,000 farmers benefited from the strong increase in production resulting from higher cropping intensities, cultivation of higher-value crops and diversification toward non-crop activities. In this case the two objectives of poverty reduction and food security could not have been achieved separately because they are highly linked to the livelihood of the rural population. More such combined approaches are needed to break the vicious cycle of disasters and low-level development. Much of the micro-economic evidence presented earlier in this chapter revealed the existence of poverty traps, whereby households fall into poverty due to a disaster (a drought or a death of the head of the household and sometimes even an illness). If these households fall temporarily into poverty because of a natural disaster, they become chronically poor. Therefore, anti-poverty schemes must be designed to help households avoid falling into poverty, with special safety-net mechanisms triggered by a natural disaster.

FINANCIAL MECHANISMS FOR COPING WITH AND PREPARING FOR NATURAL DISASTERS

When governments do not resort to higher fiscal deficit to fund relief and reconstruction costs, they generally turn to international aid or reallocation of expenditure. However, other solutions are available for spreading risks. This section discusses the strengths and weaknesses of each solution.

Fiscal Deficits

When a government is submerged by a sudden overflow of emergency needs, higher expenditures leading to bigger fiscal deficits are easy answers. Nonetheless, the long-term costs of indebtedness are well known, making this choice the last resort for the government. Benson and Clay (1998, 2004) found no impact of natural disasters on the overall budget deficit except in drought-affected Sub-Saharan economies, where five of the six case studies showed a noticeable increase in government borrowing after the drought.

Reallocation of expenditure

One of the most common ways to cope with the urgent needs of a post-disaster situation is to reallocate budgetary resources. This solution provides a rapid source of funding while keeping domestic credit and money supply under control. Still, it diverts funds from planned investments and thus hampers the development process. A main concern is that reallocation of funds after a disaster should follow a formal process rather than emergency decisions, so that funds would not be diverted from projects essential to the long-term development of the country. This is often not the case and vital long-term development is affected.

International aid

International agencies play a major role in helping countries that have limited resources to cope with the disaster. However, Benson and Clay (2004) suggest that post-disaster aid flows are not additional. In their three case studies (Dominica, Bangladesh and Malawi) they observed that disasters had little impact on the overall level of aid. Donors bring forward commitments and thus reduce the availability of aid during the subsequent years. The World Bank IEG report (2006) confirms that despite the existence of an Emergency Recovery Loan (ERL), loan reallocations are the most frequent type of responses to disasters in highly vulnerable countries, and such reallocations often do not lead to good outcomes.

Another important issue in aid-based relief and reconstruction is that considerable flows of aid from different donors raise management problems for the receiving country. They have to submit to different conditions from the various donors, which can take time and limit their sovereignty. It diminishes the government's ability to determine the allocation of reconstruction funds and setting its own priorities.

Increasingly, countries are taking greater ownership over donor coordination during the relief and recovery period. But where institutional capacities are limited, coordination can also be provided by one of the donors. After the drought in Sudan in 1989, the World Bank worked with the other donors to organize the relief effort and avoid unnecessary overlaps in coverage. Special attention is required from the international community when a natural disaster occurs in a politically unstable country or in a country with weak institutions.

Benson and Clay denounce an excessive reliance on international aid in case of disasters. Natural disasters often substantially increase the gap between commitments and actual aid disbursements. In an emergency situation, small delays may result in severe social and economic consequences. Moreover, as we look into the future, aid flows might not be able to cope with the rapid increase in the annual cost of disasters; there is a need to begin to look at alternate options. And if natural disaster management must be seen as part and parcel of economic development, then special funding mechanisms for disasters may actually lead to avoidance of the more fundamental choices that countries must make to build disaster management into their development strategy.

Financial Risk Mechanisms

Insurance

As noted by Freeman et al. (2002), in the world's poorest countries, currently less than one per cent of the losses from natural disasters is formally insured. This financial risk mitigation mechanism could certainly be developed further to reduce aid dependency for managing disasters. The expansion of insurance has been limited by its high cost: Catastrophe insurance premiums can be several times higher than the actuarially determined expected losses (Froot 1999). Furthermore, strong institutions are required to manage insurance schemes. Regulation must insure that insurance companies are sufficiently cautious and big enough to diversify the risk or be reinsured. Moreover, clear and agreed triggers are needed for insurance payouts, which are often difficult to agree on.

Because the risk is highly covariant and difficult to estimate, insurance industries always face considerable difficulties in providing insurance against natural hazard. When the risk is too low, agents have very few incentives to pay the insurance premiums. Conversely, in the most exposed regions, the soaring risk discourages insurance companies. A closer look at the developed countries points out that, in most cases, the insurance market is not fully private and the government plays a major role, generally by providing catastrophe reinsurance to the companies. As a consequence, the agents are encouraged to adopt a risky behavior, knowing that they would not bear the full costs in case of a disaster. To limit the moral hazard, insurance can be provided conditionally on the implementation of loss reduction measures and the respect of building and land use zoning codes. In that way, the insurance companies can contribute to the national effort for preparedness and mitigation by creating the appropriate incentives.

A second limit to the suggestion of a government's backstop facility is that it does not eliminate the risk, but transfers the risk from local to national level. If a rich country's government generally has the ability to absorb the costs, a poor country would not have the same capacity. In order to handle the additional pressure on its budget the government itself would need to resort to other sources of funding such as international aid.

Determination of parametric insurance trigger

A possible solution would be to establish an insurance system in which payouts would be triggered by parametric observations, such as extreme rainfall. Disbursing without damage-assessment procedures can accelerate transfers and reduce transaction costs, but it is currently difficult to find simple instruments strongly related to economic costs. Further agro-meteorological research, as well as good historical data, is necessary for the insurance companies to be able to calculate accurate rates of premium. It also requires good institutions; for example, many difficulties related to landholding titles would surge if rules of ownership are not well defined.

Because of the difficulties of implementation, few examples of insurance with a parametric trigger currently exist. The Windward Islands Crop Insurance, which covers the export of bananas in Dominica, Grenada, St. Lucia, and St. Vincent and the Grenadines, has a verification system close to the parametric trigger (Benson and Clay 2004). Evaluation of losses is easy because the insurance covers one crop against one hazard. When a disaster occurs, a 5 per cent physical survey of affected growers gives the proportion of damaged plants, avoiding lengthy damage assessment procedures. The benefit is calculated on the basis of the average deliveries during the preceding three years. The payment of premium is assured since it is directly deducted from export revenues. However, the scheme faces some difficulties, such as the high covariance risk, the fact that premiums are too low but cannot be raised because of political reasons and the long-term decline in banana prices. So far, WINCROP has been unable to extend the insurance scheme to other crops because of legislative restrictions and extremely high reinsurance rates.

In January 2006 the World Bank initiated the preparatory studies for the establishment of the Caribbean Catastrophe Risk Insurance Facility (CCRIF). The Facility will allow governments of the Caribbean Community and Common Market (CARICOM) to have access to insurance coverage at a lower rate than each state could have obtained on its own for three main reasons: (1) participating governments will pool – and thus diversify – their risk, (2) donor partners will contribute to a reserve fund in order to reduce the need of international reinsurance and (3) the use of a pre-determined parametric trigger will reduce transaction costs and moral hazard. Parametric triggers will allow immediate cash payment after the occurrence of a major earthquake or hurricane, helping governments fund immediate post-disaster recovery while mobilizing additional resources (World Bank 2007). A high exposure to natural hazard has encouraged Caribbean country governments to look for creative solutions. Table 8.1 summarizes several successful cases of catastrophic risk financing.

Table 8.1   *Recent Facilitating Countries' Access to Catastrophic Risk Financing: Some Successes*

Earthquake insurance for homeowners in Turkey.
The Turkish Catastrophe Insurance Pool (TCIP) was established in the aftermath of the 1999 Marmara earthquake. It offers efficiently priced earthquake insurance to homeowners. The World Bank provided the initial capitalization of the TCIP through a committed contingent loan facility of US$100 million, extended to US$180 million in 2004. The full risk capital requirements of TCIP are funded through commercial reinsurance (currently in excess of US$1 billion) and the build-up of surplus. The TCIP sold more than 2.5 million policies (i.e., 20 per cent penetration) in 2006, compared to 600,000 covered households when the pool was set up.

Sovereign budget insurance for Caribbean governments.
At the request of the CARICOM countries, the World Bank assisted in developing the Caribbean Catastrophe Risk Insurance Facility (CCRIF). The CCRIF allows Caribbean governments to purchase insurance, based on parametric triggers, to provide immediate liquidity and budget support after the occurrence of a major earthquake or the nearby passage of a hurricane. This Caribbean-owned, regional institution is the first regional disaster insurance facility in the world. It has 16 participating governments, with policies effective as of June 1, 2007, and is managed by the private sector. The CCRIF was able to secure US$110 million of reinsurance capacity on attractive terms prior to the current hurricane season.

Index-based livestock insurance for herders in Mongolia.
A livestock insurance program was designed and implemented by the government of Mongolia to protect herders against excessive livestock mortality caused by harsh winters and summer drought. A Livestock Insurance Indemnity Pool (LIIP) was established, whereby insurance companies build collective reserves and the government offers public reinsurance, backed by a US$5 million World Bank contingent credit facility. The viability of index-based livestock insurance is being piloted in 2005–2008 in selected areas to test the preparedness of private insurance companies to offer this product and herders' willingness to purchase. In the second sales season (April–July 2007) about 600,000 animals were insured (a 10 per cent insurance penetration).

Table 8.1   (continued)

Weather index-based insurance for farmers in India.
The government of India requested World Bank technical assistance to further improve its national agricultural insurance program (NAIS) and help the state-owned agriculture insurance company (AICI) develop innovative products such as weather-based parametric insurance. New weather-based index insurance products were piloted in the State of Karnataka during spring 2007 and more than 40,000 policies were sold.

Catastrophe bond in Mexico.
Following the successful example of Taiwan in 2003, an arm of the government of Mexico, with the technical assistance of the World Bank, issued a US$160 million three-year catastrophe bond with a historically low interest spread. Its purpose is to cover against the risk of earthquakes affecting Mexico City, as part of an overall strategy to secure US$450 million in the aftermath of a major disaster. If an earthquake above defined intensities hits in designated areas of the country within the next three years, the government will be able to draw from these funds. If no disaster occurs during the life of the fund, the money will be returned to the investors. This is the first time a sovereign entity has issued a catastrophe bond.

Contingent credit facility against natural disasters in Colombia.
The government of Colombia arranged in 2005 a US$150 million contingent credit line with the World Bank. This will provide the government with immediate liquidity in the event of a major disaster occurring in Colombia.

Source: Lester and Mahul 2007.

Instruments for spreading risks directly to the capital market

Instruments such as 'catastrophe bonds' could reduce post-disaster pressure on fiscal and external balances. The principle is very simple: the owner of the bond would receive regular payments. However, if the catastrophe occurs, an amount is taken from the principal or interest of the bond. It can provide an immediate and timely availability of funds, but because of the high transaction costs this solution is twice as expensive as insurance (Swiss Reinsurance Company 1999). When compared to post-disaster assistance, which is generally highly concessional, it is not surprising that the demand for risk-transfer mechanisms in the private market is very low in developing countries. But in countries with repeated disasters, part of the aid flows could be used to invest in market-based risk-spreading options like insurance, with part of the aid being used as a backstop facility. Turkey has developed such a scheme for earthquake insurance.

Micro-credit institutions
Micro-credit institutions can help cushion the impact of the disaster for a part of the population that is highly vulnerable and not often reached by other institutions. Natural disasters have profound impact on households, including human losses but also loss of housing, livestock, food stores and productive assets such as agricultural implements. The disaster-affected population has to replace homes and assets and meet basic needs until they are able to resume income-generating activities. In the absence of micro-credit institutions, poor households are forced to rely on money-lenders who charge considerably higher rates of interest.

However, special attention needs to be paid to micro-credit institutions, which are highly exposed. In Bangladesh, after the 1998 floods, considerable refinancing from the Bangladesh Bank prevented many micro-credit institutions from falling into bankruptcy. The government backstop is essential because, once again, the high covariance risk would result in the micro-credit agencies facing problems during a disaster. In order to avoid repercussions on the users of micro-credit, a contingent liability from the governments or donors will constantly be required. A risk-pooling arrangement with micro-credit institutions from different parts of the world could be another prospect to diversify the risk.

Increasing the flexibility of aid disbursements
The term 'moral hazard' has often been used when accusing poor countries' governments of not doing enough for disaster mitigation as part of their development strategy because of the expectation that they would rely on post-disaster external assistance. However, the cost of insurance can be so high that it could have long-run economic effects through diversion of capital from investment or any other spending with a high opportunity cost. In this case, it is not only rational to rely on international aid at a national level, but it is also rational at a collective level because international assistance would be the solution that minimizes the long-run negative economic impact of natural disasters. It is likely that a country's capacity to handle the risks linked to natural hazard without international assistance will depend heavily on its stage of development. For this reason, insurance and instruments for spreading risk linked directly to the capital market – such as catastrophe bonds – might be accessible mainly to middle-income countries. However, in the least-developed countries, where the insurance industry is reticent because of risk aversion, the

only solution might be an appropriate intervention: aid flows must be adapted to the urgent and massive needs subsequent to a disaster.

The limits of aid mentioned previously (such as delays or lack of coordination) are essentially due to the fact that the donor community tends to be reactive instead of proactive. Guillaumont (2006) suggests that aid could provide a guarantee to countries that agree to follow some predefined rules of shock management. This shift from ex-post conditionality to ex-ante conditionality could considerably reduce both delays and moral hazard. Disasters occur every year in the world, and the trend is upward. We know disasters will occur, we just don't know exactly when and where. In this case, one option would be to think of a regional or a global disaster facility. Based on recommendations from an evaluation, the World Bank has established a Global Facility for Disaster Reconstruction and Response (GFDRR), with an initial contribution of $5 million a year, and an additional $50 million from several donors. The GFDRR is assisting several countries as well as regional and international organizations in identifying the disaster risks, developing risk-mitigation and risk-financing strategies, establishing institutional and legal systems for risk reduction, and strengthening regional cooperation in early warning, knowledge sharing and emergency preparedness. If the procedures for the use of the facility are agreed upfront, then such a facility (once scaled up) would also reduce problems of donor coordination often seen in post-disaster reconstruction programs.

Even when disaster relief is reactive it can be made more effective if it is provided more flexibly. Until recently much of the aid following a disaster came in the form of donated goods and services, such as food, clothing and material donations. These often end up snarled in a logistical nightmare and are, in any case, not the most effective way to help disaster-stricken families. Cash assistance is often much better, as it allows families to make better choices on what they need, keeps families and communities intact as the men do not need to move to search for jobs to get cash, helps families who have fallen into a temporary poverty trap from disposing of all of their assets (land, jewelry, cattle, and so forth) and ensures a much faster recovery and reconstruction. Cash injections into a devastated local economy also help revive business activity and get the wheels of commerce flowing much faster, thereby creating opportunities for work within the devastated areas – a process of recovery that would normally have taken much longer. But cash assistance does not have an identified flag and is therefore not the preferred choice of most donor organizations. Many international funding agencies have now made cash assistance a key part of their toolkit to help families recover after a natural disaster, but this was not the case some years ago.

Another solution worthy of more attention, although it has already been implemented, is the use of debt relief as a way to rapidly reduce financial pressure on a country stricken by disaster. It is a way to circumvent regular delays related to fund release from the donors. This solution is particularly adapted to highly indebted poor countries, where the debt service can represent a serious burden, crowding out other important uses of scarce resources. For example, following the flood of 2000, the World Bank approved accelerated debt relief worth $10 million to the Mozambican government to cover 100 per cent of IDA debt interest over the next 12 months.

IMPROVING DISASTER PREPAREDNESS

Most of the natural hazard risks are foreseeable, in the sense that it is possible to predict where events are more likely to occur in the near future. However, it is very infrequent that they are included in country development strategies, even in highly vulnerable countries. Some of the most advanced countries in Africa, such as South Africa, spend about $5 million per year as against the economic cost of natural hazard, which are estimated at $1 billion per year. If forecasting research can make even a small contribution to better public decisions in mitigation, preparedness and crisis management, it would justify sustaining the effort in research on climatic forecast. Investments in early warning systems for flooding, tsunamis and hurricanes could also help save thousands of lives and even reduce the financial costs of disasters. There is considerable room for improvement in climate forecasting: the density of weather-watch stations is eight times lower than the minimum level recommended by the World Meteorological Organization, and reporting rates are the lowest in the world (Washington et al. 2004). But even without waiting for better forecasting, just on the basis of existing ex-post data on disasters we can classify countries into categories of vulnerability (Figure 8.4).

PLANNING RELIEF AND RECONSTRUCTION

As mentioned, it is possible to identify a number of countries that are highly exposed to natural hazards. For example, in Figure 8.4 we can classify countries as high risk where over 50 per cent of GDP is at risk, medium risk are countries where between 30–50 per cent of GDP is at risk. Some 50 countries around the world fall into this category of medium to high risk and are very vulnerable to natural disasters. Figure 8.5 notes the countries in Africa alone where at least 10 disasters occurred between 1996 and 2005, and one can see what type of risk they are exposed to. In countries in which disasters are known to occur with repeated periodicity, disaster preparedness must be a central part of their

Figure 8.4   Natural Hazard Risk Levels by Country

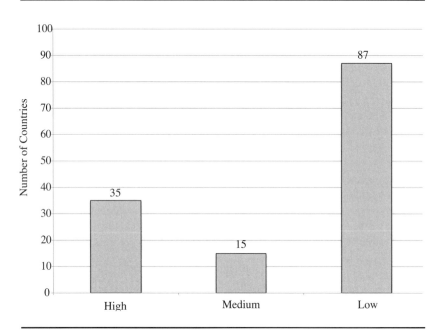

Note: High = over 50% of GDP at risk; Medium = 30-50%; Low = <30%
Source: Based on data from World Bank publication, 'Natural Disaster Hotspots: A Global Risk Analysis', 2005.

development strategy and not an afterthought. Much of their infrastructure, whether schools, roads, health-care facilities and housing stock, must be built to disaster code standards. Yet we find repeatedly that in most of these high-risk countries infrastructure built after one disaster is again being rebuilt after the next one. We also find very poor enforcement of existing codes. For example in the case of the Turkish earthquake of 1999 in Marmara where over 15,000 lives were lost, lack of housing code enforcement was a major cause of the death and destruction. Local authorities had allowed indiscriminate development without adequate enforcement mechanisms, leading to heavy damage to life and property.

Figure 8.5 also shows that floods and droughts are the most frequent types of disasters in Sub-Saharan Africa, followed by windstorms. In countries with such history, the probability that another disaster will occur during the next decade is very high. Given the huge impact of disasters on poverty and economic outcomes, it would be expected that special attention would be paid

*Figure 8.5   Countries Most Exposed To Natural Disasters in Africa
              Number and Types of Disasters (1996–2005)*

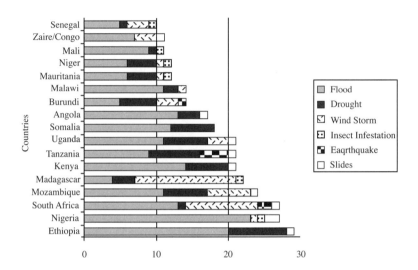

to natural hazards in these countries' development strategies. However, among all the countries represented in the preceding chart, only two have incorporated aspects of hazard risk management in their Poverty Reduction Strategy Papers.

A more ambitious agenda would involve prevention of – or reduction in – the frequency of natural disasters by designing development approaches and strategies that reduce people's vulnerability. Of course development itself, by reducing the population's exposure to agro-climatic conditions, reduces vulnerability; but more specific actions can be used as well, such as better water and land management, better infrastructure and housing and more careful attention to actions that increase people's vulnerability to natural hazards.

Disasters must be anticipated in order to make rational choices, even in emergency situations. In highly exposed countries, governments should prepare a clearly defined policy framework aimed at meeting urgent needs as well as minimizing the long-term negative consequences of disasters. It should include a system of prioritization of individual development projects and programs to ensure that any budget reallocation would not harm those with the highest development impact for the country.

The Stern report (2007) also recognizes development as a key to long-term adaptation to climate change; moreover, it points out particular areas of development that are essential to foster a country's adaptation to climate

Table 8.2   *The Negligence of Natural Disasters in Development Strategies in Africa*

Number of Disasters (1966–2005)	Number of Countries	Number of Countries including a discussion of disasters in the PRSP
21 to 29	7	1 (Mozambique)
11 to 19	6	1 (Malawi)
1 to 9	18	1 (Ghana)
TOTAL	31	3(10%)

Note: *Only includes Sub-Saharan Countries with a PRSP (Poverty Reduction Strategy Paper).
change, including

- Income and food security,
- Education and health systems,
- Urban planning and provision of public services and infrastructure, and
- Gender equality.

The cost of adaptation to climate change in the developing world is hard to estimate, but it will be tens of billions of dollars; however, it is far less costly than the consequences of inaction. Firm measures to strengthen adaptation include the integration of climate change impact in all national, sub-national and sectoral planning processes and macroeconomic projections. The implication of a core ministry, such as finance, economics or planning, which would be accountable for mainstreaming adaptation, would be an undeniable sign of government commitment (Sperling 2003).

CONCLUSIONS

The objective of this chapter is to draw attention to the growing impact of natural hazards on long-term development, as well as the reciprocal effect of development on vulnerability. After a review of the existing literature, many areas of research have emerged that will need further investigation.

First, there is currently no consensus about the long-term economic impact of natural disasters. Some authors argue that while a consequent negative impact is observed during the year of the shock, it is generally followed by an expansion, allowing a rapid return to the long-term equilibrium. Others object that the reduction of human and physical capital can hinder the long-term development of the country, especially when disasters are frequent. Because of technical difficulties, few previous studies have provided compelling empirical evidence confirming any of the two perspectives. Both theoretical and better empirical work is needed.

Second, further theoretical as well as empirical studies of the long-term impact of natural disasters will have to go into further detail into the analysis of disaster. It is very likely that the impact will differ according to the type of disaster, its frequency, the contribution of international aid and the socioeconomic conditions of the affected country. Pooling all natural disasters together would fail to consider the vast range of possible effects and could be misleading.

Third, the link between conflict and natural disasters and vulnerability needs more attention, especially in parts of Sub-Saharan Africa where population pressure is being exacerbated, and land degradation and desertification are increasing rapidly.

Fourth, the role of alternative funding mechanisms, be they market-based facilities like insurance and bonds, local funding such as micro-credit schemes to reduce vulnerability, and prearranged global or regional funding mechanisms, also need more research, including on how they could be expanded and how the inherent moral hazard and covariance could be reduced.

Fifth, more work is also needed on adaptation to climate change where the focus has been largely on technical issues, but much less attention has gone to the economic costs and benefits of different adaptation mechanisms. The manifestation of climate change will come to development largely through an increase in the frequency and intensity of natural disasters. Therefore, learning to deal with natural disasters on a more permanent and comprehensive basis and in a less reactive and more proactive manner will be the key also to a better understanding of adaptation to climate change.

Sixth, why do current development plans appear to ignore disaster risks? Is there a lack of incentives due to limited public awareness? Much more attention is needed on how economic development plans and strategies must build disaster-risk mitigation more visibly and centrally into them through the national plans.

This chapter has shown the importance of natural disasters to development and the links between disaster management and economic development. The large size of the costs of disasters, sometimes larger than aid inflows, the evidence that the intensity of disasters is determined by choices countries make on economic development, and the need to avoid considering natural disasters as one-off events are highlighted. We find that despite the frequency of disasters in many countries, very few national plans discuss them and those that do often mention them as an add-on. Finally, while most developing countries are a relatively small contributor to factors causing global warming and climate change, they are likely to be most affected by climate change, and we have offered some options for adaptation. Climate change will be the ultimate natural disaster and will begin to manifest itself through an increase in the frequency and magnitude of disasters.

NOTES

1. Based on a report on Natural Disasters prepared by the World Bank's Independent Evaluation Group.
2. Post-war reconstruction has also seen this type of feature with the rapid recovery of countries devastated by the Second World War attributed to, among other factors, new capital stock embedded with better technology.
3. A child is considered as stunting if its height given his age is two standard deviations below international norms (United Nations ACC/SCN, 2000).

REFERENCES

Abramovitz, J.N. (2001), 'Averting Unnantural Disasters', in L.R. Brown, C. Flavin and H. French (eds), *State of the World 2001: A Worldwatch Institute Report on Progress toward a Sustainable Society*, London: Earthscan, pp. 123–42.

Aghion, P. and P. Howitt (1998), *Endogenous Growth Theory*, Cambridge, MA: MIT Press.

Albala-Bertrand, J.M. (1993a), 'Natural Disaster Situations and Growth: A Macroeconomic Model for Sudden Disaster Impacts', *World Development*, **71** (9), 1417–34.

Albala-Bertrand, J.M. (1993b), *The Political Economy of Large Natural Disasters with Special Reference to Developing Countries*, New York: Oxford University Press.

Alderman, H., J. Hoddinott and B. Kinsey (2006), 'Long-Term Consequences of Early Childhood Malnutrition', *Oxford Economic Papers*, **58** (3), 450–74.

Allen, K. (2003), 'Vulnerability Reduction and the Community-Based Approach: A Philippines Study', in M. Pelling (ed.), *Natural Disasters and Development in a Globalizing World*, New York: Routledge, pp. 170–84.

Baker, R. (1987), 'Linking and Sinking: Economic Externalities and the Persistence of Destitution in Africa', in M.H. Glantz (ed.), *Drought and Hunger in Africa: Denying Famine a Future*, New York: Cambridge University Press, pp. 149–74.

Bangladesh (2000), 'Memorandum for Bangladesh Development Forum 2000–2001', Economic Relations Division, Ministry of Finance and Planning Commission, Ministry of Planning, Dhaka.

Benson, C. and E.J. Clay (1998), 'The Impact of Drought on Sub-Saharan African Economies: A Preliminary Examination', Washington, DC, World Bank Technical Paper No. 401.

—(2004), *Understanding the Economic and Financial Impacts of Natural Disasters*, Washington, DC: World Bank.

Benson, C. (2003), 'The Economy-Wide Impact of Natural Disasters in Developing Countries', draft Ph.D. diss., University of London, London.

Blaikie, P., T. Cannon, I. Davis and B. Wisner (1994), *At Risk: Natural Hazards, People's Vulnerability and Disasters*, New York: Routledge.

Carter, M.R., P.D. Little, T. Mogues and W. Negatu (2006), 'Poverty Traps and Natural Disasters in Ethiopia and Honduras', *World Development*, **35** (5), 835–56.

Chomitz, K. et al. (2007), *At Loggerheads? Agricultural Expansion, Poverty Reduction, and Environment in the Tropical Forests*, Washington: DC, World Bank.

Cochrane, H.C. (1994), 'Disasters, Indebtedness and Faltering Economic Growth', paper presented at the 9th International Seminar on Earthquake Prognostics, 9–23 September, San José, Costa Rica, and Hazards Assessment Laboratory, Colorado State University, Boulder.

Codevilla, U.R. (1993), *Antes que las Aguas nos Alcancen* [Before We Reach the Waters], Cuenca, Ecuador: Rumbos.

Cosgrave, J. et al. (2001), *Independent Evaluation of Expenditure of DEC Mozambique Floods Appeal Funds, March–December 2000*, 2 Vol., Oxford, UK: Valid International and ANSA.

Crespo Cuaresma, J., J. Hlouskova and M. Obersteiner (2008), 'Natural Disasters as Creative Destruction? Evidence from Developing Countries', *Economic Enquiry*, **46** (2), 1–13.

De Waal, A. (1997), *Famine Crimes: Politics and the Disaster Relief Industry in Africa*, London: African Rights and the International African Institute and Bloomington: Indiana University Press.

Dercon, S. (2005), 'Vulnerability: A Micro Perspective', paper prepared for the Annual Bank Conference on Development Economics, Amsterdam, Netherlands, 23–24 May.

—— (2007), 'Fate and Fear: Risk and is Consequences in Africa', paper prepared for the African Economic Research Consortium, Oxford University, Oxford.

Diamond, J. (2005), *Collapse: How Societies Choose to Fail or Survive*, New York: Penguin Books.

Dore, H.I. and D. Etkin (2003), 'Natural Disasters, Adaptive Capacity and Development in the Twenty-First Century', in M. Pelling (ed.), *Natural Disasters and Development in a Globalizing World*, New York: Routledge, pp. 75–90.

Drèze, J. and A.K. Sen (1989), *Hunger and Public Action*, New York: Oxford University Press.

Elbers, C., J. Gunning and B. Kinsey (2003), 'Growth and Risk: Methodology and Microevidence', Rotterdam, the Netherlands, Tinbergen Institute Discussion Paper No. 03-068/2.

EM-DAT: The OFDA/CRED International Disaster Database, Université Catholique de Louvain, Brussels, Belgium, at http://www.em-dat.net.

Freeman, P.K., L.A. Martin, R. Mechler and K. Warner (2002), 'Catastrophes and Development: Integrating Natural Catastrophes into Development Planning', Washington DC, World Bank, Disaster Risk Management Working Paper No. 4.

Froot, K.A. (1999), *The Financing of Catastrophe Risk*, Chicago: University of Chicago Press.

Gambia (2003), 'First National Communication of the Republic of the Gambia to the United Nations Framework Convention on Climate Change', at http://ioc3.unesco.org/accc/images/stories/File/gambia%20natcomm.pdf.

Guillaumont, P. (2006), 'Macroeconomic Vulnerability in Low-income Countries and Aid Responses', in F. Bourguignon, B. Pleskovic and J. van der Gaag (eds), *Securing Development in an Unstable World*, Washington, DC: World Bank, pp. 65–108.

Hewitt, K. (1983), *Interpretations of Calamity*, Boston: Allen and Unwin.

Kunreuther, H. (1996), 'Mitigating Disaster Losses Through Insurance', *Journal of Risk and Uncertainty*, **12** (2/3), 171–87.

Lavell, A. (1999), 'The Impact of Disasters on Development Gains: Clarity or Controversy', paper presented at the IDNDR Programme Forum, Geneva, Switzerland, 5–9 July.

Lester, R. and O. Mahul (2007), 'Facilitating Countries' Access to Catastrophic Risk Financing Some Recent Successes', mimeo, World Bank.

Lister, S. (2000), 'Power in Partnership? An Analysis of an NGO's Relationship with its Partners', *Journal of International Development*, **12** (2), 227–39.

Miguel E., S. Satyanath and E. Sergenti (2004), 'Economic Shocks and Civil Conflict: An Instrumental Variables Approach', *Journal of Political Economy*, **112** (4), 725–53.

Mortimore, M. (1998), *Roots in the African Dust*, New York: Cambridge University Press.

—— (2000), 'Profile of Rainfall Change and Variability in the Kano-Maradi Region, 1960–2000', Crewkerne, Somerset, UK, Drylands Research Working Paper No. 40.

National Climatic Center (2004), 'Mitch: The Deadliest Atlantic Hurricane Since 1780', U.S. Department of Commerce at http://lwf.ncdc.noaa.gov/oa/reports/mitch/mitch.html.

Niasse, M. (2005), 'Climate-Induced Water Conflict Risks in West Africa: Recognizing and Coping with Increasing Climate Impacts on Shares Watercourses', paper presented at the International Workshop on Human Security and Climate Change, 21–23 June, Oslo, Norway

Okuyama, Y. (2003), 'Economics of Natural Disasters: A Critical Review', Morgantown, WV, West Virginia University, Regional Research Institute Research Paper No. 2003-12.

Okuyama, Y., G.J.D Hewings and M. Sonis (2004), 'Measuring Economic Impacts of Disasters: Interregional Input-Output Analysis Using Sequential Inter-Industry Model', in Y. Okuyama and S.E. Chang (eds), *Modeling the Spatial and Economic Effects of Disasters*, New York: Springer, pp. 77–101.

Osborne, P. (2002), 'Is Zimbabwe on the Brink of Genocide?', London: Centre for Policy Studies.

Őzyaprak, S. (1999), 'Yapisal Degisim Zamani mi?' [Is it time for structural changes?], *Financial Forum* (11 August): 9.

Parker R., K. Little and S. Hueser (2007), 'Human Actions and the Rising Incidence of Disasters', Washington DC, World Bank, Independent Evaluation Group Evaluation Brief No. 4.

Pelling, M. (ed.) (2003), *Natural Disasters and Development in a Globalizing World*, New York: Routledge.

Popp, A. (2006), 'The Effects of Natural Disasters on Long-Run Growth', *Major Themes in Economics*, at http://www.cba.uni.edu/economics/themes/popp.pdf.

Quah, D. (1993), 'Empirical Cross-Section Dynamics in Economic Growth', *European Economic Review*, **37** (2/3), 426–34.

Rau, B. (1991), *From Feast to Famine*, London: Zed Books.

Sen, A.K. (1981), *Poverty and Famines: An Essay on Entitlement and Deprivation*, New York: Oxford University Press.

Shaw, T.M. (1987), 'Towards a Political Economy of the African Crisis: Diplomacy, Debates and Dialectics', in M.H. Glantz (ed.) *Drought and Hunger in Africa: Denying Famine a Future*, New York: Cambridge University Press, pp. 127–49.

Skidmore, M. and Toya H. (2002), 'Do Natural Disasters Promote Long-Run Growth?', *Economic Enquiry*, **40** (1), 664–88.

Sperling F. (ed.) (2003), 'Poverty and Climate Change: Reducing the Vulnerability of the Poor through Adaptation', Washington, DC: African Development Bank et al., available at http://www.unpei.org/PDF/Poverty-and-Climate-Change.pdf.

Stern N. (2007), *The Economics of Climate Change: The Stern Report*, New York: Cambridge University Press.

Swiss Reinsurance Company (1999), 'Alternative Risk Transfer (ART) for Corporations: A Passing Function of Risk Management for the 21st Century?', Zurich: Swiss Reinsurance Company.

Tomich, T.P. et al. (2005), 'Balancing Agricultural Development and Environmental Objectives: Assessing Tradeoffs in the Humid Tropics', in Cheryl Palm, Stephen A. Vosti, Pedro Sanchez, and Polly J. Ericksen (eds), *Slash-and-Burn Agriculture: The Search for Alternatives*, New York: Columbia University Press, pp. 415–40.

Toya, H. and M. Skidmore (2005), *Economic Development and the Impact of Natural Disasters*, Whitewater, WI: University of Wisconsin – Whitewater, Department of Economics Working Paper No. 05-04.

Uganda National Environment Management National Authority (2002), 'State of the Environment Report for Uganda'.

UNEP: Africa (annual), Vital Climate Graphics, at http://www.grida.no/climate/vitalafrica/.

UNICEF Mozambique (2002), 'Energy Preparedness and Response Plan 2002', (February).

Washington, R., M. Harrison and D. Conway (2004), 'African Climate Report: A Report Commissioned by the UK Government to Review African Climate Science, Policy and Options for Action', London: Department for International Development.

World Bank (1997), *World Disaster Report*, New York: Oxford University Press.

—— (2001), *Global Development Finance 2001: Building Coalitions for Effective Development Finance*, Washington, DC: World Bank at http://go.worldbank.org/I0IP5V2UU0.

—— (2004), 'Natural Disasters: Counting the Cost' (2 March).

—— (2005), 'Learning Lessons from Disasters Recovery: The Case of Mozambique', Washington, DC: Hazard Management Unit, Disaster Risk Management Working Paper Series No. 12.

—— (2006), *Hazards of Nature, Risks to Development, an IEG Evaluation of World Bank Assistance for Natural Disasters*, Washington, DC: Independent Evaluation Group.

—— (2007), 'Results of Preparation Work: Caribbean Catastrophe Risk Insurance Facility', Washington, DC: World Bank.

Yohe, G., N. Andronova and M. Schlesinger (2004), 'To Hedge or Not Against an Uncertain Climate Future?', *Science*, (15 October), 416–17.

9. Infectious Diseases: Responses to the Security Threat Without Borders

Mark Gersovitz

Infectious diseases, by their very nature, represent a group of classic problems in the functioning of markets, namely externalities. People who engage in risk-taking behavior that exposes them to infections, their decisions once infected and infectious themselves have consequences for other people whom the first group may infect. But it is unlikely that people, in making their decisions, consider all the costs to others of their becoming infectious, certainly not costs to people living beyond national borders. Local and national governments also typically have a too-narrow purview, focusing on the well-being of people within their borders, not the world-wide community. From a human-societal or global viewpoint, therefore, such decisions are not the best possible.

The chapter has two goals. First, it lays out how externalities arise in the health sector and how they can be mitigated. Second, it considers issues complicating research on these questions: model formulation, model conclusions and data requirements. Before proceeding to infections, externalities and public health policies, it is worth mentioning some of the other aspects of the health sector. Although not the primary focus of this chapter, these other considerations need explicit attention from time to time and always lurk in the background, conditioning how one thinks about the sector and public policy.

The health sector is inherently troublesome due to externalities and other reasons, and it is often made even more so by unwise government policies. Individuals greatly value their health. Individuals face expenditures on health that can be large relative to their incomes or wealth, raising issues of equity among people with different resources. Indeed, it is arguable whether concerns about equity in the global access to health care, rather than issues of efficiency such as externalities and public goods, should be the starting point for a discussion of the global aspect of health (Mooney and Dzator 2003). Equity considerations, however, arise for all illnesses – infectious or not – whereas externalities are specific to infectious diseases.

Furthermore, these expenditures are uncertain because people do not know what ill health they will suffer. Uncertain large expenditures make people fearful, so they want to insure themselves, but insurance presents new problems of adverse selection, moral hazard and disputes about contracts if not outright reneging. Some of these problems arise because participants in the sector – patients, different types of providers, insurers or governments – have imperfect information and, most importantly, information about different matters. Participants therefore fear not just what they do not know, but also what others may know that they themselves do not and how people 'in the know' will use their information to promote their own interests at the expense of others.

The health sector is characterized by dynamic technological change. The best way to promote health evolves as people develop new medical procedures, new medicines, new vaccines and other new methods of prevention. But achieving technological change and implementing its results in turn pose challenges. Knowledge generation is notoriously subject to the problems of a public good – how will it be funded and who will reap its benefits?

On top of all these ineluctable structural problems are problems from government policies that make the situation worse. Not all government policies do so – one hopes that government policies mitigate or can be designed to mitigate the problems inherent to the health sector, but there is plenty of experience with ones that do not – or indeed exacerbate – these problems. The very existence of problems inherent to the sector, however, ensures that one cannot easily argue for a hands-off approach by government. Finally, the balance of all these many considerations will differ among diseases.

Taken together, these factors suggest the need for an encyclopedia to discuss the threat-without-borders posed by infectious diseases. What this chapter does, however, is to focus on externalities in infectious diseases. It also considers some aspects of imperfect information, especially when these problems either have attributes of externalities, as in the case of public goods, or interact with externalities. It illustrates principles using experience from many diseases without considering all aspects of any one disease.

With so many participants, it helps to structure analysis so their modes of behavior can be discussed one at a time, or at least discussed by successively expanding the analysis to include the roles of one additional class of participant at a time. Thus, even when the threat of infection is borderless, it makes sense to group participants in clusters within consecutive rings of decision making, ranging from the narrowest to the broadest in the extent of humanity that the decision makers consider in their choices. A plausible behavioral hypothesis is that decision makers in each ring ignore the interests of the additional people represented by the decision makers located in all of the rings that enclose their ring. Several of these rings coincide with a perspective on decision making that is primarily physically interior to national borders. At the center is the individual or perhaps the family, the decision-making unit with the narrowest range of people whose interests are taken into account. The next rings are populated by different levels of local governments and then by national governments. These governments typically are principally interested in the well-being of the citizens within their borders. The outer ring would then take into account the interactions among national governments, either directly or through international organizations like the World Health Organization (WHO).

THE INDIVIDUAL AND THE FAMILY

Because individuals care about their health, they spend effort and money to avoid falling ill and to improve their health if they do fall ill. A discussion of these resource allocations needs a view of how people make decisions, and my first approximation is the rational actor: People weigh benefits against costs as they perceive them. People, therefore, take decisions to achieve the outcomes they value, subject to the constraints they encounter. Constraints include: the biology of disease, the scope for prevention and therapy, given the state of medical knowledge, people's information and incomes, and prices.

Two very general principles condition these decisions:

First, people have goals other than health and that also require resources, whether money or effort, resources that could be directed to health. In other words, tradeoffs are important to people, and they do not single-mindedly dedicate all their resources to promoting their health.

People regularly risk their health to do things they value. They want the benefits of working their farms even though such activity exposes them to schistosomiasis. They do not like sleeping under bednets to avoid malaria. They like to engage in risky sexual activity.

Second, people may spend effort and money to protect and improve the health of themselves and their family members. They are less likely to do so for unrelated people, especially ones outside their own country. In other words, people are selfish.

Self-Interest

Behavior that puts others at risk goes on all the time without, however, receiving much attention by anyone – including, most unfortunately, the people who design systematic surveys – so there is not much systematic information. People with tuberculosis are out and about and in close proximity to others all over the world every day. People with sexually transmissible diseases are sexually active and in ways that pose risks for their partners. People with schistosomiasis urinate into irrigation canals where eggs of the parasite begin the next stage on the way to infecting more people. People generate and dispose of sewage that contaminates others' drinking water.

People try to maintain their livelihood from poultry and civet cats, even when such actions put people at risk of avian flu or SARS. For instance, international smuggling of poultry products has been implicated in avian flu outbreaks in Nigeria and Egypt. Despite a ban since 2002 on poultry imports from China to the European Union, a raid at a Milan warehouse yielded three million packages of chicken smuggled from China, part of an ongoing problem (Rosenthal 2006).

So people lack the incentive to do less of things that put others at risk (negative externalities). They also lack the incentive to do more of things that lessen the risks that others face. For instance, insecticide-impregnated directly protect the people who sleep under them. They also protect others who are nearby because they cut down on the blood meals that mosquitoes need to reproduce, they prevent mosquitoes from becoming infected through the consumption of infected blood, and they kill the mosquitoes that alight on the bednets (Gamble et al. 2007; Killeen et al. 2007). But in deciding whether to sleep under nets, people derive no personal benefits from these community or mass effects (positive externalities).

Once infected, people do not take precautions that would avoid the infection of other people. Beforehand, the costs to others whom they might subsequently infect did not influence them to take extra precautions to avoid infection. And when deciding about seeking out, spending for and complying with therapy to recover, people do not take into account the benefits to others whom they might infect if they delay recovery. Thus externalities arise with respect to both prevention and therapy (Gersovitz and Hammer 2004).

Information Gaps

Information about health is important in the process of individuals' decision making. Information is of two main types: general or specific. General information includes awareness that there is a particular disease, how it is spread, how one can prevent it, how one can know if one is infected and what therapeutic options are available. Specific information would include the particular risks that a given person faces and the person's current infection status. People need to learn relevant information, but telling them the same message over and over again once they understand it is no substitute for changing the balance of benefits and costs from specific decisions that affect the dynamics of a disease.

Information campaigns about HIV in Africa illustrate well some of the complications involved in getting general information about a disease to people at risk. There is evidence that somehow most Africans know that HIV/AIDS is infectious, fatal, without a cure, sexually transmitted, and that even healthy-looking prospective partners can be infected (Gersovitz 2005). So far, so good. But what Africans know about more complex aspects of the epidemic is much less known, because the relevant studies have not been done. For instance, the risks to people depend on the overall infection rate. Information campaigns that scare people into believing that the infection rate is higher than it actually is and that any risks they take are almost certain to infect them may convince them that they might as well engage in risky behavior since anything but total isolation is ineffective. So, paradoxically, if such campaigns are successful in getting their message across, they may achieve the opposite of their ultimate aim.

By contrast, Dupas (2011) reports the results of a novel and nuanced information campaign. The study informed Kenyan teenagers in randomly selected schools that HIV prevalence was much higher among adult men and their partners than among teenage boys. It led to a 65 per cent decrease in the incidence of pregnancies by older men among teenage girls in the treatment group relative to the control, suggesting a large decrease in cross-cohort sexual activity.

There are other kinds of nuanced messages that Africans need. For instance, clinical tests for HIV infection infer infection with the virus by detecting antibodies to the virus and therefore depend on a person's immune system making detectable levels of antibodies, which only occurs about three months after infection. Within this period an infected person is infectious although negative on an antibody test. These three months are particularly dangerous because an infected person is especially infectious at this time (Butler and Smith 2007, Table 1). Indeed, if people do not abstain from risky behavior for three months before testing negative, but rather accept that a negative result means that they are safe sexual partners, it may arguably be safer to have sexual relations with someone who knows they are HIV+ and therefore outside the three months after infection period than to have relations with someone who tests negative but may be inside the highly infectious period (Butler and Smith 2007). To further complicate matters, the tests in use generate some false positives, so confirmation that someone is positive requires at least one additional test depending on the protocol.

These two characteristics of the test, the highly infectious period of negative tests and false positives, must be understood by people at risk of HIV infection.

But there is very little evidence on whether these concepts important to understanding the meaning of an HIV test are widely known in Africa. People must have this knowledge for the test results to be useful – if not actually dangerous – because of a misunderstanding of the window and false positives.

In general, the need for information by individual decision makers raises many issues for policymakers associated with externalities. Information and the methods to disseminate it may be costly to develop, but once these costs are paid it may be relatively costless to provide information.

It is usually not possible to charge for information, so all the stages required to develop and provide information need funding by a non-market mechanism, such as some level of government. And when information acquisition is not costless, it is worthwhile to faciliate the acquisition of information by people who can help to spread it to others in ways that they, in turn, cannot charge for, such as by word of mouth.

LOCAL AND NATIONAL GOVERNMENTS

To the extent that individuals do not choose levels of prevention and therapy based on the consequences to other people, there is an externality associated with infections, levels of prevention and therapy are not socially optimal, and there is at least one justification for government intervention.

Subsidies and Taxes

In the abstract, government interventions should involve subsidies or taxes. Such policies are well established in the cases of pollution charges based on environmental damage or traffic fees to diminish the costs of congestion otherwise ignored by people choosing to use their cars, for instance in central London. In principle, to deal with the threat of infection, subsidies would encourage people to avoid infecting others or taxes would penalize them if they did so. So much for rudiments of the classic theory. In practice, behaviors that affect whether people become and remain infectious are difficult to subsidize or tax because they relate to intimate activities that are difficult or impossible to monitor and therefore not easy to tax or subsidize. Policy makers may adopt interventions that they think may substitute for the infeasible optimal tax/ subsidy packages. But such approximations mean inefficiencies and, if not carefully designed, can even worsen the situation when all costs are taken into account (the classic lesson of the economic literature on the general theory of the second best).

By way of example, consider again the prevention of HIV/AIDS. In this case, the optimal policy is to tax risky sexual activity and to subsidize safe sexual activity. In actuality, what can be done is to subsidize condoms or HIV tests or to provide information to people about the risks they face. But none of these activities is the equivalent of the optimal policy. It could well be that even with free condoms people do not want to use them. Paying people to take away condoms is certainly not then the solution. Paying people to *use* condoms would be the optimal policy and in most cases it would be infeasible. Thailand and some other Asian countries, however, do seem to have at least managed to get condoms used within brothels, settings more susceptible to enforcement than elsewhere (Rojanapithayakorn 2006). But at the same time, it is conceivable that enough prostitutes and their customers avoid condom use by moving to less-well-regulated venues, with the side effect of more disease transmission and a situation that is worse than before.

In fact, enforcement is almost always an important complement to any subsidy/tax interventions to deal with externalities. For instance, health authorities try to overcome the selfish inclinations of individuals by enforced quarantine of people who have been exposed to the possibility of infection and isolation of people who show symptoms of infection. Quarantine has little benefit for the people involved and clear costs so it is not surprising that it is resisted.

During the SARS (Severe Acute Respiratory Syndrome) epidemic of 2003, Taiwan quarantined more than 150,000 people from 10 to 14 days each. To ease the costs imposed on these individuals and presumably justified by the more than commensurate public benefit, public health nurses brought the quarantined people three meals per day and sometimes helped with odd jobs (Hsieh et al. 2005). In this way, subsidies were combined with enforcement. Other experiences with quarantine during the SARS outbreak were not so happy. Twenty-five hospital staff fled confinement in Taiwan, and people rioted against plans to set up quarantine centers in two Chinese provinces (Teo et al. 2005).

Isolation

Isolation of the infected has the mitigating benefit from the individual's perspective in that it is usually associated with treatment, although there are exceptions. For instance, tuberculosis is both a life-threatening disease and one that can be caught from casual contact with an infected person, so isolation of patients combined with treatment is a natural public health tool.

Nonetheless, patients may resist isolation perhaps when there is limited prospect of successful treatment. Thus, on 19 December 2007, the BBC reported, 'Twenty-three patients with incurable, highly infectious and drug-resistant tuberculosis have escaped from a South African hospital...' Apparently, they wanted to 'spend Christmas with family'. Certainly, the South African situation is grim: the disease is terrifying, isolation is extremely unpleasant under the best of conditions and the prospects for cure uncertain, while close contact with patients who have extremely drug-resistant tuberculosis has dire implications for others in the same facility who only have the multi-drug resistant variant (Dugger 2008). Similarly, Frosch (2007) reported on a U.S. patient who 'caused a furor when, knowing he had drug-resistant tuberculosis, he flew to Europe for his wedding and honeymoon. While overseas, he learned that the strain was more serious, and, fearing he would be quarantined in Italy, he and his wife flew from Rome to Prague to Montreal before driving across the United States border to New York City'.

In the case of zoonoses, the culling of animals is an important method of control. Avian flu and SARS are two recent examples. Compensation to animal owners plays an important role in gaining their cooperation both in surveillance and in the actual culling (World Bank 2006).

Compensation

Compensation is justified by the benefits from disease control to people beyond the animal owners. But compensation is tricky. Offer too little, and people have incentives to hide potentially diseased animals, slaughter and sell them or move them outside the cull zone. In these cases, culling may actually help spread the disease. By contrast, if compensation is too generous, animal owners may move them into the cull zone and could even have an incentive to court infection of their animals, thereby extending the zone of infection. The correct amount of compensation is therefore hard to determine, especially when animals have different monetary values. For instance, there were special problems with domesticated songbirds in Vietnam, kampong chickens in Indonesia and fighting cocks in Thailand (World Bank 2006, 43). The way to solve this problem is to view compensation as part of a package that includes administratively enforced barriers to the movement of animals, thereby imposing a cost to evading the cull.

Direct Observation

In the case of tuberculosis, the strategy of Directly Observed Treatment Short Course (DOTS) tries to encourage patients to take their medicine as prescribed by having health care workers monitor patients' adherence, although there is controversy about the success of DOTS in achieving its goal (Frieden and

Munsiff 2005; Garner and Volmink 2006; Khan et al. 2005; Radilla-Chavez and Laniado-Laborin 2007). One important barrier to DOTS in poor countries is the cost of travel to the DOTS observer, which is paid by the patient in time and money. In addition to the patient's own welfare, there are two benefits of DOTS associated with externalities that the patient would not be expected to take into account. First, a patient who is cured cannot spread TB to others. Second, incomplete compliance by patients promotes drug-resistant populations of the bacillus, which make it more difficult and costly to cure other people who become infected by these strains. If efficacious, the expense of DOTS is justified by its utility in offsetting these two externalities of infections, as would be the additional subsidization of transport costs.

DOTS is not, however, a strategy that can be transferred automatically to other seemingly similar situations. HIV is a life-long infection that therapies do not cure and that may be associated with discrimination. It is even unclear whether compliance that is less than optimal from the patient's viewpoint is likely to generate more or less drug resistance, given the tendency for drug resistance to arise during the course of fully compliant therapy (Liechty and Bangsberg 2003). In any case, daily visits for the life of the patient will be extremely expensive and likely make others aware that the patient is HIV infected, something many HIV+ people want to avoid. Again, a focus on information helps in understanding motives and designing interventions.

Externalities

The classic conception of an externality presumes that government interventions must be sustained. To a first approximation, the discrepancy between the social and private net benefits of prevention and therapy are ongoing. Therefore, public actions must likewise somehow induce individuals on an ongoing basis to take into account the social benefits and costs that they would otherwise ignore. To believe differently is generally wishful thinking, but exceptions could arise:

First, epidemics are dynamic processes, and at different stages the discrepancies between the private and social considerations may be in a different balance. Hence the optimal rates of subsidies and taxes to offset the externality vary over time. Similarly, the expenditure on prevention or therapy (the subsidy/tax base) will change over time. An extreme example when public efforts would not have to be sustained is when a disease is eradicated, but the presumption is that most infectious diseases cannot be eradicated and will remain endemic; therefore, so will the need to sustain interventions. In general, not much can be said here, but a dynamic approach of intertemporal social optimization subject to private behavior, using the models of mathematical epidemiology, can shed light on this question once these models are realistically parameterized for any specific disease (Gersovitz and Hammer 2004, 2005).

Second, in some cases the public intervention has a teaching component – seeing is believing. Learning may even occur when the public intervention is not primarily about providing information. For instance, Kremer and Miguel (2007) consider whether a de-worming program in Kenya might have taught people about the private benefits of a lower worm burden, thereby leading to a diminished need for subsidies to individuals to sustain de-worming therapy.

Third, local communities may somehow come to a sense of 'ownership' of public health programs and continue them. It is not clear, at least in economists' terms, why this should be so or even what ownership of this kind means. If the benefits and costs are contained within the locality, then ownership is just another name for the realization that government at the relevant local level is the right level of decision making to achieve the optimal outcome. In any case, the program that Kremer and Miguel (2007) studied seemingly produced large social benefits because they estimate that when one person is de-wormed most of the benefits actually accrue to others through decreased transmission by the person who has been cured. But once the subsidized treatment was ended the program turned out not to be sustainable – neither learning nor community ownership sustained it.

Modeling Infection

So far, the discussion has been qualitative: I have suggested how discrepancies between individual choices and socially desirable choices that affect the level of infection arise and how the discrepancies can be mitigated. Design of an implementable policy requires quantification, i.e., an explicit mathematical model of infection, the costs of a disease and the costs of activities to deal with it, individual behavior and government interventions. Such an approach must draw firmly from mathematical epidemiology (e.g., Anderson and May 1991; Keeling and Rohani 2008) marrying these tools to those of classical welfare economics, most especially the concept of the externality.

From mathematical epidemiology come methods of modeling the dynamics of infection. A simple formulation of how new infections occur for an infection that passes directly from person to person, as opposed to one that is mediated by a vector such as a mosquito in the case of malaria, is the classic random-matching model. In this case, the chance that a single match (or meeting) with another person by a susceptible person is with an infected person is the proportion of people who are infected in the population, i. The number of susceptibles (S) who have such matches is therefore the product, Si. The number of such matches that lead to infection depends on the ease with which infection occurs and the number of such matches per susceptible per period, both embodied in the parameter.

At present, research on combining epidemiology and economics is just beginning, and many of the results so far are only qualitative. Certainly, one general lesson is that optimal strategies to control infectious diseases typically will involve a coordinated package of subsidies and other interventions to deal with the externality. For instance, in the case of diseases that are passed from person to person and from which people recover to be again susceptible, one result is that preventive activities and therapies should be subsidized at equal rates. Private choices about either prevention or therapy equally keep someone in the pool of infected people longer than is socially optimal (Gersovitz and Hammer 2004). Vector-borne infections provide scope for more elaborate packages. For instance, an optimal program to control malaria could include all sorts of subsidized activities: controlling breeding places, residual spraying of homes, killing mosquitoes through treated bed nets, directly preventing people from being infected by infected mosquitoes, such as through bed nets, blocking mosquitoes from becoming infected by infected people or helping people to recover through therapies. Suitably parameterized models can help to design these packages.

Vaccines, when available, are an important part of a disease control strategy. Table 9.1 presents the sort of explicit formula that can be derived for a subsidy to vaccination, justified by the externality associated with infection in a model based on the random matching formulation of mathematical epidemiology. This calculation proceeds under rather simple assumptions, and it is not yet clear how far it can be generalized while preserving a simple formula for the optimal subsidy to deal with the externality. My hunch is that there is a good deal of complication that can be introduced into the model before it becomes intractable algebraically, and one has to fall back on numerical methods of solution for particular sets of parameter values.

The externality arises because people do not take into account that if they get vaccinated they will not be able to infect other people. They only care about the private benefit to themselves of being personally immune to infection. The subsidy gives them an additional incentive to choose to be vaccinated, inducing them to decide as though they cared about other people. The subsidy increases alongside the population growth rate (more people who benefit after someone is vaccinated), the higher is the cost of infection, the lower is the cost of the vaccine, the lower is the interest rate (which raises the future cost of the externality relative to the current cost of being vaccinated) and the lower is the death rate (which is the depreciation of the investment in vaccination). The subsidization of a vaccine in this way is an application of the concept of the externality that is relatively conventional: There is a service that is observed

Table 9.1   Formula for the Optimal Subsidy for a Vaccine

Assumptions:
1. People are either susceptible, infected and infectious or vaccinated.
2. People are born uninfected and susceptible.
3. People die at a fractional rate and therefore can in principle live foreverregardless of whether infected or not.
4. Once infected, people never recover, continue to bear the costs of infection and remain infectious.
5. Vaccination is 100% effective in preventing illness.
6. Infection occurs through random matching of susceptibles and infecteds.
7. People deciding on vaccination take into account only their private costs.

The Optimal Subsidy:

$$t_q^* = \frac{-\in\left[p_I - p_q(r+\delta)\right]}{(r+\delta)(p_I - \in p_q)} < 0$$

(9.1)

in which:

1. t_q^* is the optimal rate of subsidy expressed as a negative tax on the price of the vaccine.
2. ε is the rate of population growth.
3. δ is the rate of death.
4. r is the interest rate.
5. p_I is the cost of being infected per year.
6. p_q is the cost of provision of the vaccine.
7. $(1 + t_q^*)p_q$ is the price of the vaccine to the person being vaccinated.

Source: Gersovitz 2003.

and that private markets would price. Uptake occurs in front of other people and so can plausibly be observed, being vaccinated is very much the specific activity that is at issue and in the extreme people could even be paid to be vaccinated i.e., subsidized more than 100 per cent, so long as there is some way to prevent people from being paid for unnecessary vaccinations.

Some considerations just discussed arise principally at the local or national levels because people are more likely to infect their neighbors and fellow citizens than people living in other countries. But infections move across borders, sometimes quite rapidly as the case of SARS brings to mind, sometimes quite broadly as the case of HIV illustrates and a new endemic disease becomes established among the worldwide population of humans. Thus, local or national governments only have an incomplete motivation to communicate the worldwide social costs of infection to their citizens – some of these social costs arise abroad. Furthermore, some expenditures have the characteristics of public goods at the level of the world – once a fixed investment has been made, benefits are available throughout the world but there is no way for the funders of such expenditures to ensure that they get reimbursed by the beneficiaries for the initial fixed cost. These considerations lead to the need for multinational and supranational coordination in dealing with the threats of infection without borders.

MULTINATIONAL AND SUPRANATIONAL CONSIDERATIONS

Generalization of the externality argument to the international level seems clear. For instance, foreign governments might want to subsidize prevention in another country where a disease is likely to first emerge before spreading to other countries so that the disease does not in fact do so. Some complications might arise as governments behave strategically, trying to foist expenditures on other governments that generate benefits for the citizens of their own countries. The international organizations concerned with global health, such as the WHO or, when zoonosises are involved, the Food and Agriculture Organization (FAO) or the World Animal Health Organization (OIE), act to coordinate the interests of countries as a whole. Working through their budgets and activities provide scope for the international sharing of the costs of disease containment in countries where outbreaks occur. But, these organizations cannot compel the cooperation of their member countries nor can they even undertake surveillance within national boundaries without permission. The controversy that erupted over researchers' access to samples of the avian flu virus from Indonesia and Vietnam are indicative of problems of coordination among countries with different interests (Normile 2005, 2007).

Basic Science

Public goods arise at the international level when everyone in the world can share in benefits without additional costs. First of all is basic science. The results of such scientific understanding enter the public domain and are shared broadly at little cost and are essentially impossible to charge for. They therefore have to be funded by a government or a consortium of governments or perhaps some not-for-profit foundations or universities with charitable funding.

The natural equilibrium would seem to be for funding from sources in the rich countries, with small poor countries able to free ride. A similar conclusion would seem to obtain for the somewhat more applied science specific to a particular disease, such as HIV/AIDS, at least if it affects the citizens of rich countries. For a disease that primarily or exclusively affects the citizens of poor countries there may be less interest in the rich countries, especially to the extent that interest is self-interest, and there is the risk that the science of such diseases will be ignored. There is, however, always the possibility of specialized interests arising within the rich countries, such as the armed forces, whose members may be concerned about preparing for military or other activities outside their home countries.

New Drugs

The next more applied activity is the development of preventive and therapeutic drugs. In these cases, there are real prospects for cost recovery because the income from sales of a drug can be controlled by patents and the drug itself in its immediate effects is a private good, one that potentially infected or infected people are willing to pay for. Of course, the patent that makes cost recovery possible also conveys market power to the patent holder with consequent inefficiencies as the fixed costs of drug development are amortized by the users of the drugs who pay more than the narrow costs of manufacturing the drug.

Changing Behaviors

The preceding sketch provides some of the economic issues that arise in generating knowledge in the biosciences, and they have been given much attention elsewhere (e.g., for vaccine development, see Kremer and Glennerster 2004; Berndt et al. 2007; Salant 2007). Much less attention has been given to the corresponding issues in the generation of knowledge in the social sciences, including epidemiology. Diseases in human populations are social phenomena, and the extent of infection is fundamentally determined by human behavior as well as by biology.

Arguably, the more promising approach to disease control is through altering behavior rather than through scientific discoveries. Regardless, it is at least likely that the two approaches are complementary and both need support. Research findings on behavior are potentially just as much public goods as findings from the biophysical sciences. Their lessons are available freely in the same way as the findings of other basic scientific research. But such research needs resources, particularly systematic data. Unfortunately, efforts to facilitate research often have poor records.

Data Collection

A well-documented case is HIV/AIDS and, more generally, sexually transmitted diseases. Data on the prevalence of these diseases is weak. It took more than 20 years from the start of the HIV epidemic for nationally representative, anonymous sero-status surveys linked to socio-demographic variables on individuals in the heavily infected countries of Africa and elsewhere to be undertaken and made publicly available through the Demographic and Health Surveys (DHS). In the meantime, with few exceptions, researchers had to rely on samples of convenience, such as samples of antenatal clinic attendees or blood donors.

This neglect of systematic data collection has many consequences. Most basic has been ignorance about the true extent of the epidemic, as witnessed by the significant revisions to prevalence figures by UNAIDS and WHO (2007). The current prevalence, however, is just one piece of an understanding of the HIV/AIDS situation. There is now no way to recover the history of prevalence in these countries over a quarter century, so it is not now possible to benefit from systematically documented experience to understand the dynamics of the epidemic. In one of the most studied cases, Uganda, debate rages over the regularities of the epidemic and the worldwide lessons for control, but participants argue in a miasma that could have been much thinned by the systematic collection of data (Allen 2006; Gray et al. 2006; Green et al. 2006 and the references therein). Unfortunately, while large amounts of money were spent in all kinds of ways, no one saw fit to fund the basic survey research that could have let people understand what was happening.

Accurate estimates of aggregate prevalence are just one use of data on sero-status. In the 1990s, samples of convenience were providing evidence that sero-discordant couples were just as likely to be female HIV+/male HIV– as female HIV–/male HIV+ (see references in Gersovitz 2001 and 2005). Such a finding calls into question the core group model, the conventional workhorse of HIV/AIDS epidemiology, in which a man becomes infected through commercial sex outside marriage and then infects his wife (Anderson and May 1991; Over and Piot 1993). What one believes about model specification has implications for how to devise information campaigns and other interventions to control the epidemic, and it seems that ignorance about the pattern of discordant couples has sent people off on in the wrong direction. A correct understanding is a public good – an incorrect understanding is the reverse. Without systematic data from randomly representative national surveys, however, one could not rule out that the bias of the epidemiological studies somehow produced this conclusion about discordant couples.

With the newly available sero-status DHS surveys, however, it can be seen that this finding on discordant couples and the core group model characterizes large, national samples that have tried to be randomly representative. Furthermore, with such large samples, publicly available and linked to other basic socio-economic variables, additional analysis is possible. Using DHS data, de Walque (2007) shows that even for couples that have been together for 10 years, the proportions of HIV+ female and HIV+ male discordant couples remain roughly equal.

This finding, in turn, suggests that these women were unlikely to have been infected prior to marriage because the mean time to death from AIDS without anti-retrovirals is 10 years. Because researchers have not had the resources to document these characteristics of the epidemic, it is not surprising that getting information out to the affected populations has been inadequate. For instance, Bunnell, Nassozi and Marum interviewed discordant couples and counselor trainers recruited through the AIDS Information Centre in Kampala, one of the oldest and largest testing organizations in Africa. They found that a 'majority of both clients and counselors explained discordance by denying it was possible' (Bunnell et al. 2005, 1003), a dangerous misunderstanding that stands in the way of preventing transmission within discordant couples.

Prevalence data alone are one thing, but the main goal is to understand behavior. In the case of the HIV epidemic, the relevant behavior includes much that is intimate. Unsurprisingly, therefore, surveys of sexual behavior have many problems; but without trying to deal with these difficulties through a refinement of the surveys, analysts continue to work in the dark. Contemporary with the first uses of scientifically random surveys for any purpose at all, there was the work on sexual behavior in the United States by the Kinsey Institute (1948, 1953). It was clear that a reliable survey had two necessary requisites that are both particularly challenging given the topic: (1) respondents must answer accurately and (2) the group of respondents must be statistically representative of the population. Kinsey put emphasis on accuracy, believing that only highly adept interviewers could gain the confidence of respondents. Without representativeness, however, it is hard to know how to make inferences, and the Kinsey studies did not use random sampling to choose the respondents (Cochran et al. 1954), thereby fundamentally compromising the inferences that could be drawn.

The same concerns dominate contemporary work on the determinants of sexual behavior. They manifest themselves in various statistical anomalies. One widespread problem is that surveys of sexual behavior typically report more presumably heterosexual activity by men than by women. Of course, this finding violates the basic fact that every heterosexual act has to have participation by a man and a woman. As with the original Kinsey surveys, there are the twin problems of inaccurate responses and unrepresentative respondents (for instance, Morris 1993; Gersovitz et al. 1998; Brown and Sinclair 1999; Nnko et al. 2004). If there is to be a confident understanding of the behavioral determinants of the HIV epidemic, this anomaly needs to be understood and overcome.

Another type of anomaly occurs in comparisons of reports of sexual behavior over time. Table 9.2 provides some information from the Ugandan DHS reports for 1995 and 2000. A comparison between the proportions of both men and women who report not having had sex before age 16 and age 19 shows an increase in these proportions for the youngest cohorts that can be compared, except in the case of men for sex before age 16, which is essentially constant (cols. 1 vs. 3, 4 vs. 6, 7 vs. 9 and 10 vs. 12). (Note that these youngest cohorts in each survey were born in different years and are not the same cohorts, but rather are of the same age at the time of the two different surveys.) The inference about behavior might be that information campaigns promoting abstinence worked and contributed to the containment of the Ugandan HIV epidemic. By contrast, when one compares what cohorts are saying in 2000 (cols. 3, 6, 9 and 12) to what the same cohorts were saying in 1995 (cols. 2, 5, 8 and 11), one finds that the proportions who say they had not had sex by a fixed age are also increasing. But they should not be if the surveys are consistent. Because these two sets of columns of the table only report on people who are either older than 16 or 19 in 1995, whether members of the same cohort had sex before these ages cannot change between the dates of the surveys. Either people are changing what they say or the samples are not equally representative of the underlying population. In any case, inferences about the adoption of abstinence are undermined (Gersovitz 2007).

Finally, surveys of behavior have consistently omitted variables that are important to the design of interventions to promote public health. One group of omitted variables is basic economic data: incomes of respondents and the prices that they face. Without this information it is not possible to analyze demand for such interventions as condoms and HIV testing, and without demand information it is not possible to understand how demand responds to subsidies designed to offset externalities or how to target interventions to people with different incomes, a standard variable used to condition equitable interventions.

Understanding and correcting these anomalies and other shortcomings in the data are of fundamental importance in devising interventions to control the epidemic. Because the benefit in devising interventions from solving these problems for even one country could be of value to many others, the solution is

Table 9.2   Comparison of Sexual Behavior over Time in Uganda

	Ugandan Men						Ugandan Women					
	Fraction No Sex before 16			Fraction No Sex before 19			Fraction No Sex before 16			Fraction No Sex before 19		
	1	2	3	4	5	6	7	8	9	10	11	12
		Check			Check			Check			Check	
Age	1995	2000	2000	1995	2000	2000	1995	2000	2000	1995	2000	2000
16–18	0.733		0.727				0.570		0.697			0.173
19–21	0.654		0752	0.271		0.380	0.537		0.630	0.134		0.149
22–24	0.672	0.696	0.845	0.268		0.393	0.556	0.548	0.606	0.149		0.182
25–27	0.635	0.671	0.724	0302	0.262	0.351	0.501	0.556	0.608	0.121	0.142	0.158
28–30	0.672	0.639	0.732	0.314	0.281	0.314	0.431	0.521	0.570	0.120	0.130	0.116
31–33	0.634	0.679	0.707	0.233	0.313	0.379	0.468	0.479	0.517	0.097	0.110	0.171
34–36	0.701	0.618	0.781	0.234	0.293	0.397	0.458	0.444	0.597	0.164	0.135	0.165
37–39	0.647	0.673	0.786	0.216	0.204	0.388	0.412	0.459	0.563	0.124	0.104	0.134
40–42	0.713	0.696	0.817	0.298	0.234	0.377	0.425	0.429	0.510	0.130	0.149	0.150
43–45	0.617	0.687	0.871	0.288	0.292	0.385	0.479	0.457	0.546	0.178	0.149	0.156
46–48	0.625	0654	0.841	0.238	0.255	0.468	0.415	0.402	0.586	0.120	0.102	

Source: Gersovitz 2007.

close to being a worldwide public good. So would be devising and implementing comprehensive surveys of behavior related to other diseases, some of which involve information on behavior that is fundamentally anti-social and therefore something that respondents likely find sensitive to answer about. For instance, hiding chickens and ducks, in the case of avian flu, or civet cats, in the case of SARS, are things people are likely to be reticent about even when promised anonymity in surveys. People are unlikely to volunteer that they have diverted DDT made available for malaria control to agricultural use with implications for vector resistance and environmental damage. Compliance with therapies for infectious diseases such as tuberculosis is a similarly sensitive topic. As bad as things are with regard to data on sexually transmitted diseases, we can at least be grateful for the DHS reports. For other diseases the worldwide community is short of even a starting point for the documentation of behavior that generates health-related externalities, the determinants of such behavior and the scope for deterring such behavior.

There are additional international spillovers with negative effects. They arise because the priorities of poor countries are affected by decisions made in the rich countries and international organizations and in ways that are not necessarily positive. For instance, for a long time the WHO, among other organizations, promoted the Voluntary Counseling and Testing (VCT) approach to HIV testing. Testing was to be undertaken at the initiative of the person to be tested, hence voluntary. Any person wanting to be tested was to be counseled before and after being tested, hence counseling. This protocol was widely adopted by government testing sites and by non-governmental organizations in Africa. But it is controversial because it is expensive and because many people who might consider a test find it offputting, and, seemingly as a result, uptake has been low and few people know their HIV status. Beginning in 2004 with Botswana (Steen 2007), some African governments have been moving to complement VCT with an alternative protocol – routine testing (De Cock et al. 2006). People using most medical services, including antenatal, tuberculosis and sexually transmitted disease clinics, would be tested unless they chose to opt out. Counseling would be available before and after testing but need not be mandatory for receiving results. Although the reasons why the VCT protocol was given such impetus in Africa are speculative, it is at least arguable that part of the motive arose from considerations that are domestic to the HIV situation in the rich countries and their particular constellation of interest groups and ethical concerns, rather than the needs of African countries facing widespread HIV epidemics.

DDT use to control malaria presents another instance in which the valuation of costs and benefits, means and ends differ between poor countries and interest groups in rich countries (Rosenberg 2004; Schapira 2006). In this case, there are many activist environmentalist groups, usually based in rich, malaria-free countries, that want a complete ban on the use of DDT.

Opposed to them are the WHO and many people in countries where malaria is endemic and associated deaths are high. At present, DDT is approved for residual spraying of residences for malaria control. This debate and advocacy continue.

CONCLUSIONS

Economists are neither the only nor, doubtless, the first observers to remark that infectious processes mean that one person's infection status and the actions that determine it have implications for others. Epidemiologists use terms such as mass or community effects and herd immunity. What distinguishes these notions from the externality is that the economic concept of an externality is anchored in an explicit comparison between the incentives faced by rational individuals and the policymaker. Furthermore, the policymaker takes account of individuals' valuations of outcomes while recognizing that individuals' actions, taken together, have consequences for people's well-being, but people lack the incentives to affect these through their individual decisions. These ideas of welfare economics help to design socially desirable policies in the health sector as elsewhere and give the economists' discussion structure, one that even holds out the hope of the precision contained in Table 9.1. Thus, these economic concepts can move the discussion on health policy beyond what everyone else already knows. They can provide guidance on the ideal way to modify individual incentives to achieve the social good as well as an understanding of (1) how to approximate these ideal modifications (theory of the second best), (2) when such welfare-improving approximations may not be practical and (3) when well-intentioned interventions may actually worsen the situation.

Thus, the specifics of policy formulation to deal with any particular disease require a careful dissection of the exact manifestations of the principle of the externality. Individuals take most of the immediate decisions about health, but governments can try to make these individuals' decisions approximate the calculus of social benefits and costs. When the effects of infection are dispersed beyond any borders, different levels of government take into account differing fractions of the total worldwide social benefits and costs. There is a hierarchy of decision makers that need to be induced to make all decisions with regard to the full social benefits and costs to all of humanity. Global public health should be about making sure that this outcome happens to the greatest degree possible.

REFERENCES

Allen, T. (2006), 'AIDS and Evidence: Interrogating Some Ugandan Myths', *Journal of Biosocial Sciences*, **38** (2), 7–28.

Anderson, R.M. and R.M. May (1991), *Infectious Diseases of Humans*, New York: Oxford University Press.

BBC (2007), 'Hunt on for Escaped TB Patients', (19 December) at http://news.bbc.co.uk/2/hi/africa/7152855.stm.

Berndt, E.R. et al. (2007), 'Advance Market Commitments for Vaccines against Neglected Diseases: Estimating Costs and Effectiveness', *Health Economics*, **16** (5), 491–511.

Brown, N.R. and R.C. Sinclair (1999), 'Estimating Number of Lifetime Sexual Partners: Men and Women do it Differently', *Journal of Sex Research*, **36** (3), 292–97.

Bunnell, R.E., J. Nassozi and E. Marum (2005), 'Living with Discordance: Knowledge, Challenges and Prevention Strategies of HIV-discordant Couples in Uganda', *AIDS Care*, **17** (8), 999–1012.

Butler, D.M. and D.M. Smith (2007), 'Serosorting Can Potentially Increase HIV Transmissions', *AIDS*, **21** (9), 1218–20.

Cochran, W.G. et al. (1954), *Statistical Problems of the Kinsey Report on Sexual Behavior in the Human Male*, Washington, DC: American Statistical Association.

De Cock, K.M. et al. (2006), 'Unfinished Business: Expanding HIV Testing in Developing Countries', *New England Journal of Medicine*, **354** (5), 440–42.

de Walque, D. (2007), 'Sero-Discordant Couples in Five African Countries: Implications for Prevention Strategies', *Population and Development Review*, **33** (3), 501–23.

Dugger, C.W. (2008), 'TB Patients Chafe under Lockdown in South Africa', *New York Times* (25 March).

Dupas, P. (2011), 'Do Teenagers Respond to HIV Risk Information? Evidence from Field Experiment in Kenya', *American Economic Journal: Applied Economics*, **3** (1), 1–36.

Frosch, D. (2007), 'Traveler with TB is Released after Treatment in Denver', *New York Times* (27 July).

Frieden, T.R. and S.S. Munsiff (2005), 'The DOTS Strategy for Controlling the Global Tuberculosis Epidemic', *Clinics in Chest Medicine*, **26** (2), 197–205.

Gamble, C. et al. (2007), 'Insecticide-Treated Nets for the Prevention of Malaria in Pregnancy: A Systematic Review of Randomized Controlled Trials', *PloS Medicine*, **4** (3), 506–15.

Garner, P. and J. Volmink (2006), 'Families Help Cure Tuberculosis', *The Lancet* (24 June), 878–79.

Gersovitz, M. (2001), 'Human Behaviour and the Transmission of Infectious Disease: An Economist's Perspective', in K. Anderson, *Australia's Economy in the International Context: The Joseph Fisher Lectures*, Vol. 2, Adelaide: Adelaide University.

Gersovitz, M. (2003), 'Births, Recoveries, Vaccinations and Externalities', in R.J. Arnott et al. (eds), *Essays in Honor of Joseph E. Stiglitz*, Cambridge, MA: MIT, pp. 469–83.

Gersovitz, M. (2005), 'The HIV Epidemic in Four African Countries Seen through the Demographic and Health Surveys', *Journal of African Economies*, **14** (2), 191–246.

Gersovitz, M. (2007), 'HIV, ABC and DHS: Age at First Sex in Uganda', *Sexually Transmitted Infections*, **83** (2), 165–68.

Gersovitz, M. and J.S. Hammer (2004), 'The Economical Control of Infectious Diseases', *Economic Journal*, **114**, (492), 1–27.

Gersovitz, M. and J.S. Hammer (2005), 'Tax/Subsidy Policies Toward Vector-Borne Infectious Diseases', *Journal of Public Economics*, **89** (4), pp. 647–74.

Gersovitz, M. et al. (1998), 'The Balance of Self-Reported Heterosexual Activity in KAP Surveys and the AIDS Epidemic in Africa', *Journal of the American Statistical Association*, **93** (443), 875–83.

Gray, R.H. et al. (2006), 'Uganda's HIV Prevention Success: The Role of Sexual Behavior Change and the National Response. Commentary on Green et al (2006)', *AIDS and Behavior*, **10** (4), 347–50.

Green, E.C. et al. (2006), 'Uganda's HIV Prevention Success: The Role of Sexual Behavior Change and the National Response', *AIDS and Behavior*, **10** (4), 335–46.

Hsieh, Y.-H. et al. (2005), 'Quarantine for SARS, Taiwan', *Emerging Infectious Diseases*, **11** (2), 278–82.

Keeling, M.J. and P. Rohani (2008), *Modeling Infectious Diseases in Humans and Animals*, Princeton, NJ: Princeton University Press.

Khan, M.A. et al. (2005), 'Tuberculosis Patient Adherence to Direct Observation: Results of a Social Study in Pakistan', *Health Policy and Planning*, **20** (6), 354–65.

Killeen, G.F. et al. (2007), 'Preventing Childhood Malaria in Africa by Protecting Adults from Mosquitoes with Insecticide-Treated Nets', *PloS Medicine*, **4** (7), 1246–58.

Kinsey, A., W. Pomeroy and C. Martin (1948), *Sexual Behavior in the Human Male*, Bloomington: Indiana University Press.

Kinsey, A., W. Pomeroy, C. Martin and P. Gebhardt (1953), *Sexual Behavior in the Human Female*, Bloomington: Indiana University Press.

Kremer, M. and R. Glennerster (2004), *Strong Medicine: Creating Incentives for Pharmaceutical Research on Neglected Diseases*, Princeton, NJ: Princeton University Press.

Kremer, M. and E. Miguel (2007), 'The Illusion of Sustainability', *Quarterly Journal of Economics*, **122** (3), 1007–64.

Liechty, C.A. and D.R. Bangsberg (2003), 'Doubts about DOT: Antiretroviral Therapy for Resource-Poor Countries', *AIDS*, **17** (9), 1383–87.

Mooney, G. and J. Dzator (2003), 'Global Public Goods for Health: A Flawed Paradigm?', in R. Smith, R. Beaglehole, D. Woodward and N. Drager (eds), *Global Public Goods for Health*, New York: Oxford University Press, pp. 233–45.

Morris, M. (1993), 'Telling Tails Explain the Discrepancy in Sexual Partner Reports', *Nature* (30 September), 437–40.

Nnko, S. et al. (2004), 'Secretive Females or Swaggering Males? An Assessment of the Quality of Sexual Partnership Reporting in Rural Tanzania', *Social Science and Medicine*, **59** (2), 299–310.

Normile, D. (2005), 'Vietnam Battles Bird Flu... And Critics', *Science* (15 July), 368–73.

——— (2007), 'Indonesia to Share Flu Samples Under New Terms', *Science* (6 April), 37.

Over, M. and P. Piot (1993), 'HIV Infection and Sexually Transmitted Diseases', in D.T. Jamison et al. (eds), *Disease Control Priorities in Developing Countries*, New York: Oxford University Press, pp. 455–527.

Radilla-Chávez, R. and R. Laniado-Laborin (2007), 'Results of Directly Observed Treatment for Tuberculosis in Ensenada, Mexico: Not all DOTS Programs are

Created Equally', *International Journal of Tuberculosis and Lung Disease*, **11** (3), 289–92.

Rojanapithayakorn, W. (2006), 'The 100% Condom Use Programme in Asia', *Reproductive Health Matters*, **14** (28), 41–52.

Rosenberg, T. (2004), 'What the World Needs Now is DDT', *New York Times Magazine*,(11 April).

Rosenthal, E. (2006), 'Bird Flu Virus May Be Spread by Smuggling', *New York Times* (15 April).

Salant, S. (2007), 'Review of M. Kremer and R. Glennerster, Strong Medicine: Creating Incentives for Pharmaceutical Research on Neglected Diseases', *Economic Development and Cultural Change*, **55** (4), 848–52.

Schapira, A. (2006), 'DDT: A Polluted Debate in Malaria Control', *The Lancet* (16 December), pp. 2111–12.

Steen, T.W. (2007), 'Two and a Half Years of Routine Testing in Botswana', *Journal of Acquired Immune Deficiency Syndromes*, **44** (4), 484–88.

Teo, P. et al. (2005), 'SARS in Singapore: Surveillance Strategies in a Globalising City', *Health Policy*, **72** (3), 279–91.

UNAIDS and WHO (2007), *AIDS Epidemic Update*, Geneva: UNAIDS and WHO.

World Bank (2006), *Enhancing Control of Highly Pathogenic Avian Influenza in Developing Countries through Compensation*, Washington, DC: World Bank.

Index

ADI 40, 83
Afghanistan,
    international intervention 153, 156, 160
    opium farmers 151
    police,
        disarmament 156
        people view as predatory 157
        provincial police liaison boards 159
        training 157, 162
        security sector reform programs 157
        warlords 160, 162
Africa,
    50 per cent live in marginal lands 181
    armed conflict,
        civil 11
        cost of 1
        state and non-state wars 88
        study of 72
    climate change 38
    French informal security guarantees in 61
    HIV information 212
    natural disasters, planning for 202
    peace in 89
African countries,
    disasters between 1996 and 2005 199–200
    horizontal inequalities widespread 83
    internally displaced persons 74
    negative growth increased likelihood of conflict 178
    structural conditions for war present in most 88
    terms of trade losses 35
    variety of problems 27
Aggregate Differential Index *see* ADI
aid,
    cash assistance much better than goods and services 198
    management problems for receiving country 192
    post-conflict context 67
    post-Cold War allocation 5, 7
    post-disaster 198
AIDS 94, 223
AIDS Information Centre in Kampala (Uganda) 223
Algeria 105, 116, 121
AMELIA program 44
Andes (Peru), coca farmers 151
Angola 75
    aid 100
    food shortage 184
    civil wars in 45, 46, 48, 73
    GDP higher after war 75, 80, 84, 86
    peace settlement 57–8
    UNITA 12
Arab world,
    population under age 15 37
    World Bank Group and 40
Aristotle, better to be ruled by laws than by men 135
armed conflict,
    source of poverty 87
Armed Conflict Dataset 71, 89, 102
armed conflicts in sub-Saharan Africa 71
    conclusions 88–9
    consequences on poverty and development 75–9
    policy responses to addressing risk factors 86–7
    structural conditions and war risks 79
    chronic poverty 79–80
    demographic youth bulge 85
    environmental pressure related to migration 85
    history of war 86
    horizontal inequalities 83–4
    neighborhood spillovers 84–5